From Abortion to Reproductive Freedom

Transforming a Movement

Marlene Gerber Fried
editor

South End Press
Boston, MA

Grateful acknowledgement is made to all the authors who have contributed previously published material. For copyright information, please see the individual chapters.

Any properly footnoted quotation of up to 500 sequential words may be used without permission, as long as the total number of words quoted does not exceed 2,000. For longer quotations or for a greater number of total words, please write for permission to South End Press or to the original publisher.

Cover design by Dan Spock
Text design and production by the South End Press collective
Printed in the U.S.A. on acid-free paper
First edition, first printing

Library of Congress Cataloging-in-Publication Data
From abortion to reproductive freedom: transforming a movement/ edited by Marlene Gerber Fried.
p. cm.
Includes index.
ISBN 0-89608-388-8 (cloth): $30.00.—ISBN 0-89608-387-X (paper) $14.00
1. Abortion—Social aspects—United States. 2. Abortion—Government policy—United States. 3. Pro-choice movement—United States. 4. Women's rights—United States. I. Fried, Marlene Gerber.
HQ767.5.U5F77 1990   90-40541
363.4'6'0973—dc20   CIP

South End Press, 116 Saint Botolph Street, Boston, MA 02115
98 97 96 95 94 93 92 91 90   1 2 3 4 5 6 7 8 9

From Abortion to Reproductive Freedom: Transforming a Movement

Acknowledgments vii

Introduction ix

THE POLITICS OF THE ABORTION RIGHTS MOVEMENT

Transforming the Reproductive Rights Movement:
The Post-*Webster* Agenda 1
  Marlene Gerber Fried

Racism, Birth Control, and Reproductive Rights 15
  Angela Davis

From Privacy to Autonomy:
The Conditions for Sexual and Reproductive Freedom 27
  Rhonda Copelon

Key United States Supreme Court
Abortion and Privacy Cases 45

Mobilizing Against the State and International
"Aid" Agencies: "Third World" Women
Define Reproductive Freedom 49
  Jacqui Alexander

Abortion and Sterilization in the Third World 63

The Right to Life:
What Can the White Man Say to the Black Woman? 65
  Alice Walker

SPEAKING OUT FOR WOMEN: CHOOSING OURSELVES

Before *Roe v. Wade* 71
  Sharon Cox

Exits and Entrances 73
  Joan Fishbein

A Question of Survival/A Conspiracy of Silence:
Abortion and Black Women's Health 75
    Byllye Avery

Choosing Ourselves: Black Women and Abortion 83
    Beverly Smith

Hidden History: An Illegal Abortion in 1968 87
    Margaret Cerullo

The Abortion 91
    Susan Tracy

Just call "Jane" 93
    "Jane"

The Politics of Menstrual Extraction 101
    Laura Punnett

Abortion Without Apology 113
    Lynn S. Chancer

Breaking Silences: A Post-Abortion Support Model 121
    Sarah Buttenweiser and Reva Levine

Who Has Abortions in the United States? 129

Putting Women Back into the Abortion Debate 131
    Ellen Willis

Raising Our Voices 139
    Loretta Ross

DEFENDING ABORTION RIGHTS: CONFRONTING THREATS TO ACCESS

Emergency Memorandum to Women of Color 147
    Loretta Ross, Sherrilyn Ifill, Sabrae Jenkins

Abortion Rights, Poor Women, and Religious Diversity 151
    Sabrae Jenkins

The Reproductive Health of Black Women 157

Kathy's Day in Court 161
    Angela Bonavoglia

Reproductive Issues Are Essential Survival Issues
for the Asian-American Communities 175
    Connie S. Chan

Pro-Choice Activism Springs from Many Sources 179
    Ann Baker

Operation Oppress You: Women's Rights Under Siege 185
    Dázon Dixon

Every Sperm Is Sacred 187
    Cynthia Peters

Clinic Violence and Harassment of Abortion Providers 195

RU-486 197
    Judy Norsigian

Fighting Back to Save Women's Lives 205
    Brenda Joyner

The Female War Saga 213
    Sharon Cox

EXPANDING THE AGENDA:
BUILDING AN INCLUSIVE MOVEMENT

Survival, Empowerment, and Activism 217
    Roxanna Pastor

La Mujer Puertorriqueña,
Su Cuerpo, y Su Lucha por La Vida:
Experiences with Empowerment in Hartford, Connecticut . . . 221
    Cándida Flores, Lani Davison, Enid Mercedes Rey,
    Migdalia Rivera, María Serrano

Shared Dreams: A Left Perspective
on Disability Rights and Reproductive Rights 233
    Adrienne Asch and Michelle Fine

Abortion/Baby Doc Controversy 241
    Marian Blackwell-Stratten, Mary Lou Breslin,
    Arlene Byrnne Mayerson, Susan Bailey

Women's Reproductive Rights in the Age of AIDS 245
    Hortensia Amaro

Court-Ordered Caesareans:
A Growing Concern for Indigent Women 255
    Janean Acevedo Daniels

Pregnancy and Drug Use: Incarceration Is Not the Answer . . 263
    Jacqueline Berrien

Punishing Women in the Name of Fetal Rights 269

Gender Difference, Fetal Rights,
and the Politics of Protectionism: Workplace Issues 271
    Cynthia Daniels

"Together We Will Get Somewhere": Working Together
for Lesbian/Gay Liberation and Reproductive Freedom 281
    Shelley Mains and Stephanie Poggi

Reproductive Rights Position Paper:
the National Black Women's Health Project 291

Vision Statement: Women of Color Partnership Program 293

Statement of Asian-Pacific Women on Reproductive Health . . 295

A Reproductive Rights Agenda for the 1990s 297
    Kathryn Kolbert

Reproductive Rights and Coalition-Building 307
    Byllye Avery

Notes on Contributors 309

Index 313

ACKNOWLEDGMENTS

I want to thank the many people who helped, encouraged, and supported me during this project. I want to acknowledge the women whose contributions make up this collection. Their work—both activist and intellectual—deepens my understanding of the meaning of reproductive freedom and inspires my activism.

My own political commitments have been primarily shaped by the many women with whom I have worked politically, especially those in the Reproductive Rights Network (R2N2) which has been my organizational home for over a decade. R2N2's collective commitment to feminism, to grassroots activism, and to a multi-racial, multi-issue movement has been a critical influence in my political development. At the same time, the collapse of National R2N2—because of a failure to adequately address racism within the organization—made painfully clear to me the need for new leadership and new organizations.

In recent years, several organizations and conferences have taken the lead in developing an expanded vision of reproductive freedom and in asserting the leadership role of women of color within the movement. Among these, I am especially indebted to the National Black Women's Health Project; the Women of Color Partnership Program of the Religious Coalition for Abortion Rights; Women of Color and Reproductive Rights Conference in 1988; the conference, "In Defense of Roe," in April 1989; and the "Sisters and Allies" conference in November 1989. I am grateful to Sabrae Jenkins, Loretta Ross, and Lynn Paltrow for enabling me to be part of these activities which are transforming the abortion rights movement. These are also the networks through which I learned about the work of many of the contributors to this volume. A special thanks goes to Sabrae Jenkins, editor of the Women of Color Partnership Program newsletter, "Common Ground—Different Planes," the source of several articles included here.

I could not have done this project without the personal support of my friends, my children Danny and Michael, and my husband Bill Fried whose support, love, and encouragement, not to mention his willingness to do much more than his fair share of child care, made it possible. In addition, Bill has been the editor's editor, patiently working through many drafts of my article and consulting on others in the book.

Barry Lefsky typed the entire manuscript onto disk, often at very short notice and with amazing accuracy. Judith Liben and Diane Raymond gave editorial assistance. Anne Deutsh helped with correspondence in the early stages. Leslie Hannigan did the index.

Many thanks to Loie Hayes, Ellen Herman, and Cynthia Peters from South End Press. It was their idea to do a book in response to the abortion crisis. Their enthusiasm and encouragement drew me to the project, and I am appreciative of their ongoing commitment and support as the book grew in length and breadth. I also thank Ellen Herman for her editorial work and the entire South End Press collective for production.

Finally, but not insignificantly, I want to acknowledge my debt to Hampshire College and to Toni Huber for his generosity and support of the Civil Liberties and Public Policy Program which not only enabled me to undertake this project, but has made it possible for me to bring together my political commitments and my academic interests. I am very grateful to have had this opportunity.

INTRODUCTION

Marlene Gerber Fried

Abortion rights are in danger, the most serious since legalization in 1973 when the U.S. Supreme Court decided *Roe v. Wade*. Not only has the existing Court shown itself willing to strike at the very core of the Constitutional right to abortion, but every state legislature will have a shot at it.

This is a crisis, but one which is full of possibilities. The ongoing attacks at abortion clinics and the gutting of Constitutional protections for abortion by the Supreme Court in the *Webster* decision (July 3, 1989) have created strong general support for "choice." Ironically, the willingness of the Supreme Court to seriously curtail abortion access may have been the spark needed to prevent further erosion. Thousands of women and men, many of whom have never been active before, have become involved. The membership of large national groups like NOW (National Organization for Women) and NARAL, (National Abortion Rights Action League), as well as that of independent grassroots groups and coalitions, has soared. The public has been galvanized. But for what—freedom of choice circumscribed by race and class, removed from feminist demands about women's autonomy, and shrouded in "privacy," or reproductive freedom for all women? Will it be a movement that confines itself to the legal right to abortion or one that fights for all of the rights needed to make reproductive choice a reality? What will be the politics of this movement?

Answering these questions involves us in turmoil, confusion, and political struggle. We have an opportunity to move ahead with a positive reproductive rights agenda. Doing so requires that we build the kind of movement we have not had in the past—one that is broad-based in its membership, its leadership, and its politics; a movement that goes beyond reaffirmation of *Roe* to demand access not just to abortion, but to the full range of reproductive rights; a movement that is based on a class- and race-conscious feminism.

I have been an activist in this movement for almost 15 years, and while I am critical of much of our past, I am hopeful about our future. I think we can broaden the base of the movement and widen our agenda. I am also convinced that in order to do so we need to change our strategies and our goals.

At the November 1989 "Mobilization for Women's Lives" in Washington D.C., amidst a sea of pro-choice banners and speeches, I saw only one physical testament to a broader agenda—a T-shirt which read: "Abortion is not the only issue" and listed demands for access to safe, legal abortion, effective birth control, sex education and AIDS treatment, full economic rights for all women, an end to sterilization abuse, and reproductive freedom for lesbians, gays, and bisexuals.

Even that list is incomplete. Needs such as child care, freedom from violence, good jobs, safe workplaces, and many more belong on that shirt. Our demands should be nothing short of everything we need for every woman's freedom.

Transforming the abortion rights movement from a relatively narrow one focused on defending the legal right to abortion to a movement for reproductive freedom, from a movement whose membership and leadership is predominantly white to an inclusive movement with a broad and diverse grassroots base, these are key political tasks facing reproductive rights activists. And these are the issues that motivated this book.

For too long, white mainstream women's groups have undervalued the participation of women of color in the reproductive rights movement, and, with the exception of abortion, have ignored the issues of primary concern to women of color. To paraphrase Brenda Joyner, long-time activist and co-director of the Tallahassee Feminist Women's Health Center (see her article "Fighting Back to Save Women's Lives" in this collection), this narrow vision of choice has prevented them from seeing that work with pregnant teenagers, and prenatal care advocacy; activism to reduce the high infant and maternal death rate for Black women; organizing to end hazardous workplaces, racism, sterilization abuse, and violence; AIDS activism, and the expansion of gay and lesbian rights and child care access...are all part of the reproductive rights struggle.

> Perhaps the question is not really where are women of color in the abortion rights and reproductive rights movement. Rather, where is the primarily white middle-class movement in our struggles for freedom? Where was a white middle-class movement when the Hyde Amendment took away Medicaid funding of abortions for poor women?[1]

Her perspective is echoed in many of the articles here. The message is clear: the reproductive rights movement must change in order to represent the interests of *all* women.

In selecting articles I have tried to bring together as many voices and issues as I could to deepen our understanding of the meaning of reproductive freedom and to present a broad political agenda. I hope this book will contribute to the consciousness-changing process necessary to transform the movement, as well as to the strategy debates that accompany our struggle.

While I am acutely aware of the many voices and constituencies that are not represented, I am also excited by this collection. There is tremendous diversity here. The women whose articles appear are all part of the transformation process. They are activists committed to reproductive freedom and to creating a movement which reflects that commitment in its agenda, its participants, and its leaders. These articles are a clear reflection of both the need to transform the abortion rights movement and the fact that this process is already happening.

From Abortion to Reproductive Freedom is organized into four sections:

The Politics of the Abortion Rights Movement

In this section the articles examine the prevailing politics, strategies, and language of the abortion rights movement, currently and historically. My essay examines the dominant political tendencies which are barriers to building an inclusive movement. Angela Davis addresses the issue of racism in the abortion rights and birth control movements; in this piece she focuses on eugenics, population control, and sterilization abuse. Rhonda Copelon looks at the key Supreme Court cases involving abortion rights and analyzes the limitations and possibilities of privacy. Jacqui Alexander situates the meaning of reproductive freedom for third world women within the broader international context. Alice Walker's piece is an eloquent and powerful reminder of the violence committed by white men against women and children of color.

Speaking Out for Women: Choosing Ourselves

Faced with an unwanted pregnancy, women do what they must, constrained only by the circumstances of their lives. Themes explored in this section include: experiences of abortion both illegal and legal; the value of women's lives; women taking control through collective action; and the place of women in the abortion debate.

The poems by Sharon Cox and Joan Fishbein invoke the fear, the shame, and the inequities which defined illegal abortion. Byllye Avery describes her experiences helping women gain access to abortion both before and after legalization. Her article goes on to place abortion in the context of the survival needs of Black women and the empowerment strategy of the National Black Women's Health Project. Beverly Smith recalls the days of illegal abortion and the difficulties Black women have in choosing to take care of themselves. She also discusses the participation of Black women in the abortion rights struggle. Margaret Cerullo's article, and the poem by Susan Tracy are first-person accounts of illegal abortion. Both remind us that the abortion struggle is over the value placed on women's lives. "Just Call Jane" is the story of an illegal, feminist abortion service, a story of women taking control of abortion and taking care of other women. This is the first time a former "Jane" has herself written about the experience.

Another form of women's control of their reproductive capacity—self-help—is the topic of Laura Punnett's essay. She discusses the politics of menstrual extraction and the importance of using it to enable women to control their own fertility as opposed to its being used as an instrument of population control. Lynn Chancer focuses on the way in which the current abortion debate is framed. She is particularly concerned about the defensiveness of pro-choice supporters. Sarah Buttenweiser and Reva Levine write about the toll anti-abortion politics takes on women who have had abortions. Ellen Willis is critical of the effort to disengage abortion from feminism and sexual politics. She demands that women's lives and needs be seen as the central issue in the abortion debate. Loretta Ross focuses on the need for the Black community to break its silence on the abortion issue and to provide support for Black women who are making this choice. She also argues that alliances are needed between the civil rights, abortion rights, and feminist movements.

Defending Abortion Rights: Confronting Threats to Access

Attacks on abortion access by the anti-abortion movement are part of an overall strategy which seeks, in the short run, to make abortion more and more difficult for increasing numbers of women and, in the long run, aims to criminalize abortion—for any woman, for any reason. The articles in this section discuss these attacks and ways in which our movement has responded.

The most vulnerable women in our society—poor women, of whom a disproportionate number are women of color, and young women—have borne the brunt of the legislative attacks on access. The Emergency Memorandum and the articles by Sabrae Jenkins and Angela Bonavoglia address the impact that the erosions in access have had on these women. Connie Chan talks about the interrelation of classism, sexism, and language barriers all resulting in lack of access to reproductive counseling, education, and abortion within Asian-American communities.

The attacks on abortion clinics are very direct challenges to women's access to abortion. The articles by Ann Baker, Dázon Dixon, and Cynthia Peters discuss Operation Rescue and report on pro-choice responses.

Judy Norsigian's article updates us on RU-486 as an alternative method of abortion. Brenda Joyner's article emphasizes the importance of fighting back against all threats to abortion access. Cox's poem "The Female War Saga" reflects the pain and anger of the battle and the determination to resist.

Expanding the Agenda: Building an Inclusive Movement

Safe, legal, and funded abortion is crucial for reproductive choice. So too are many other rights which we have never had. The struggle for reproductive rights takes different forms in different communities. The pursuit of a full reproductive freedom agenda is necessary if we are to build a movement of and for all women. Women's survival needs are being threatened in so many ways and women are mobilizing in their communities both to resist the attacks and to demand more. The voices in this section address some of these other issues which are key to building an inclusive movement.

Roxanna Pastor talks about Latina women and the struggle for survival. Cándida Flores, et al., describe and analyze a self-help model of empowerment for Latina women which addresses these survival issues.

The reproductive rights movement must insure that abortion rights will not be won at the expense of the rights of any group of women. The article by Adrienne Asch and Michelle Fine, and the excerpt on the Baby Doe case link the issue of disability rights to the struggle for abortion rights. These authors are especially concerned to block efforts by the anti-abortion movement to exploit the disability issue in the service of oppressing women. Hortensia Amaro looks at the impact of AIDS on women of color and new threats to reproductive choice

"Fetal rights" have become central in challenging abortion rights and as justifications for other efforts to control women's behavior. The articles by Janean Daniels and Jacqueline Berrien focus on fetal abuse/neglect charges, forced Caesareans, and the impetus to punish pregnant women. They point out that women of color and poor women are overwhelmingly the targets. Cynthia Daniels argues that "fetal protection" policies harm working women and focus attention away from remedying hazardous workplaces.

Transforming the abortion rights movement involves linking issues and movements. Stephanie Poggi and Shelley Mains talk about links between the abortion rights and lesbian/gay liberation movements. The vision statements of the Black Women's Health Project, the Women of Color Partnership Program of the Religious Coalition for Abortion Rights, the statement by Asian-American women to the "In Defense of Roe" conference, and the article by Kathryn Kolbert all articulate a broad reproductive rights agenda. The final selection is Byllye Avery's speech to the historic "In Defense of Roe" conference. It is a call for coalition-building in the reproductive rights movement based on respect for the reproductive choices of all women.

Notes

1. Brenda Joyner, "The Fight for Abortion Rights and Reproductive Freedom," conference, Hampshire College, April 1990.

THE POLITICS OF THE ABORTION
RIGHTS MOVEMENT

Transforming the Reproductive Rights Movement: The Post-Webster Agenda[1]

Marlene Gerber Fried

At 6 o'clock in the morning, January 13, 1990, dozens of pro-choice activists assembled at each of four abortion clinics in Boston. Our goal was to enable women seeking abortions to get inside. We knew anti-abortionists from Operation Rescue were going to blockade; we did not know where. By 8:00 a.m. their target was clear, and most of us were directed to that clinic where pro- and anti-forces shoved and chanted. Pro-choice demonstrators made a human chain reinforcing police barricades set up to create an access corridor. Police on the inside of the barricades had, in previous Operation Rescue assaults, permitted the anti-abortionists to effectively block clinic doors. We were there to prevent the Operation Rescue people from crawling under, going over, or breaking through the barricades, and we did whatever was necessary to keep the corridor open. This included pushing, kicking, and verbal abuse. Escorts pushed women through the hostile blockers to get them into the clinic. We were literally squeezed between the cops and the anti-abortionists. The "rescuers" were trying to break through our line. The role of the police was less clear.

Once again, we had won. Women had their abortions. Operation Rescue had been significantly outnumbered. We had demonstrated our commitment to women and our ability to mobilize the pro-choice majority. We had kept the clinic open. Yet I left five hours later profoundly disturbed both by the day's events, which have come to typify clinic defense, and by the response and politics of the pro-choice movement.

No matter how we try to control the clinic battles, we remain in a structurally defensive position. In the year and a half since Operation Rescue came to town, we have tried nearly everything—from holding a demonstration away from the clinics; to counter-demonstrating on the

other side of the street; to interposing our bodies between the anti-abortionists and the clinic. Our level of organization at the clinics is impres-
sive—a 3,000-person phone tree; hundreds of trained escorts and clinic
coordinators who communicate with beepers and special codes. Despite
all of this, it is not our show. Our efforts have been directed at figuring
out what they are doing and how to foil them. It is not surprising, then,
that even when we "win," it doesn't feel like victory. Most disturbing,
however, is the siege mentality at the clinics. It is painful to witness what
women must face in order to exercise their right to make reproductive
choices. Some women will not push their way through demonstrators to
get into a clinic. Some will not even come at all if they anticipate
harassment by anti-abortionists. It is painful even when the women are
undaunted by the harassment, even when they and we fight back: a
young man accompanying his girlfriend for an abortion escorts her to
the clinic wielding a baseball bat. He says to the anti-abortionists, "You
mess with her, you're in trouble." The girlfriend of a woman coming to
the clinic punches one of the blockaders who tries to stop her. It is painful
even when the effects are radicalizing—often women having abortions
become politically active after having had to confront anti-abortion
demonstrators. It is still disturbing and angering.

Is this "safe and legal" abortion? Is this what it means to defend a
woman's right to choose? I am not just angry. I am frightened by those
who participate in the "rescues." These anti-abortionists are fanatics, and
I don't use this word lightly. I have watched as they exorcised the clinic;
they are told that we are "Satanic." Is there any limit to what they would
do to stop us? I have watched as they become increasingly more violent.
I know that bombings of clinics are on the rise. When will one of them
have a gun? Maybe this morning? A man in Montreal just murdered 13
female college students because he is angry at feminists. How different
is this? If long-time abortion rights activists feel the fear, what about those
newer to the movement?

Despite the violence of some anti-abortionists, despite the fact that
they are breaking the law, despite the fact that we see them as threatened,
angry, scary people, they have made inroads into the public consciousness. They have helped create the climate in which legal abortion itself
is up for grabs. The Supreme Court is validating their views, not ours.

The point of all this is not just to air my frustrations, but to raise
questions which our movement must address. These questions are
crucial not just to the more narrow issue of Operation Rescue, but to
articulating our broader goals.

The pro-choice movement has followed strategies which I see as
barriers to these wider goals. In this article I will discuss the ones I see
as most problematic: framing the issue in terms of privacy and civil rights

rather than in terms of women's liberation and sexual freedom; shaping strategy and politics in accordance with the concerns of white middle-class women and ignoring the diverse needs of other groups of women; relying on those in power to create change rather than pursuing grass-roots empowerment strategies; and isolating abortion from other issues. I conclude by suggesting that the current crisis gives us the chance to tackle these strategic problems, to get back on the offensive, and to transform our movement.

The Anti-Abortion Offensive: Opposing Women's Liberation

Since 1973, when abortion was legalized through *Roe v. Wade*, the anti-abortion movement has worked to limit the ability of women to "choose" abortion. These efforts became part of a larger backlash which opposed gains made in the late 1960s and early 1970s by the women's liberation movement. Legalized abortion was fought for and won by that movement as part of a new and comprehensive vision of women's potential. In the 1970s and 1980s, abortion came to symbolize that vision as the New Right, driven by anti-feminism, made opposition to abortion the centerpiece of its own social and political program. The attack on abortion was part of an overall attack on women's freedom. This included a successful campaign to defeat the Equal Rights Amendment; efforts to constrain the rights of teenage girls through "Squeal Laws" which would force providers to notify parents if a minor sought contraception or a pregnancy test; the "Chastity Bill," which provided 30 million federal dollars to promote chastity among teens; gutting of affirmative action programs; and, most recently, efforts to control women's behavior during pregnancy by incarceration and other punitive measures.

In both the propaganda and policies of the Right, hostility to women's autonomy is the unifying link between opposition to abortion and opposition to other feminist goals. Abortion rights are central to and have come to symbolize women's control. The Right opposes that control in the broadest sense. That is why they oppose sex education, government-funded contraception and family planning clinics, gay rights, and government programs directed at the battering of women and children within their homes. But their fight against abortion is the most virulent, and they have made real gains.

Abortion Rights Eroded

The anti-abortion challenge has been serious and continuous at both the state and national levels. There has been a steady chipping away of the right to choose, both in its limited meaning of the legal right to abortion, and in its broader meaning, which encompasses a range of rights, all of which are necessary to support reproductive choices.

Abortion has become increasingly less accessible. Poor women, women of color, young women, and federal and state employees have borne the brunt of the limitations in access. The Hyde Amendment, first passed in 1976, prohibits federal Medicaid funding for abortions except in cases where the life of the pregnant woman is at risk. It was followed by campaigns in many states to prohibit state funding. Today only 13 states continue to fund abortions.

The 1989 Supreme Court *Webster* decision went beyond cutting off access to public funding by prohibiting abortions in public facilities and in private hospitals that receive public funds. In the late 1970s, the first laws were passed requiring parental consent/notification for minors seeking abortions. Today, 35 states have such laws. Restrictions on the abortion rights of young women continue to be in the forefront of the struggle both in the courts and in state legislatures.

Spousal consent has been resurrected again after having been declared unconstitutional in 1976. Increasingly, men—spouses, ex-spouses, boyfriends—have been seeking control over women's abortion decisions through the courts. In the wake of *Webster,* the Pennsylvania legislature passed a broadly restrictive law which contains a husband notification provision. Under threat of criminal penalties, women would have to sign statements that they had told their husbands of their abortion decision. This would then become part of the medical record. There is currently a federal court injunction against this and other provisions of the law, and a lawsuit is pending. It is not at all clear how the courts will rule on this. With a majority of all federal judges and almost half the Supreme Court Justices having been appointed by the Reagan/Bush administrations, we are learning we can no longer count on the courts to protect abortion rights.

Other legislation has been proposed in an effort to re-criminalize abortion: at the federal level, there have been many versions of a so-called Human Life Amendment which would constitutionally outlaw abortion. This has been an official strategy of the Republican Party since the late 1970s. (Although recently, seeing this as a political liability, even some conservative Republicans have begun to call it into question.) While initial efforts to pass an amendment have failed, it has not been abandoned and has also been pursued at the state level. In the wake of *Webster,* a state by state battle covering all ways of restricting and ultimately criminalizing abortion has already begun.

The anti-abortion movement has also used illegal and increasingly violent tactics. Picketing of clinics and harassment of clinic personnel have become routine. Cases of clinic bombings and arson have been steadily rising. Since 1987, Operation Rescue has pursued its strategy of blockading clinics in 165 cities. The stated goal of this strategy has been to shut down abortion clinics. While this goal has not been met, the "Rescue" demonstrations have succeeded in revitalizing the anti-abortion movement and in gaining press coverage. It is difficult to judge how successful they have been in intimidating clinic workers, women seeking abortions, and the general public. I think they have done some real damage. While there appears to be a groundswell of support for legal abortion, there also seems to be slippage. Polls on abortion are notoriously murky depending upon the way the question is asked, i.e., whether they have lumped together those who support a woman's right to abortion under all circumstances and those who support a more restricted right. The former is a much smaller category, and my sense is that the anti-abortionists have succeeded in shrinking it further as well as undermining the confidence of many supporters of choice. The notion that abortion is morally problematic is growing. Fear, intimidation, and difficulty surround the abortion issue. This climate made it possible for the Supreme Court Justices to retreat as far as they did from *Roe* to *Webster.*

Judicial protection for legalized abortion is now shaky at best. While the most recent Supreme Court decision, *Webster v. Reproductive Health Services,* claims to leave *Roe v. Wade* and the legal right to abortion intact, the restrictions it permits are wide-ranging. Further, the Court has made clear that it has not finished the job of circumscribing abortion rights. From the 7-2 decision in *Roe v. Wade* (1973), through the 5-4 *Thornburgh* decision narrowly re-affirming *Roe* (1986), to the 5-4 *Webster* decision for greater restrictions (1989), the trajectory is disturbingly clear.

This, then, is the context within which to look at the pro-choice movement.

Politics of the Pro-Choice Movement: On the Defensive

The abortion rights movement essentially folded after abortion became legal. While more radical segments of the movement mobilized in 1977 after the Hyde Amendment prohibited federal Medicaid funding of abortion, it was not until the threat of a constitutional amendment that would ban all U.S. abortions was posed in 1981 that a visible mainstream abortion rights movement re-emerged.

The 1980s movement formed as a reaction to the backlash, and was shaped by the need to respond to an all-out anti-choice campaign, one with initiatives in legislatures, in the courts, and in the streets. In an effort to hold the line, the new abortion rights movement rarely dared talk about abortion or women's rights, preferring instead to focus on the intolerance and extremism of the other side. The pro-choice movement attempted to sanitize its own demands. Insisting on abortion rights as a necessary condition of all women's sexual freedom continues to be seen as too threatening, too risky, too selfish. Instead, the movement turned to the more innocuous and ambiguous language of "choice" and "personal freedom." The women's movement fought to bring women's reproductive lives out of the private sphere, arguing that our personal choices were political. How ironic that the pro-choice movement now argues that abortion is private and personal, not political.

In trying to hold onto past gains, the pro-choice movement has failed to pursue new ones, either by solidifying its own membership or speaking out to the public. *Roe v. Wade* was not the first step of a feminist agenda for reproductive control; it turned out to be the *only* step, defended by appeals to the right to privacy—the importance of keeping the government out of our personal lives—and to religious tolerance.

Those activists who have argued for a radical reproductive rights approach have had to struggle simply to put abortion and women's lives back into the debate. There seems to be no place at all in the ideology of "choice" for public discussion of women's needs for autonomy and sexual freedom and for the societal changes that would make these possible.

This defensive posture is problematic in many ways. While the pro-choice movement must respond to the attacks on abortion and does not control the timing or place of the attacks, it *can* control the terms of the response. A defensive stance implies that we will settle for less. The decision to fight for choice rather than justice is itself a decision to appeal to those who already have choices. This keeps the visible movement primarily white and middle-class despite the fact that the abortion rights of poor women, of whom a disproportionate number are women of color, have been, and continue to be, the most vulnerable.

Abortion campaigns offer unprecedented opportunities for alliances between activists and groups fighting for the rights of poor women, yet many of these opportunities have been missed. The women's movement has a history of trading away the rights of women of color and working-class women in favor of gains for more privileged women. Because of this history, we must consciously and aggressively make clear that we are not about to repeat this pattern in the present or future. Steps must be taken to develop a multi-racial and class-conscious movement for abortion rights. One way to do this is to acknowledge the fact that poor women have consistently borne the brunt of the attack on abortion rights. For poor women, the legal right to abortion is empty, and choice an abstraction. Without access to abortion services, it is as if *Roe v. Wade* never happened. Until the *Webster* decision, the pro-choice movement had been weak in its defense of access. There was no broad pro-choice organizing and outcry in opposition to the Hyde Amendment, nor has there been a strong pro-choice voice for social welfare funding in general. Worse yet, our movement has shown a willingness to trade away the rights of poor women when it argues that abortion is cheaper than paying for the birth and upbringing of poor children or that abortion is necessary because there are already too many of "them."

The *Webster* decision did mark a turning point for the pro-choice movement. For the first time, mainstream pro-choice organizations put the abortion rights of poor women in the center of their agenda. This is because *Webster* made the link between access and legality frighteningly clear. In *Webster,* the Court simultaneously curtailed access to abortion for poor women and passed restrictions that will apply to all women seeking abortions. The Court made clear that legal abortion itself was not secure.

In the aftermath of *Webster,* fear of further losses is causing some mainstream pro-choice groups to continue the defensive posture that has characterized the pro-choice movement since *Roe v. Wade.* They argue that if we fail to compromise, we will lose everything. The political implications of this stance are already being felt.

In the absence of federal constitutional protections, and with anti-abortion offensives, many pro-choice organizations and individuals are proposing legislation to "safeguard" abortion rights. Massachusetts provides a clear example. The mainstream Coalition for Choice (the decision makers in this group are: Planned Parenthood, League of Women Voters, Religious Coalition for Abortion Rights, Civil Liberties Union of Massachusetts, Mass Choice, and NOW) is pursuing an amendment which protects a woman's choice only until the 24th week of pregnancy. The Coalition chose to pursue this option over legislation that would codify unrestricted abortion rights.

Supporters of this strategy are on the run. They insist on the need to draw on so-called "soft supporters," those who support abortion only under some circumstances. They see this as a way to defuse anti-abortion advocates who often target late abortions in their rhetoric and graphics. The question of viability is dominating the public debate, arising not just in the abortion arena, but in the area of reproductive technologies. (In 1989, a Tennessee judge ruled in favor of a woman suing for custody of frozen embryos on the grounds that these "babies" had a right to life.) Legal experts and professional pollsters say the restricted proposals are the only ones that can win right now.

While I understand the urgency individuals and groups feel about the need to protect some ground, this is a dangerous approach. It is a strategy that trades away the most basic aspect of abortion rights—the fact that abortion is fundamentally a woman's right to decide, at any point in pregnancy, for any reason. Going for what we think we can get right now helps to legitimize the view that there are morally acceptable and morally unacceptable abortions and that those decisions are best made by someone other than the pregnant women. Feminists need instead to be arguing for the right of every woman to make her own decision.

Anything less puts every abortion up for grabs. Further, it is a strategy which concedes the anti-abortionists' contention that the fetus ought to be the focus of legislative and constitutional protection. For years, the abortion rights movement has been trying to re-frame the political debate so that women's lives come first. We cannot afford to pull back now.

Legislation like that proposed in Massachusetts would immediately have adverse effects on the lives of women. Those who seek late abortions are usually women in desperate circumstances, living on the margins with few protections and many obstacles in their lives—youth, poverty, physical and mental disabilities. The anti-abortion movement has consistently pursued policies which target the most vulnerable women and segregate them from women with more "choices." The abortion rights movement must not do the same. Yes, it is true that there are very few third-trimester abortions. But this does not mean that protecting abortion rights throughout pregnancy is merely a symbolic fight. We need to advocate for the rights of *all* women, refusing to make any into bargaining chips.

The rush to compromise ignores, or doubts the power of, political education and organizing. It seems clear that while there is widespread support for legal abortion, there is not adequate support for women's right to abortion under all circumstances. Building support for this is one of our political tasks. The kind of compromise described above undermines our ability to do so. Instead, we need a political vision that moves people forward.

Abortion Is Not the Only Issue: The Trap of Single-Issue Politics

Many interpret the *Webster* loss as a failure of those who care about abortion rights to be as single-minded as their opponents. Vowing to correct this error, pro-choice activists are being encouraged, for example, to view abortion rights as the only basis on which to support electoral candidates.

Single-issue politics is not new in the abortion struggle. It has in fact been the politics of NARAL (National Abortion Rights Action League) and Planned Parenthood, mainstream groups which dominate the pro-choice movement. What is different is the claim that *Webster* vindicates the single-issue approach of the anti-abortion movement. The threat that we could totally lose the constitutional right to abortion is being used to argue for single-issue, pro-choice politics.

Should this argument be any more compelling now than at other times? I don't think so. My reading of the political losses we have suffered in this area is that abortion rights can neither be won nor preserved by themselves. For the most part, the struggle to defend abortion rights has been waged by a movement very different from that which won legal abortion in 1973. Unlike the broad women's liberation program, the pro-choice movement has been dedicated to a single issue: "choice" equated with legal abortion. In the face of the challenges to abortion rights, the pro-choice movement has narrowed the agenda. Doing so, however, has narrowed the movement's base of support and has alienated the very constituencies necessary to defend abortion rights. Those fighting for gay rights and against the cutbacks in social welfare programs and in education (to name just a few) cannot be expected to support an agenda that ignores their concerns.

The pro-choice movement is more vulnerable when abortion is isolated from other issues. While the pro-choice movement has contributed to its own isolation, it has also been made into something of a pariah by those who might have been allies. As progressive movements have been challenged, many decided to go it on their own, believing that linking issues to others would weaken the chances of winning anything. Abortion has been one of the main casualties of this mentality. It is an issue that other movements have sought to avoid.

At the same time, the anti-abortion movement has made links between abortion and sexual freedom, school prayer, crime, and many more issues, allowing them to create links to other right wing organizations. This has allowed the anti-abortion movement to challenge a broad range of reproductive freedoms. The Right has clearly understood the power of making these connections while our side avoids them and attempts to reduce reproductive choice to legal abortion.

The Politics of Defending Abortion Clinics

Differences over effective political strategies have divided the pro-choice movement. The need for grassroots education, mobilization, and direct action is something that, until very recently, the mainstream pro-choice movement thought unnecessary. Even now, the message from the mainstream leadership is that the real fight for abortion rights is in the electoral arena, in combatting *Webster*-type regulations and advancing pro-choice legislation, in electing pro-choice candidates, and in making abortion an issue in every election. Our movement has been consistently polarized not just in terms of ideology, but in strategy as well. At the same time, the anti-abortion movement has been gathering strength from direct action strategies and finding ways for diverse organizations to work together.

Without question, the *Webster* decision has mobilized pro-choice support. But activism was already intensifying in response to the Operation Rescue attacks on abortion clinics. The face-to-face confrontations at abortion clinics—escorting clients, counter-demonstrations, human chains to keep anti-abortionists out—have mobilized and radicalized the rank and file of the pro-choice movement.

The activists who are flocking to the movement are receptive to a more radical politics than those being offered by the mainstream organizations. This has both tactical and ideological implications. These clinic actions present some of the greatest challenges our movement faces. While passionately committed to reproductive choice, we are not fanatics. Our movement is not built on secrecy, menace, and threat. It is built on the affirmation of women's lives and choices. How many Saturday mornings in rain, cold, and snow will we have to stand in the streets outside clinics? Is this a viable tactic? How can we protect women's rights without acceding to and legitimizing repression by the police?

In many cities, activists find themselves caught among a variety of political tendencies. Abortion clinics are not political organizations although they have become the key political battlefield. Clinic workers have taken on heroic qualities, since going to work sometimes involves fighting one's way through an angry mob. Nonetheless, their stake in this is to continue providing services, some for profit, others not. There are many clinic directors who view pro-choice demonstrators in almost the same way they view anti-abortion militants—as disruptions to their business as usual. While clients and clinic escorts have been generally supportive of pro-choice demonstrators, we have been told repeatedly by some clinic directors that the safety and privacy of their patients and their ongoing ability to operate are compromised by direct confrontations with anti-abortionists.

These clinic directors prefer internal security and the police. They accept advice from the police about what to do to keep clinics open. Not surprisingly, the police reinforce the message that pro-choice people should stay away. At a meeting of clinic directors, pro-choice activists, town government, and police leaders in Brookline, Massachusetts, the police said they consider pro-choice people to be blockading and subject to arrest if laws are broken. Outraged as we were at this construction of the facts, they get to decide who gets arrested.

How can we stay away from the clinic confrontations, one of the most visible and direct challenges to our right to choose abortion? So much of the abortion debate has occurred in courtrooms and legislatures

remote from those of us most affected by the outcome. We ask supporters to call their legislators, to give money, to vote, to commemorate legal
abortion every January 22, to demonstrate for access to abortion on
October 3, etc. Yet all of these activities are quite removed from those
whose actions erode our rights. Does it make sense to ask us to go to
Washington but to remain distant when the threat is right here, just a
subway ride away? The prominence of the police is problematic for us
in other ways. We do want to keep the clinics open. We do want the
police to uphold the constitutional rights of women seeking abortion
services. We do not want to obstruct them in this task. Because the
anti-abortion strategy at the clinics is one of civil disobedience and arrest,
our own goals already involve us in some amount of cooperation with
the police. But how much? How do we avoid taking political direction
from them? Are we supporting police brutality of anti-abortionists?

What do we want the police to do? We are often frustrated at what
appears to us to be at best incompetence and at worst political favoritism
toward anti-abortionists. Abortion rights activists who are veterans of
civil disobedience marvel at the seemingly endless amount of time it
takes the police to remove/arrest anti-abortionists. Pro-choice activists
actually have had to get injunctions against Operation Rescue before the
police would even attempt to open clinics, so concerned were they to
protect the First Amendment rights of the blockaders. We can't help but
feel outraged that their rights carry greater weight than the rights of
women seeking abortions and the pro-choice demonstrators who come
to support them.

Finally, it is infuriating that keeping an abortion clinic open is seen
almost as a favor the police are performing, while clearing demonstrators
away from nuclear power plants is a civic duty.

What should we make of these feelings of anger and frustration?
What do we want? Some on our side cheer for the police while others
cringe—more identified with law breakers than with the "peacekeep-
ers." After all, most of our political lives have been devoted to challenging
the status quo, putting us in direct opposition to those whose job is to
preserve it. At one pole we have pro-choice organizations seeking
injunctions against anti-abortion demonstrators. At the other are activists
who do not see this as the most effective political tactic, and who
articulate a "no more nice girls" politics. They argue that we need to take
the gloves off to show that we are as serious about supporting women's
lives and rights as our opponents are about challenging them. The divide
here is not how much we loathe the anti-abortionists but how much
legitimacy we accord the police.

Many of those participating in ongoing clinic defense are discour-
aged by having to rely on the "legitimate authorities" to protect abortion

rights. The prominence of the police, while inevitable when the anti-choice tactics are ones of civil disobedience, is especially problematic for us. When abortion rights counter-demonstrators cheer the police, the ambiguity of our position becomes painfully clear. When clinics try to get injunctions against demonstrators to constrain their protest and attempt to use the RICO (Racketeering-Influenced and Corrupt Organizations Act) law to impose huge fines on protestors, the degree of complicity with the status quo is highly problematic.

We want to stop the anti-abortion movement, but using the very tactics which are so often used against progressive movements does not really bring satisfaction. Instead it makes us uneasy about the way the battle has been shaped. Counting on the police to keep the clinics open, counting on the courts to preserve abortion rights, counting on the medical establishment to provide abortion services make us complicit with an oppressive system, a system which should be challenged, not relied upon.

Political Implications: Transforming the Movement

I have been raising questions about the strategies and politics of the pro-choice movement. I want to turn now to the possibilities for change within our own movement. Can we defend abortion rights without becoming a defensive movement—one that settles for less out of fear of losing more? Can we go from a movement focused primarily on the narrow right of legal abortion to a movement for reproductive freedom? Can we become an inclusive movement whose politics and leadership reflect the diversity of women's lives and needs?

The current political scene provides many opportunities for the pro-choice movement to link abortion to other reproductive rights issues. The attack on abortion is part of a larger attack on sexual freedom. The effort to curtail abortion rights, like the effort to manipulate fears about AIDS, is an attempt to suppress sexual freedom. The *Webster* decision links defense of abortion rights to defense of public health care and facilities and to the struggle for economic justice. As in the *McRae* case (1981, the Supreme Court upheld the Hyde Amendment) the Court has made painfully obvious that poor women will bear the brunt of erosions in abortion rights. In the past, however, the pro-choice movement has failed to connect the defense of abortion rights to the struggle for better health care and economic conditions of poor women and women of color. Is it possible now to orient the politics of the pro-choice movement in this direction? I think so.

Women of color, poor women, gay men and lesbians, union activists, and civil rights activists have all participated in the struggle for reproductive rights. The amicus brief for *Webster* had broad support from groups representing many diverse constituencies.

In April 1989, a group of about 150 grassroots activists from all over the country, a majority of whom were women of color, came to a conference in Washington, D.C. called "In Defense of Roe." The messages from that meeting were significant and clear: women of color are participating in the struggle for reproductive rights; women of color are prepared to take the leadership in the struggle for abortion rights so long as that struggle is not separated from other aspects of reproductive freedom. The struggle must be seen to be about women's survival in all of its breadth.

This means having a wider vision of women's reproductive, social, and economic needs, reflecting that vision in policies and practices, and sharing financial and organizational resources. We must also challenge our assumptions about who is and can be active around reproductive rights. For white women, this implies challenging a self-image as "the leaders" in the movement. As currently organized, the movement does not speak for all women nor does its leadership reflect broader commitments.

The abortion rights movement is coming together in an effort to re-focus the debate so that women's lives become the central issue. In doing so, more radical demands are emerging. Women are calling for not only the right to choose among existing options, but are questioning why they lack the power to create the options themselves. There is a re-awakening of interest in women-controlled health care and abortion. There is a call for women to control the development and distribution of abortifacient drugs like RU-486. Women are saying they will take on the task of keeping the clinics open regardless of the legal status of abortion. Millions of women seem prepared not only to have abortions even if abortion is criminalized, but to publicly announce their intentions to do so.

Civil disobedience and other forms of direct action are being widely discussed. The refusal to allow abortion to go underground in the way that it was pre-*Roe* is striking. The women's movement has permanently changed the consciousness of many women. Young women feel entitled to abortion rights, birth control, jobs, and other aspects of equality. And now they seem prepared to fight to secure these rights.

This is a time for our movement to be aggressive. On this and other political and strategic questions, the issue of leadership is a crucial one. While mainstream groups are somewhat divided on all of these points, their membership and leadership remain predominantly white and middle-class. This is also true of more radical, local, grassroots reproductive rights groups and left-wing groups active on the issue. While it may be tempting to move at once to rebuild national Left-feminist networks, which were dominated by white women, these efforts will fail if they do not insure women of color equal partnership in the movement.

Reproductive rights activists need to engage in a dialogue so we can set a post-*Webster* agenda to take us beyond where we have ever been. The need to deepen understandings of choice and reproductive rights is as acute within the pro-choice movement as outside of it. Political development has been one of the casualties of the need to constantly defend the bottom line. We have seen the fragility not only of our court-granted rights, but of public consciousness. Even as pro-choice electoral support is booming, the climate is shaky because it is taken as a given that abortion is a necessary *evil*, morally problematic, something to be avoided. This way of thinking is common not just among our enemies, but also among our friends.

This book was conceived in the period when the *Webster* decision was pending. At that point, both the threats and the possibilities were clear. We are now in the earliest phases of the post-*Webster* period. Pollsters, politicians, and pundits on all sides of the abortion issue are still vacillating about who has won this round. The only clear agreement is about the inadvertent boost given to the pro-choice movement and the momentum it has gained.

While I have been focusing on problematic areas of the abortion rights struggle, I am also excited by the possibilities. Grassroots activists can take heart from the emergent radical tendencies and re-focus the struggle for abortion rights on women's lives and needs, incorporating a broad definition of what it takes for all women to be able to make uncoerced reproductive decisions. The abortion rights movement will grow stronger through this effort. And in this process, the women's movement as a whole will become a more unified, powerful force for all women's liberation.

Notes

1. Thanks to Liz Hill, Shelly Mains, and Hilary Roberts. Many of my ideas were developed through discussions with them and work on co-authored pieces.

Racism, Birth Control, and Reproductive Rights[1]

Angela Davis

When nineteenth-century feminists raised the demand for "voluntary motherhood," the campaign for birth control was born. Its proponents were called radicals and they were subjected to the same mockery as had befallen the initial advocates of woman suffrage. "Voluntary motherhood" was considered audacious, outrageous, and outlandish by those who insisted that wives had no right to refuse their husbands' sexual urges. Eventually, of course, the right to birth control, like women's right to vote, would be more or less taken for granted by U.S. public opinion. Yet in 1970, a full century later, the call for legal and easily accessible abortions was no less controversial than the issue of "voluntary motherhood" which had originally launched the birth control movement of the United States.

Birth control—individual choice, safe contraceptive methods, as well as abortions when necessary—is a fundamental prerequisite for the emancipation of women. Since the right of birth control is obviously advantageous to women of all classes and races, it would appear that even vastly dissimilar women's groups would have attempted to unite around this issue. In reality, however, the birth control movement has seldom succeeded in uniting women of different social backgrounds, and rarely have the movement's leaders popularized the genuine concerns of working-class women. Moreover, arguments advanced by birth control advocates have sometimes been based on blatantly racist premises. The progressive potential of birth control remains indisputable. But in actuality, the historical record of this movement leaves much to be desired in the realm of challenges to racism and class exploitation.

The most important victory of the contemporary birth control movement was won during the early 1970s when abortions were at last declared legal. Having emerged during the infancy of the new women's liberation movement, the struggle to legalize abortions incorporated all

15

the enthusiasm and the militancy of the young movement. By January 1973, the abortion rights campaign had reached a triumphant culmination. In *Roe v. Wade* (410 U.S.) and *Doe v. Bolton* (410 U.S.), the U.S. Supreme Court ruled that a woman's right to personal privacy implied her right to decide whether or not to have an abortion.

The ranks of the abortion rights campaign did not include substantial numbers of women of color. Given the racial composition of the larger women's liberation movement, this was not at all surprising. When questions were raised about the absence of racially oppressed women in both the larger movement and in the abortion rights campaign, two explanations were commonly proposed in the discussions and literature of the period: women of color were overburdened by their people's fight against racism, and/or they had not yet become conscious of the centrality of sexism. But the real meaning of the almost lily-white complexion of the abortion rights campaign was not to be found in ostensibly myopic or underdeveloped consciousness among women of color. The truth lay buried in the ideological underpinnings of the birth control movement itself.

The failure of the abortion rights campaign to conduct a historical self-evaluation led to a dangerously superficial appraisal of Black people's suspicious attitudes toward birth control in general. Granted, when some Black people unhesitatingly equated birth control with genocide, it did appear to be an exaggerated—even paranoiac—reaction. Yet white abortion rights activists missed a profound message, for underlying these cries of genocide were important clues about the history of the birth control movement. This movement, for example, had been known to advocate involuntary sterilization—a racist form of mass "birth control." If ever women would enjoy the right to plan their pregnancies, legal and easily accessible birth control measures and abortions would have to be complemented by an end to sterilization abuse.

As for the abortion rights campaign itself, how could women of color fail to grasp its urgency? They were far more familiar than their white sisters with the murderously clumsy scalpels of inept abortionists seeking profit in illegality. In New York, for instance, during the several years preceding the decriminalization of abortions in that state, some 80 percent of the deaths caused by illegal abortions involved Black and Puerto Rican women.[2] Immediately afterward, women of color received close to half of all the legal abortions. If the abortion rights campaign of the early 1970s needed to be reminded that women of color wanted desperately to escape the back-room quack abortionists, they should also have realized that these same women were not about to express pro-abortion sentiments. They were in favor of *abortion rights,* which did not mean that they were proponents of abortion. When Black and Latina women resort to abortions in such large numbers, the stories they tell are not so much about the desire to be free of their pregnancy, but rather about the miserable social conditions which dissuade them from bringing new lives into the world.

Black women have been aborting themselves since the earliest days of slavery. Many slave women refused to bring children into a world of interminable forced labor, where chains and floggings and sexual abuse for women were the everyday conditions of life. A doctor practicing in Georgia around the middle of the last century noticed that abortions and miscarriages were far more common among his slave patients than among the white women he treated.

***

Why were self-imposed abortions and reluctant acts of infanticide such common occurrences during slavery? Not because Black women had discovered solutions to their predicament, but rather because they were desperate. Abortions and infanticides were acts of desperation, motivated not by the biological birth process but by the oppressive conditions of slavery. Most of these women, no doubt, would have expressed their deepest resentment had someone hailed their abortions as a stepping stone toward freedom.

During the early abortion rights campaign, it was too frequently assumed that legal abortions provided a viable alternative to the myriad problems posed by poverty. As if having fewer children could create more jobs, higher wages, better schools, etc. This assumption reflected the tendency to blur the distinction between *abortion rights* and the general advocacy of *abortions*. The campaign often failed to provide a voice for women who wanted the *right* to legal abortions while deploring the social conditions that prohibited them from bearing more children.

The renewed offensive against abortion rights that erupted during the latter half of the 1970s has made it absolutely necessary to focus more sharply on the needs of poor and racially oppressed women. By 1977, the passage of the Hyde Amendment in Congress had mandated the withdrawal of federal funding for abortions, causing many state legislatures to follow suit. Black, Puerto Rican, Chicana, and Native American Indian women, together with their impoverished white sisters, were thus effectively divested of the right to legal abortions. Since surgical sterilizations, funded by the Department of Health, Education and Welfare [now the Department of Health and Human Services], remained free on demand, more and more poor women have been forced to opt for permanent infertility. What is urgently required is a broad campaign to defend the reproductive rights of all women—and especially those women whose economic circumstances often compel them to relinquish the right to reproduction itself.

***

While women have probably always dreamed of infallible methods of birth control, it was not until the issue of women's rights in general became the focus of an organized movement that reproductive rights could emerge as a legitimate demand. In an essay entitled "Marriage," written during the 1850s, Sarah Grimke argued for a "...right on the part of woman to decide *when* she shall become a mother, how often and under what circumstances."

***

Sarah Grimke advocated women's right to sexual abstinence.

***

The notion that women could refuse to submit to their husbands' sexual demands eventually became the central idea of the call for "voluntary motherhood." By the 1870s, when the woman suffrage movement had reached its peak, feminists were publicly advocating voluntary motherhood.

***

It was not a coincidence that women's consciousness of their reproductive rights was born within the organized movement for women's political equality. Indeed, if women remained forever burdened by incessant childbirths and frequent miscarriages, they would hardly be able to exercise the political rights they might win. Moreover, women's new dreams of pursuing careers and other paths of self-development outside marriage and motherhood could only be realized if they could limit and plan their pregnancies. In this sense, the slogan "voluntary motherhood" contained a new and genuinely progressive vision of womanhood. At the same time, however, this vision was rigidly bound to the lifestyle enjoyed by the middle classes and the bourgeoisie. The aspirations underlying the demand for "voluntary motherhood" did not reflect the conditions of working-class women, engaged as they were in a far more fundamental fight for economic survival. Since this first call for birth control was associated with goals which could only be achieved by women possessing material wealth, vast numbers of poor and working-class women would find it rather difficult to identify with the embryonic birth control movement.

Toward the end of the 19th century the white birth rate in the United States suffered a significant decline. Since no contraceptive innovations had been publicly introduced, the drop in the birth rate implied that women were substantially curtailing their sexual activity. By 1890, the typical native-born white woman was bearing no more than four children.[4] Since U.S. society was becoming increasingly urban, this new birth pattern should not have been a surprise. While farm life demanded large families, they became dysfunctional within the context of city life. Yet this phenomenon was publicly interpreted in a racist and anti-working-class fashion by the ideologues of rising monopoly capitalism. Since native-born white women were bearing fewer children, the specter of "race suicide" was raised in official circles.

In 1905, President Theodore Roosevelt concluded his Lincoln Day Dinner speech with the proclamation that "race purity must be maintained."[5] By 1906, he blatantly equated the falling birth rate among native-born whites with the impending threat of "race suicide." In his State of the Union message that year, Roosevelt admonished the well-born white women who engaged in "willful sterility—the one sin for which the penalty is national death, race suicide."[6] These comments were made during a period of accelerating racist ideology and of great waves of race riots and lynchings on the domestic scene.

***

How did the birth control movement respond to Roosevelt's accusation that their cause was promoting race suicide? The President's propagandistic ploy was a failure, according to a leading historian of the birth control movement, for, ironically, it led to greater support for its advocates. Yet, as Linda Gordon maintains, this controversy "...also brought to the forefront those issues that most separated feminists from the working class and the poor."[7]

> This happened in two ways. First, the feminists were increasingly emphasizing birth control as a route to careers and higher education—goals out of reach of the poor with or without birth control. In the context of the whole feminist movement, the race-suicide episode was an additional factor identifying feminism almost exclusively with the aspirations of the more privileged women of the society. Second, the pro-birth control feminists began to popularize the idea that poor people had a moral obligation to restrict the size of their families, because large families create a drain on the taxes and charity expenditures of the wealthy and because poor children were less likely to be "superior."[8]

The acceptance of the race-suicide thesis, to a greater or lesser extent, by women such as Julia Ward Howe and Ida Husted Harper reflected the suffrage movement's capitulation to the racist posture of Southern women. If the suffragists acquiesced to arguments invoking the extension of the ballot to women as the saving grace of white supremacy, then birth control advocates either acquiesced to or supported the new arguments invoking birth control as a means of preventing the proliferation of the "lower classes" and as an antidote to race suicide. Race suicide could be prevented by the introduction of birth control among Black people, immigrants, and the poor in general. In this way, the prosperous whites of solid Yankee stock could maintain their superior numbers within the population. Thus class bias and racism crept into the birth control movement when it was still in its infancy. More and more, it was assumed within birth control circles that poor women, Black and immigrant alike, had a "moral obligation to restrict the size of their families."[9] What was demanded as a "right" for the privileged came to be interpreted as a "duty" for the poor.

***

During the first decades of the 20th century, the rising popularity of the eugenics movement was hardly a fortuitous development. Eugenic ideas were perfectly suited to the ideological needs of the young monopoly capitalists. Imperialist incursions in Latin America and in the Pacific needed to be justified, as did the intensified exploitation of Black workers in the South and immigrant workers in the North and West. The pseudo-scientific racial theories associated with the eugenics campaign furnished dramatic apologies for the conduct of the young monopolies. As a result, this movement won the unhesitating support of such leading capitalists as the Carnegies, the Harrimans, and the Kelloggs.[10]

By 1919, the eugenic influence on the birth control movement was unmistakably clear. In an article published by Margaret Sanger in the American Birth Control League's journal, she defined "the chief issue of birth control" as "more children from the fit, less from the unfit."[11] Around this time the American Birth Control League (ABCL) heartily welcomed the author of *The Rising Tide of Color Against White World Supremacy* into its inner sanctum.[12] Lothrop Stoddard, Harvard professor and theoretician of the eugenics movement, was offered a seat on the ABCL board of directors. In the pages of the ABCL's journal, articles by Guy Irving Birch, director of the American Eugenics Society, began to appear. Birch advocated birth control as a weapon to

> ...prevent the American people from being replaced by alien or Negro stock, whether it be by immigration or by overly high birth rates among others in this country.[13]

By 1932, the Eugenics Society could boast that at least 26 states had passed compulsory sterilization laws and that thousands of "unfit" persons had already been surgically prevented from reproducing.[14] Margaret Sanger offered her public approval of this development. "Morons, mental defectives, epileptics, illiterates, paupers, unemployables, criminals, prostitutes and dope fiends" ought to be surgically sterilized, she argued in a radio talk.[15] She did not wish to be so intransigent as to leave them with no choice in the matter; if they wished, she said, they should be able to choose a lifelong segregated existence in labor camps.

Within the ABCL, the call for birth control among Black people acquired the same racist edge as the call for compulsory sterilization. In 1939, its successor, the Birth Control Federation of America, planned a "Negro Project." In the Federation's words,

> [t]he mass of Negroes, particularly in the South, still breed carelessly and disastrously, with the result that the increase among Negroes, even more than among whites, is from that portion of the population least fit, and least able to rear children properly.[16]

Calling for the recruitment of Black ministers to lead local birth control committees, the Federation's proposal suggested that Black people should be rendered as vulnerable as possible to their birth control propaganda. "We do not want word to get out," wrote Margaret Sanger in a letter to a colleague,

> that we want to exterminate the Negro population and the minister is the man who can straighten out that idea if it ever occurs to any of their more rebellious members.[17]

This episode in the birth control movement confirmed the ideological victory of the racism associated with eugenic ideas. It had been robbed of its progressive potential, advocating for people of color not the individual right to *birth control,* but rather the racist strategy of *population control.* The birth control campaign would be called upon to serve in an essential capacity in the execution of the U.S. government's imperialist and racist population policy.

The abortion rights activists of the early 1970s should have examined the history of their movement. Had they done so, they might have understood why so many of their Black sisters adopted a posture of suspicion toward their cause. They might have understood how important it was to undo the racist deeds of their predecessors, who had advocated birth control as well as compulsory sterilization as a means of eliminating the "unfit" sectors of the population. Consequently, the young white feminists might have been more receptive to the suggestion that their campaign for abortion rights include a vigorous condemnation of sterilization abuse, which had become more widespread than ever.

It was not until the media decided that the casual sterilization of two Black girls in Montgomery, Alabama, was a scandal worth reporting that the Pandora's box of sterilization abuse was finally flung open. But by the time the case of the Relf sisters broke, it was practically too late to influence the politics of the abortion rights movement. It was the summer of 1973 and the Supreme Court decision legalizing abortions had already been announced in January. Nevertheless, the urgent need for mass opposition to sterilization abuse became tragically clear. The facts surrounding the Relf sisters' story were horrifying simple. Minnie Lee, who was 12 years old, and Mary Alice, who was 14, had been unsuspectingly carted into an operating room, where surgeons irrevocably robbed them of their capacity to bear children.[18] The surgery had been ordered by the HEW-funded Montgomery Community Action Committee after it was discovered that Depo-Provera, a drug previously administered to the girls as a birth prevention measure, caused cancer in test animals.[19]

After the Southern Poverty Law Center filed suit on behalf of the Relf sisters, the girls' mother revealed that she had unknowingly "consented" to the operation, having been deceived by the social workers who handled her daughters' case. They had asked Mrs. Relf, who was unable to read, to put her "X" on a document, the contents of which were not described to her. She assumed, she said, that it authorized the continued Depo-Provera injections. As she subsequently learned, she had authorized the surgical sterilization of her daughters.[20]

In the aftermath of publicity exposing the Relf sisters' case, similar episodes were brought to light. In Montgomery alone, 11 girls, also in their teens, had been similarly sterilized. HEW-funded birth control clinics in other states, as it turned out, had also subjected young girls to sterilization abuse. Moreover, individual women came forth with equally outrageous stories. Nial Ruth Cox, for example, filed suit against the state of North Carolina. At the age of 18—eight years before her suit—officials had threatened to discontinue her family's welfare payments if she refused to submit to surgical sterilization.[21] Before she assented to the operation, she was assured that her infertility would be temporary.[22]

Nial Ruth Cox's lawsuit was aimed at a state which had diligently practiced the theory of eugenics. Under the auspices of the Eugenics Commission of North Carolina, so it was learned, 7,686 sterilizations had been carried out since 1933. Although the operations were justified as measures to prevent the reproduction of "mentally deficient persons," about 5,000 of the sterilized persons had been Black.[23] According to Brenda Feigen Fasteau, the ACLU attorney representing Nial Ruth Cox, North Carolina's recent record was not much better.

> As far as I can determine, the statistics reveal that since 1964, approximately 65 percent of the women sterilized in North Carolina were Black and approximately 35 percent were white.[24]

As the flurry of publicity exposing sterilization abuse revealed, the neighboring state of South Carolina had been the site of further atrocities.

Eighteen women from Aiken, South Carolina, charged that they had been sterilized by a Dr. Clovis Pierce during the early 1970s. The sole obstetrician in that small town, Pierce had consistently sterilized Medicaid recipients with two or more children. According to a nurse in his office, Dr. Pierce insisted that pregnant welfare women "will have to submit [sic] to voluntary sterilization" if they wanted him to deliver their babies.[25] While he was "...tired of people running around and having babies and paying for them with my taxes,"[26] Dr. Pierce received some $60,000 in taxpayers' money for the sterilizations he performed. During his trial he was supported by the South Carolina Medical Association, whose members declared that doctors "...have a moral and legal right to insist on sterilization permission before accepting a patient, if it is done on the initial visit."[27]

Revelations of sterilization abuse during that time exposed the complicity of the federal government. At first the Department of Health, Education and Welfare claimed that approximately 16,000 women and 8,000 men had been sterilized in 1972 under the auspices of federal programs.[28] Later, however, these figures underwent a drastic revision. Carl Shultz, director of HEW's Population Affairs Office, estimated that between 100,000 and 200,000 sterilizations had actually been funded that year by the federal government.[29] During Hitler's Germany, incidentally, 250,000 sterilizations were carried out under the Nazis' Hereditary Health Law.[30] Is it possible that the record of the Nazis, through the years of their reign, may have been almost equaled by U.S. government-funded sterilizations in the space of a single year?

Given the historical genocide inflicted on the native population of the United States, one would assume that Native American Indians would be exempted from the government's sterilization campaign. But according to Dr. Connie Uri's testimony in a Senate committee hearing, by 1976 some 24 percent of all Indian women of childbearing age had been sterilized.[31] "Our blood lines are being stopped," the Choctaw physician told the Senate committee, "Our unborn will not be born...This is genocidal to our people."[32] According to Dr. Uri, the Indian Health Services Hospital in Claremore, Oklahoma, had been sterilizing one out of every four women giving birth in that federal facility.[33]

***

The domestic population policy of the U.S. government has an undeniably racist edge. Native American, Chicana, Puerto Rican and Black women continue to be sterilized in disproportionate numbers. According to a national fertility study conducted in 1970 by Princeton University's Office of Population Control, 20 percent of all married Black women have been permanently sterilized.[34] Approximately the same percentage of Chicanas have been rendered surgically infertile.[35] Moreover, 43 percent of the women sterilized through federally subsidized programs were Black.[36]

The astonishing number of Puerto Rican women who have been sterilized reflects a special government policy that can be traced back to 1939. In that year President Roosevelt's Interdepartmental Committee on Puerto Rico issued a statement attributing the island's economic problems to the phenomenon of overpopulation.[37] This committee proposed that efforts be undertaken to reduce the birth rate to no more than the level of the death rate.[38] Soon afterward, an experimental sterilization campaign was undertaken in Puerto Rico. Although the Catholic Church initially opposed this experiment and forced the cessation of the program in 1946, it was converted during the early 1950s to the teachings and practice of population control.[39] In this period, over 150 birth control clinics were opened, resulting in a 20 percent decline in population growth by the mid-1960s.[40] By the 1970s, over 35 percent of all Puerto Rican women of childbearing age had been surgically sterilized.[41]

***

The prevalence of sterilization abuse during the latter 1970s may be greater than ever before. Although the Department of Health, Education and Welfare issued guidelines in 1974, which were ostensibly designed to prevent involuntary sterilizations, the situation has nonetheless deteriorated. When the American Civil Liberties Union's Reproductive Freedom Project conducted a survey of teaching hospitals in 1975, it discovered that 40 percent of those institutions were not even aware of the regulations issued by HEW.[42] Only 30 percent of the hospitals examined by the ACLU were even attempting to comply with the guidelines.[43]

The 1977 Hyde Amendment added yet another dimension to coercive sterilization practices. As a result of this law passed by Congress, federal funds for abortions were eliminated in all cases but those involving rape and the risk of death or severe illness. According to Sandra Salazar of the California Department of Public Health, the first victim of the Hyde Amendment was a 27-year-old Chicana woman from Texas. She died as a result of an illegal abortion in Mexico shortly after Texas discontinued government-funded abortions. There have been many more victims—women for whom sterilization has become the only alternative to the abortions, which are currently beyond their reach. Sterilizations continue to be federally funded and free, to poor women, on demand.

Over the last decade the struggle against sterilization abuse has been waged primarily by Puerto Rican, Black, Chicana and Native American women. Their cause has not yet been embraced by the women's movement as a whole. Within organizations representing the interests of middle-class white women, there has been a certain reluctance to support the demands of the campaign against sterilization abuse, for these women are often denied their individual rights to be sterilized when they desire to take this step. While women of color are urged, at every turn, to become permanently infertile, white women enjoying prosperous economic conditions are urged, by the same forces, to reproduce themselves. They therefore sometimes consider the "waiting period" and other details of the demand for "informed consent" to sterilization as further inconveniences for women like themselves. Yet whatever the inconveniences for white middle-class women, a fundamental reproductive right of racially oppressed and poor women is at stake. Sterilization abuse must be ended.

Notes

1. This article is excerpted from Angela Y. Davis, *Women, Race, & Class*, Chapter 12, (New York: Random House, 1981). Reprinted by permission.

2. Edwin M. Gold *et al.*, "Therapeutic Abortions in New York City: A Twenty-Year Review," *American Journal of Public Health*, Vol. LV (July, 1965), pp. 964-972. Quoted in Lucinda Cisler, "Unfinished Business: Birth Control and Women's Liberation," in Robin Morgan, ed., *Sisterhood Is Powerful: An Anthology of Writings From the Women's Liberation Movement* (New York: Vintage Books, 1970), p. 261. Also quoted in Robert Staples, *The Black Woman in America* (Chicago: Nelson Hall, 1974), p. 146.

3. Gerda Lerner, *The Female Experience: An American Documentary* (Indianapolis: Bobbs-Merrill, 1977), p. 91.

4. Mary P. Ryan, *Womanhood in America from Colonial Times to the Present* (New York: Franklin Watts, Inc., 1975), p. 162.

5. Melvin Steinfeld, *Our Racist Presidents* (San Ramon, California: Consensus Publishers, 1972), p. 212.

6. Bonnie Mass, *Population Target: The Political Economy of Population Control in Latin America* (Toronto, Canada: Women's Educational Press, 1977), p. 20.

7. Linda Gordon, *Woman's Body, Woman's Right: A Social History of Birth Control in America* (New York: Penguin Books, 1976), p. 157.

8. *Ibid.*, p. 158.

9. *Ibid.*

10. Mass, *op. cit.*, p. 20.

11. Gordon, *op. cit.*, p. 281.

12. Mass, *op. cit.*, p. 20.

13. Gordon, *op. cit.*, p. 283.

14. Herbert Aptheker, "Sterilization, Experimentation and Imperialism," *Political Affairs*, Vol. LIII, No. 1 (January, 1974), p. 44.

15. Gena Corea, *The Hidden Malpractice* (New York: A Jove/HBJ Book, 1977), p. 149.

16. Gordon, *op. cit.*, p. 332.

17. *Ibid.*, pp. 332-333.

18. Aptheker, "Sterilization," p. 38. See also Anne Braden, "Forced Sterilization: Now Women Can Fight Back," *Southern Patriot*, September, 1973.

19. *Ibid.*

20. Jack Slater, "Sterilization, Newest Threat to the Poor," *Ebony,* Vol. XXVIII, No. 12 (October, 1973), p. 150.

21. Braden, *op. cit.*

22. Les Payne, "Forced Sterilization for the Poor?" *San Francisco Chronicle,* February 26, 1974.

23. Harold X., "Forced Sterilization Pervades South," *Muhammed Speaks,* October 10, 1975.

24. Slater, *op. cit.*

25. Payne, *op. cit.*

26. *Ibid.*

27. *Ibid.*

28. Aptheker, "Sterilization," p. 40.

29. Payne, *op. cit.*

30. Aptheker, "Sterilization," p. 48.

31. Arlene Eisen, "They're Trying to Take Our Future—Native American Women and Sterilization," *The Guardian,* March 23, 1972.

32. *Ibid.*

33. *Ibid.*

34. Quoted in a pamphlet issued by the Committee to End Sterilization Abuse, Box A244, Cooper Station, New York 10003.

35. *Ibid.*

36. *Ibid.*

37. Gordon, *op. cit.,* p. 338.

38. *Ibid.*

39. Mass, *op. cit.,* p. 92.

40. *Ibid.,* p. 91.

41. Gordon, *op. cit.,* p. 401. See also pamphlet issued by the Committee to End Sterilization Abuse.

42. Rahemah Aman, "Forced Sterilization," *Union Wage,* March 4, 1978.

43. *Ibid.*

From Privacy to Autonomy: The Conditions for Sexual and Reproductive Freedom[1]

Rhonda Copelon

Thus, "not with a bang, but a whimper," the plurality discards a landmark case of the last generation, and casts into darkness the hopes and visions of every woman in this country who had come to believe that the Constitution guaranteed her the right to exercise some control over her unique ability to bear children...For today, at least, the law of abortion stands undisturbed. For today, the women of this Nation still retain the liberty to control their destinies. But the signs are evident and very ominous, and a chill wind blows.

—*Justice Harry Blackmun, dissenting,*
Webster v. Reproductive Health Services, *July 3, 1989.*[2]

Recognition by the Supreme Court in *Roe v. Wade*[3] that women have a qualified right to abortion has fueled a controversy that remains dangerously unresolved. At the center is the question of whether women are entitled to be self-determining, for to be denied control over reproduction or sexuality is to be denied full personhood and reduced to dependence. The explosive response to *Roe* attests to the deeply radical nature of the demand, first by feminists and then by lesbians and gays, for a power so fundamental in our traditional liberal constitutional scheme as control over one's body.

As Justice Blackmun warned in *Webster v. Reproductive Health Services,* the new majority on the Supreme Court is chillingly hostile to ceding this power, for its denial is a cornerstone of patriarchal power whether expressed in the enslavement of African-American people, the reproductive servitude of women, or the denial to gays and lesbians of the right to love. Given the need to stave off further erosion in the Supreme Court as well as to secure these fundamental rights in Congress and state courts and legislatures throughout the country, it is important that we understand the limitations of the rights heretofore recognized by the Court, in this case the right of privacy. At the same time as we applaud the progressive impact and symbolism of the Court's recognition of a right to abortion, it is also essential to recognize its weaknesses. Against the backdrop of a brief history of the attacks on the privacy right and a brief summary of the Court's recent decisions in *Hardwick* and *Webster,* this article examines both the negative character and the positive potential of the privacy right.

My hope for this next phase of the movement for procreative and sexual rights is that we will not limit ourselves simply to winning back what we have lost, but rather set our sights to win what we need: recognition of an affirmative right of self-determination, one rooted in equality and societal responsibility. This requires not simply the protection of choice but the provision of the material and social conditions that render choice a meaningful right rather than a mere privilege. It is essential that we recognize the inextricable interrelationship between reproductive and sexual decision making and the broader demand for equality. In a world riddled by racism, sexism, homophobia, poverty, and exploitation, choice cannot be fully free.

Dismantling the Privacy Right

Since 1973 the Court's decision in *Roe v. Wade* has survived numerous assaults. For about a decade following the 1973 decision, the "fetal personhood" campaign, spearheaded by the Catholic Church and later joined by Protestant New Right fundamentalists, held center stage.[4]

Right-to-life advocates argue for the subservience of woman to the fetus, pitting images of innocent and helpless souls against those of selfish, unnatural, and murderous femininity.[5] Their goal is not simply to save fetuses but to return woman to her "proper place"—to assure that motherhood remains her primary preoccupation. Their campaign has had some terrible successes in the Court, particularly in the decisions in *Harris v. McRae,* permitting legislatures to deny abortion funding to poor women[6] and *Baird v. Bellotti,* predicating a teenage girl's rights on parental approval or a judicial shaming ceremony.[7] In 1983, however, a number of fetal rights efforts initiated at the outset of the Reagan administration to nullify or at least challenge the constitutional foundations of *Roe* were defeated in Congress.[8] At the same time, the Court rejected the Reagan administration's effort to have the Court water down *Roe,* although its position was substantially adopted by Justice Sandra Day O'Connor in her dissenting opinion.[9]

Despite the defeat of these efforts to overrule *Roe v. Wade* at the federal level, the opposition persisted and had sufficient political clout to obtain repeated endorsements in the Republican platform of a human life amendment. The Reagan Presidency provided the mechanism for the ultimate attack on *Roe v. Wade*—the appointment of over one-half of the federal judiciary and almost one-half of the Justices of the Supreme Court who were chosen because of their allegiance to the overruling of *Roe* and the dismantling of the modern right of privacy, as well as most of the rights protected by the Bill of Rights.

The Reagan administration cloaked its right wing agenda in the argument that the Court had no power to protect rights not articulated in the text of the Constitution or intended by the framers. While parading as the "jurisprudence of original intent," the practical implications of resuscitating the framers' intent as the measure of the Constitution explain its popularity on the Right. When the "founding fathers" are sacralized as the fount of wisdom, we are not reminded that they lived in a thoroughly patriarchal society, preserved slavery in the Constitution, and mocked the idea of the vote for women. Even the Radical Republicans who framed the principle of equality after the Civil War did not envision school desegregation or the equality of women. In contrast to the originalist school, defenders of the modern Court's decisions argue that the Constitution is a document for the ages and that the broad principles it expresses are to be given new meaning in light of the historical evolution of the society as well as of the new, lived meaning of human rights. This means that just as we have expanded the concept of equality to include women, so the original set of rights must be expanded if women are to be admitted to full citizenship under the Constitution. The "originalist" attack on the Constitution is thus primarily an attack on the human rights decisions of the last 40 years. Abortion and the right of privacy are, not surprisingly, a centerpiece in that attack.[10]

From *Hardwick* to *Webster*

The Court's 1986 decision in *Bowers v. Hardwick*[11] signaled the growing success of the Reagan strategy in the privacy sphere. By a 5:4 vote, the Court rejected a challenge to Georgia's criminal sodomy law which punished sodomy with a potential 20 years in prison. The *Hardwick* decision is homophobic in the extreme—it rejects the analogy between gay sex and familial, procreative, and childrearing concerns as "facetious."[12] It analogizes gay sexual intimacy to incest, assault, and the possession of firearms and drugs rather than understanding it as intimacy, love, connection, pleasure, and transcendence, and as an essential part of the familial relations of lesbians and gay men.[13] In so doing, the majority indicated its hostility to any interpretation of privacy that would protect activity that has previously been criminalized. In its hostility to protecting privacy for rights not enumerated in the text and previously subject to criminal laws, the majority provided the blueprint for overruling *Roe v. Wade* as well as the contraception cases that preceded it. By 1989 when *Webster* was decided, Reagan had weathered the Bork hearings and succeeded in appointing Anthony Kennedy, the fifth member of the new conservative majority. The Court was ready to carry the right wing attack to procreative rights. And it did.

The *Webster* decision did not pronounce the demise of *Roe v. Wade,* but it assured it. It is not necessary to announce the elimination of abortion from the roster of protected rights to make abortion essentially inaccessible to most women. *Webster* has taken a giant step in this direction. It extended the rationale of the Medicaid decisions—that the state can choose to favor the fetus over the woman, and indirectly coerce childbirth over abortion where the state is paying the medical bill—to permit states to close down hospitals to paying patients simply because the facility is on land leased from the state. In so doing, the Court allowed states to interfere with relationships that have been traditionally deemed private. The consequence for women's access is profound. Hospitals are used by women who often have no alternative: poorer women, women of color, rural women, as well as women needing late abortions. Excluding abortions from any hospital with a public connection will also marginalize the practice of abortion, and threatens to remove it from the curriculum of medical schools which conduct their training in hospitals tangentially related to the state.

Webster also began the undoing of the framework of *Roe*, which prevents medical regulations that unnecessarily increase the cost and burden or decrease the accessibility of abortion. *Roe v. Wade* is significant not simply because of the recognized right to abortion but because *Roe* refused to treat the right as absolute. The key to availability is "strict scrutiny"—the requirement that the state prove a compelling reason for any restriction on the right. The changing balance between the woman's right and the state's interest is expressed in the trimester trilogy which both restricted and unfortunately permitted some regulation and even prohibition of abortion. In the first trimester, this standard has been applied to invalidate all regulations except the requirement that a doctor perform the abortion. In the second, it has resulted in invalidating unnecessary or costly medical regulations. In the third trimester, however, the Court declared the state to have a compelling interest in the protection of viable fetal life and, therefore, enabled it to prohibit abortion, except where the woman's life or health is at stake. The Court's tradeoff for fetal life was the Achilles' heel in the original *Roe* decision.

Webster expands the dangerous potential of the viability limitation. In upholding a provision of the statute requiring tests for viability during the last third of the second trimester, it collapsed a scientifically valid distinction between the viable and non-viable fetus and greatly increased the cost and medical burden of abortion. In so doing, the majority announced its frontal assault on the "rigid trimester analysis," the "virtual Procrustean bed."[14] It called explicitly into question earlier decisions striking medical regulations as unnecessary or unjustifiable and asserted that the interest in fetal life should be treated as compelling throughout pregnancy.

Justice Rehnquist's opinion for the majority was denied the full force of law only because Justice O'Connor was temporizing and considered it unnecessary to re-examine the *Roe* trilogy. While she indicates some reluctance to join in the elevation of the fetus to a compelling interest (a position which she had personally advocated),[15] she sees regulation as acceptable so long as it does not "unduly burden" the abortion right.[16] Under this highly manipulable standard, O'Connor had previously approved a law requiring hospitalization for abortion[17]—a requirement that can easily quadruple the cost of abortion. Thus, unless she has a change of heart, it can be expected that expensive regulations will be easily sanctioned and legal abortion will be placed beyond the reach of most women. In other words, O'Connor's solution preserves the appearance of a right to abortion, but not the reality.[18]

Finally, an aspect of *Webster* that has gotten little attention, despite the fact that Justice Stevens focused his dissent on it, is the Court's refusal to invalidate the statute's preamble, which finds that "the life of every human being begins at conception," and requires that the Missouri laws be interpreted to provide unborn children with the same rights accorded other persons so long as not in violation of the federal constitution or the Supreme Court's interpretation.[19] Because the statute does not require the unconstitutional application of state laws, the majority of the Court declined to rule on the constitutionality of the preamble. In doing so, it knowingly let slip by the enshrinement of a theological view of the fetus into state law against the first amendment's purpose to preserve the separation of church and state.[20] Indeed, on the basis that the preamble states the premise and purpose of the Missouri law, the entire statute should have been declared unconstitutional on this ground alone.

Hardwick and *Webster* thus teach us that constitutional protection for reproductive autonomy is quite fragile and that antagonism toward sexual freedom is quite deep. Not only has the Court upheld the criminalization of gay sexuality, but the accessibility as well as legality of abortion is up for grabs. Moreover, in the abortion case currently pending in the Supreme Court, the Solicitor General's brief on behalf of the Bush administration not only reiterates the Reagan administration's call for the complete overruling of *Roe v. Wade*, but also calls into question the contraception cases.[21] To move forward effectively, we must better understand our past.

Feminist Advocacy and Privacy

The first challenge to the criminal abortion laws through litigation and reform bills in state legislatures envisioned abortion as a doctor's professional prerogative. Then in 1969 in New York, the first feminist challenge to the criminal abortion laws was filed,[22] putting women's right to control their bodies and lives at center stage. Whereas in the legislatures women had to break into an ongoing dialogue between male legislators and experts, in the courts it was easier to focus attention on their experience, need, and entitlement to control reproduction. The second wave of the mostly white feminist movement coalesced around the demand for legal abortion and the effort to win constitutional protection for women's decisions about reproduction. This transformed a social reform movement for legal abortion led by doctors, family planners, and population controllers into a human rights struggle. As Ellen Willis wrote: "It was the feminist demand for an *unconditional right to abortion* that galvanized women and *created effective pressure for legislation.*"[23]

The claim of privacy played a central role in early abortion rights advocacy. The first legal cases involved doctors who challenged the imposition of criminal sanctions as an interference with the privacy of the doctor-patient relationship. The appeal to privacy also reflected the more liberal orientation of some feminist abortion advocates and a more cautious approach to litigation.

More radical feminist attorneys, echoing the movement's insistence on the right of women to control childbearing, sought abortion rights not simply as a matter of privacy but as a fundamental aspect of women's liberty. The movement made the analogy between forced pregnancy and slavery. Feminist attorneys argued that criminal abortion laws imposed a formal servitude that violated the Thirteenth Amendment. They emphasized the disparate impact of the criminal abortion laws on poor women. And they elaborated the idea that the choice of whether to have an abortion is essential to gender equality and women's capacity to participate equally in society as full persons.[24]

The right to terminate an unwanted pregnancy was linked, in the popular resistance to the criminal laws, to the right of women to be sexual, free of either the patriarchal constraints of uncontrolled pregnancy or the mandate to be heterosexual. In court, only a few pressed this argument and emphasized the differential punishment women suffered as a consequence of sexual activity enjoyed at least as much by men.[25] Most abortion rights advocates, however, have been wary of this sexuality argument, even though antagonism to women's sexual freedom is the core of the attack on abortion.

Given this array of possible frameworks, it is significant and not surprising that, in *Roe,* the Court chose privacy as the vehicle for protecting abortion. Privacy was compatible with a legal tradition of non-interference in marriage; a tradition that denied women legal relief from economic and physical abuse by their husbands; a tradition that had long served to reinforce male dominance in the home. Privacy buttresses the conservative idea that the personal is separate from the political, and that the larger social structure has no impact on private, individual choice. The privacy framework assumes that the society bears no affirmative responsibility for individual choice or action.

This notion of privacy appealed to a broad constituency favoring contraception and abortion: doctors, who urged decriminalization on the basis of the privacy of the physician-patient relationship; family planners, who fought constraints on reproductive control and sought, among other things, to rationalize marriage and childbearing; the population controllers, who wanted to discourage childbearing; and libertarians, who hold that in exchange for being left alone, a person should ask nothing from society by way of support.

Until *Bowers v. Hardwick* in 1986, the right to privacy also figured prominently in gay rights litigation in part because the doctrine of privacy was well established and in part because the lesbian/gay movement, like the mainstream women's and abortion rights movement, had given privacy a significant place in its own advocacy. Privacy arguments, partly because of their success and partly because of their broad appeal, have until now been the predominant argument for reproductive and sexual rights. But *Hardwick,* which upheld a Georgia law making homosexual sex a criminal act, has forced gay and lesbian advocates to rethink the reliance on privacy, just as *Webster* must generate reassessment among supporters of reproductive rights.

The core idea of the right to abortion—that women should be in control of decision making over their reproduction—employs the notion of non-interference by the state to reinforce rather than undermine women's autonomy. In this respect it is a progressive demand. But, as it has been elaborated by many pro-choice advocates and by the Court, it is still a limited and deeply flawed basis for reproductive freedom. There has emerged a sharp tension between two notions of privacy: the liberal idea of privacy as the negative and qualified right to be left alone (so long as nothing too significant is at stake), and the more radical ideal of privacy as the positive liberty of self-determination and an aspect of equal personhood. Both practically and theoretically, the privacy doctrine is double-edged, having within it the tendency to constrain as well as to expand reproductive rights.

The Progressive Impact of Privacy

There is probably no decision that has had as profound and pragmatic impact on women's daily lives as *Roe v. Wade*. Since 1973, over 25 million women have had legal abortions. Legalization of abortion transformed unwanted pregnancy from a potentially life-shattering event into one over which a woman could take rightful control. Abortion, though a significant and potentially painful decision, was no longer a dangerous, desperate, criminal, and stigmatizing experience, but rather a safe, legitimate health care option.

Constitutional recognition of the right to abortion has profound symbolic importance as well. It is the precondition for women's passage from chattel to full personhood. At least in principle, it acknowledged women's power to be self-determining, to refuse to be the object of someone else's desire for procreation, whether it be on the part of the state, the husband, the progenitor, or the self-styled guardians of embryonic life.

Roe had even broader, although guarded, implications for sexual freedom. Even though the Court was never willing to recognize a right to be sexual, both contraception and abortion are necessary preconditions for liberating female sexuality. By removing the duty or terror of unwanted pregnancy for many heterosexual women, legal abortion alleviated some of the repression and shame imposed on female sexual desire.[26] By permitting the separation of sexuality and reproduction, the right to abortion indirectly protects the right of lesbians to be sexually self-determining. The right to abortion is thus a bottom line issue—it is the difference between women being full persons or criminals.

Privacy doctrine, while exceedingly limited, has evolved in several important respects. It has been 25 years since the notion of an independent right of privacy was first suggested in *Griswold v. Connecticut*[27] to protect the use of contraceptives in marriage. Although a significant innovation in constitutional law, the notion of marital privacy drew upon the principle (and illusion) of non-intervention in the family, which has operated historically to reinforce patriarchal power over the resources and the person of the wife. *Griswold* could be read in diametrically opposed ways: as an endorsement of the decidedly anti-feminist notion of marriage as specifically insulated from state intervention, or as a cornerstone of a broader right to sexual and intimate association. Until now, it has been the latter.

The subsequent recognition in 1972 of the right of unmarried people to obtain contraception in *Eisenstadt v. Baird*[28] was a critical step. In constitutional law, it marked the transformation of the family from a corporate body or unit, with privacy rights protecting the male-controlled entity, into an association of separate individuals, with separate claims to constitutional protection. The journey from familial privacy to individual autonomy was further consolidated with the Court's rejection of the power of a husband or father to veto an abortion,[29] a decision that has more recently been challenged by husbands and putative "fathers" seeking to force women to remain pregnant.

A similar evolution in privacy doctrine occurred in relation to a woman's role in the abortion decision. When the Court first recognized the right to abortion in *Roe,* it characterized the decision as belonging to physicians. While the women's movement interpreted *Roe* as giving women the right to make the decision, this did not legally occur in the Court until 1977.[30] Although doctors still exercise considerable control over the conditions under which abortion is performed,[31] the need for medical legitimation of the decision itself has diminished. Cutbacks on the constitutional right, however, are likely to resuscitate medical control to enforce limited exceptions (life, health, rape, incest, or fatal defect) to abortion prohibitions. Historically, these exceptions provided emotionally costly access to those women with substantial connections and funds; for the poor, they were a virtual dead-letter.[32]

The Court's most forceful articulation of the right to abortion came in response to the most serious challenge to its legitimacy: the Reagan administration's request in *Thornburgh v. American College of Obstetricians and Gynecologists* that the Court completely overrule *Roe v. Wade.* In response Justice Blackmun wrote for a majority of five:

> Few decisions are more personal and intimate, more properly private, or more basic to individual dignity and autonomy, than a woman's decision—with the guidance of her physician and with the limits specified in *Roe*—whether to end her pregnancy. A woman's right to make that choice freely is fundamental. Any other result, in our view, would protect inadequately a central part of the sphere of liberty that our law guarantees to all.[33]

Formulating the abortion right in this way is doubly significant because it places the right to make autonomous decisions about childbearing in the context of equality. That women should have the right to abortion is not an instance of special treatment; it is instead an extension to women of the traditional liberal constitutional values of liberty, possession of the self, and opportunity to participate as producer and citizen. This opinion reflects, for the first time, a deeply feminist understanding of the necessity of the abortion right to women's full personhood.

The positive meaning of privacy was further elaborated by Justice Blackmun in his dissent in *Bowers v. Hardwick,* recognizing the right to choose one's intimate relationships:

Only the most willful blindness could obscure the fact that sexual intimacy is a "sensitive, key relationship of human existence, central to family life, community welfare, and the development of the personality." The fact that individuals define themselves in a significant way through their intimate sexual relationships with others suggests, in a Nation as diverse as ours, that there may be many "right" ways of conducting those relationships, and that much of the richness of a relationship will come from the freedom an individual has to choose the form and nature of these intensely personal bonds.[34]

He suggested that privacy means more than toleration of "offensive" conduct. Rather, the Constitution should protect sexual intimacy affirmatively and respect sexual difference because the process of sexual and familial self-definition is central to authenticity and self-realization.

The Constraints of Privacy

Despite these eloquent efforts to transform privacy into positive liberty, the prevailing opinions—with the exception of the now defunct majority in *Thornburgh*—have seen it as the more limited right to be left alone. The fact that this traditional idea of privacy as negative and defensive prevails makes it a weak vehicle for challenging traditional, gendered reproductive and sexual norms. Further, it denies the relationship of social conditions and public responsibility to the ability of the individual to exercise autonomy.

The limitations of privacy have consequences both for the development of constitutional protection and for the progress of a movement that relies too heavily upon it. The privacy argument is attractive because it seems easier to sell—it does not require a court to renounce society's prejudices. Instead it can assume a seemingly neutral attitude: "Even though homosexuality is disgusting or abortion is murder, we must allow it," or, "It's okay to be homosexual as long as it doesn't show in public." But these are not neutral positions, and privacy is not a neutral doctrine.

The fact that abortion rights have been qualified by fetal viability since *Roe v. Wade* is attributable, of course, to political compromise but also to the combined defects of a negative theory of privacy and a truncated view of women's personhood. To limit a woman's right—whether it be to decide on an abortion or refuse Caesarean surgery in childbirth—in the interest of viable yet still physically dependent potential life denies her full moral and physical autonomy. To recognize a countervailing weight in fetal life, whether after viability in *Roe* or through pregnancy as suggested in *Webster,* denies the fundamental material condition of pregnancy. It burdens the pregnant woman with a duty to save fetal life at an enormous cost to herself—a cost that, as a society, we ask of no man, not even the parent of a child.[35]

Women must be seen as having the moral authority to make their own abortion decisions not because they are victims who are suffering, but because doing so is integral to being able to chart one's own destiny. When pregnancy is finally viewed as a voluntary gift of life to another, not a woman's duty, the abortion debate will not turn on the question of when life begins. When women who refuse childbearing are understood to be responsible rather than reprehensible, there will be no incentive to place fetal viability or any other restrictions on their decision making. And when women are accorded a right to be sexual, the sanctification of fetal innocence and the urge to punish with unwanted pregnancy or illegal abortion will abate.

Just as the failure of privacy theory in the abortion cases is, in part, a function of viewing women's full sovereignty as a threat, so also the majority's opinions in *Hardwick* make clear that same-sex intimacy failed the negative privacy test because it is experienced as threatening— threatening to gender identity and differentiation, the expectation of heterosexuality, and the power relations it embodies. A heterosexist culture goes to elaborate lengths to construct distinct gender identities as well as the propensity toward heterosexuality.[36] It may be that the very fragility of the channeled sexual self heightens the danger presented by crossing the line, that precisely because sexual identity and heterosexuality are not ordained but choosable,[37] those who deviate from the heterosexual norm must be stigmatized and excluded.

Same-sex relationships also threaten the traditional hegemony of men in the sexual pecking order. Just as Justice Burger thinks homosexual sodomy worse than rape, the possibility of homosexual solicitation is treated more harshly than the sexual harassment of women.[38] However, the potential for women to have sexual pleasure and to construct relationships and communities without men changes the balance of sexual power in familial relations, precisely the arena most resistant to egalitarian intervention.[39]

The sense in which the *Hardwick* majority is right highlights the shortsightedness of relying on a negative right of privacy. Sexual self-definition must cross the bounds of privacy, for autonomy cannot be realized apart from social interaction. While privacy implies secrecy and shame, the choice of sexual partners of the same sex is no more intrinsically private than the identity of a person's spouse. Nor is this choice easily confined to the private realm of the bed or the closet. It involves not only sexual but also familial and social identity—who one is in public as well as in private and what the legal norms are. To accept mere tolerance of sexual difference is not only degrading; it is ultimately self-defeating.

Privacy is also inadequate as a theory for reproduction and sexual self-determination because it perpetuates the myth that the right to choose is inherent in the individual, a given of private life, rather than acknowledging that choices are shaped, facilitated, or denied by social conditions. The negative right of privacy not only dissociates the individual from the broader context; it also exempts the state from responsibility for contributing to material conditions and social relations that facilitate autonomous decision making.

Nowhere is this negative aspect of privacy more clearly or cruelly demonstrated than in the Court's 1980 decision in *Harris v. McRae* permitting the state to deny Medicaid funding for abortion and, more recently, in *Webster's* approval of the closing of private hospitals receiving any public funds. The decisions recognize that by funding or facilitating childbirth and not abortion, the state is seeking to influence private choice. The Court also recognized that the absence of funding will make it "difficult if not impossible"[40] for some poor women to implement their choice. However, the Court saw this as constitutionally irrelevant. The inability to obtain an abortion did not result from an obstacle created by the state but rather from the fact that the woman is poor, or, in the case of *Webster*, cannot find a purely private facility. A negative right of privacy carries no corresponding obligation on the part of the state to facilitate choice. The integrity of a woman's decision making process is not even protected against purposeful manipulation through the selective provision of state resources for childbirth only.

To treat a woman's poverty and her inability to exercise choice as a consequence of personal failure, rather than of public policy and the market conditions it produces, is a dangerous fiction. Not only does the state escape responsibility for the conditions of people's lives, but the ideology of private responsibility makes it possible to blame the poor, who are overwhelmingly women, for being consigned to poverty. It is a small step, as the Medicaid cases indicate, from blame to control. The Court is explicit that where exercise of the right of privacy depends on public resources, moralistic disapproval or population control will justify its destruction.[41] If abortion were a matter of affirmative liberty or equality, it would be impermissible for the state to manipulate decision making through selective support.

The gap between a private right of choice and the necessary conditions for autonomy widens when we consider the broad range of factors that influence, and in many cases determine, women's choices about reproduction. The prevalence of economically influenced abortions and the sterilization campaigns against poor, minority, and disabled women show us that autonomy is impossible without eradication of discrimination and poverty. Racism, sexism, and poverty can make the difference between abortions that reflect choice and those reflecting bitter necessity.[42] Privacy rights do not magically endow women, gay men, or lesbians with choice in the full sense that their liberation intends. Privacy rights do not in themselves guarantee autonomy.

A viable conception of autonomy would presuppose a society in which both the workforce and the family were restructured to value the work and the gift of procreation and to encourage gender-neutral, same- or hetero-sex, and communal participation. Autonomy would also require a positive, needs-oriented concept of rights that guarantees the preconditions for self-realization, including shelter, food, day care, health care, education, and the possibility of meaningful work, relationships, and engagement in political and social life.[13]

Autonomy with regard to sexual self-determination is likewise inseparable from material and ideological conditions. It requires redistributing power between the sexes as well as dismantling heterosexism.[44] The continuing economic and social realities of male power and female dependency, as well as their translation into male aggression and female passivity in the sexual realm, complicate the ability of women to make autonomous choices about their intimate sexual and familial relations.[45] The possibility of choosing to live one's life as gay or lesbian did not emerge until social conditions permitted independence from the traditional family,[46] and this choice will not be fully guaranteed until the right to express one's sexual identity is recognized, accepted, and materially supported to the same extent as heterosexual intimacy.

Assuring reproductive autonomy also requires affirmative initiatives on the part of the state. It requires the state to address the broad threats to reproduction stemming from toxicity in the workplace and the environment, from AIDS, and from the simple and unforgivable failure of this society to provide adequate prenatal care. These are threats not only to reproductive autonomy but to human survival itself. Ultimately even money and the objectifying "state-of-the-art" technology that it can buy cannot provide protection. These are problems that can only be solved societally; individual rights like privatized solutions cannot avert the danger.

Thus, to protect a "right to choose" without assuring the social conditions necessary to foster an autonomous choice provides equality of opportunity in form but not in fact. Worse, this idea of privacy obscures the necessity for public responsibility to bring this transformation about.

The Future Struggle for Equality

An extensive social transformation is required to guarantee autonomy, one that cannot be accomplished solely through judicial recognition or enforcement of rights. Instead, we need a multifaceted strategy involving litigation, legislation, collective bargaining, grassroots activism, and, ultimately, cultural change in order to eradicate discrimination and restructure the nature of the family and the market as well as the relationship between them. Constitutional change is an important part of this strategy because it reflects desirable social policy and an ethical bottom line.

How a movement articulates its demands and its vision can make a difference to constitutional development. While the notion of a right of privacy has advanced reproductive and sexual autonomy, it has also permitted these rights to be disconnected from the broader vision of equality that women's and lesbian/gay liberation requires. The danger is that the Court's mediated version of rights will become the measure of the movement's goals, even as attention is turned to state courts and legislatures.

In both legal and political advocacy, privacy must be transformed into an affirmative right to self-determination and grounded in the broader principle of equality and in the concrete conditions of people's lives. We must articulate these arguments in the public sphere before they can have resonance in the courts and legislatures. And we must recognize the interplay between limited doctrine and broader visions as well as between social activism and legal reform.[47]

Abortion and sexual rights are elemental conditions for liberation, necessary although not sufficient. They are the bottom line. And this is precisely what is frightening about the Supreme Court's dismantling of these rights: they are making us fight to save the bottom line. Justice Scalia complained in *Webster* that the Court had only removed the door jamb instead of dismantling the whole structure.[48] But, it is more apt to describe the Court as taking out the floor—the floor of decency and respect for the person.

What is frightening, and also poses the central challenge to all of us, is that the Court is doing this in every area of civil rights. There is no favored group, no preferential treatment. We are all deeply threatened, and in that terrible prospect lies our hope. The breadth of the Court's attack on human rights can help us build an unprecedented coalition and movement that joins the issues essential to human freedom.

Notes

1. This article develops from and draws on portions of two of my previous articles: "Unpacking Patriarchy: Reproduction, Sexuality, Originalism, and Constitutional Change," (in *A Less Than Perfect Union*, J. Lobel, ed., Monthly Review Press, 1988) and "Beyond the Liberal Idea of Privacy: Toward a Positive Right of Autonomy," (in *Judging the Constitution: Critical Essays on Judicial Lawmaking,*

Michael W. McCann and Gerald L. Houseman, eds., Scott, Foresman and Company, 1989).

2. 109 S.Ct. 3040, 3077-3079 (1989).

3. *Roe v. Wade*, 410 U.S. 113 (1973).

4. The religious basis of the fetal rights position is extensively documented in the District Court opinion and appendix in *McRae v. Califano*, 491 F. Supp. 630 (E.D.N.Y. 1980).

5. Rosalind Petchesky, *Abortion and Woman's Choice: The State, Sexuality and Reproductive Freedom* (New York: Longman, 1984).

6. *Harris v. McRae*, 448 U.S. 297 (1980); *Maher v. Roe*, 432 U.S. 464 (1977).

7. *Baird v. Bellotti*, 443 U.S. 622 (1979), upheld parental consent statutes so long as they provided for judicial review for minors who chose not to seek the consent of their parents. The trauma this produces for teen women is documented in *Hodgson v. State of Minnesota*, 648 F. Supp. 756 (D. Minn. 1986), reversed on appeal, 853 F.2d 1452 (8th Cir. 1989), appeal pending No. 90, U.S. S.Ct.

8. The first attempt to enact a constitutional amendment died in the Senate Judiciary Committee in 1976. In 1980, Jesse Helms introduced the "Human Life Statute," a blatantly unconstitutional effort to overturn *Roe* by majoritarian vote. In the same period a number of constitutional amendments were under active consideration. Both efforts were defeated in the Senate in 1983.

9. *City of Akron v. Akron Center for Reproductive Health*, 462 U.S. 416 (1983). See also *Thornburgh v. American College of Obstetricians & Gynecologists*, 476 U.S. 747 (1986).

10. For fuller discussion of a feminist critique of originalism, see R. Copelon, "Unpacking Patriarchy," in J. Lobel, ed., *A Less Than Perfect Union* (New York: Monthly Review Press, 1988).

11. *Hardwick*, 478 U.S. 186 (1986).

12. *Ibid*. at 194.

13. *Ibid*. at 196.

14. *Webster*, 109 S.Ct. at 3044.

15. *City of Akron*, 462 U.S. at 453-459 (O'Connor, J. dissenting).

16. *Webster*, 109 S.Ct. at 3063 (O'Connor, J. concurring).

17. *City of Akron*, 462 U.S. at 427-470.

18. For an excellent examination of the impact of the "unduly burdensome" standard on poor women, see Brief Amicus Curiae on behalf of National Council of Negro Women et al. in *Webster v. Reproductive Health Services*, available from Center for Constitutional Rights, NYC or from author.

19. *Webster*, 109 S.Ct. at 3049-50.

20. *Ibid*. at 3079-85 (Stevens, J. concurring and dissenting).

21. Brief for the United States as Amicus Curiae, in *Hodgson v. Minnesota*, No. 88-1125 and 88-1309, at 13 (1990). Ironically, despite its proclaimed hostility to the creation of new rights by the Court, the brief suggests that the parental notice statute at issue might even be justified as advancing the parental right to direct the upbringing of their children. *Ibid*. at 16.

22. The case, *Abramowicz v. Lefkowitz*, filed by 300 women plaintiffs in January 1970 in Federal District Court, was withdrawn after the New York state legislature, by a margin of one, voted on April 3, 1970, to repeal restrictions on abortion within the first 24 weeks of pregnancy. The work in this case provided the foundation for other feminist challenges to criminal abortion laws. The testimony is excerpted in D. Schulder and F. Kennedy, *Abortion Rap* (New York: McGraw-Hill, 1971).

23. Ellen Willis, *Village Voice*, March 3, 1980, p. 8. See also R. Petchesky, *Abortion and Woman's Choice*, pp. 125-129.

24. See, e.g., Amicus Brief on Behalf of New Women Lawyers, in *Roe v. Wade;* New Women Lawyers Amicus on behalf of New Jersey Coalition for Battered Women et al. in *Right to Choose v. Byrne,* reprinted in 7 *Women's Rights Law Reporter* 286 (1982); See S. Law, "Rethinking Sex and the Constitution," 132 *U. Pa. L. Rev.* 955 (1984).

25. See New Women Lawyers Amicus; Right to Choose Amicus.

26. One strand of late twentieth-century feminism rejects the contribution of contraception and abortion to a more liberated female sexuality, holding that heterosexual sexual relations, in a gender unequal society, are by definition oppressive (see, e.g., MacKinnon, *Feminism Unmodified,* Harvard University Press, 1987, pp. 93-102). This view is a flat and dangerous stereotype, for it precludes exploration and appreciation of women's capacity for sexual agency, power, and desire. Even accepting, as I do, that many women are vulnerable to sexual coercion as a product of inequality, abortion does not increase their abuse. At the very least, abortion enables them to relieve the further degrading and potentially life-destroying consequences thereof. For many, it is an act of self-affirmation, even in the face of victimization and despair.

27. *Griswold,* 381 U.S. 479 (1965).

28. *Eisenstadt,* 405 U.S. 438 (1972).

29. *Planned Parenthood of Central Missouri v. Danforth,* 420 U.S. 918 (1975).

30. *Whalen v. Roe,* 429 U.S. 589 (1977).

31. See, e.g. *City of Akron v. Akron Center for Reproductive Health,* 462 U.S. 416 (1983).

32. See Women of Color Brief in *Webster, supra* n. 17.

33. *Thornburgh v. ACOG,* at 2185.

34. *Bowers v. Hardwick* 478 U.S. at 205 (1986).

35. See, e.g., Regan, "Rethinking *Roe v. Wade,*" 77 *Michigan L. Rev.* 1569 (1977); Thomson, "A Defense of Abortion," 1 *Phil. & Pub. Affairs* 1 (1971).

36. See J. Money and A. Ehrhardt, *Man and Woman, Boy and Girl: The Differentiation and Dimorphism of Gender Identity from Conception to Maturity* (Baltimore: Johns Hopkins University Press, 1972); A. Rich, "Compulsory Heterosexuality and Lesbian Existence," in Snitow et al., eds. *Powers of Desire* (New York: Monthly Review Press, 1983), p. 177; G. Rubin, "The Traffic in Women: Notes on the 'Political Economy' of Sex," in R. Reiter, ed., *Toward an Anthropology of Women* (New York: Monthly Review, 1975), p. 157.

37. Although some lesbians and gay men experience their sexual orientation as determined and immutable, others are very clear that it is a matter of choice. To reduce self-definition to biological, psychological, or cultural determinism, as the medical model does, argues for tolerance of the pathetic, not respect for the authentic. Nor does it help people who don't identify as gay to examine sexual hypocrisy or desire in their own lives. See Halley, "The Politics of the Closet: Towards Equal Protection for Gay, Lesbian and Bisexual Identity," 36 *UCLA L. Rev.* 915 (1989).

38. See, e.g., *Dronenburgh v. Zech,* 741 F.2d 1388, rehearing denied 746 F.2d 1526 (D.C. Cir 1984). Judge Bork wrote that the disruption from potential sexual solicitation justified the total exclusion of homosexuals from the military.

39. "Even women who had not the slightest inclination to cross the threshold of taboo reaped some benefits in their heterosexual negotiations from the general acknowledgement that lesbianism was not within the realm of the imaginable," *Powers of Desire, op. cit.,* p. 34.

40. *Harris v. McRae* 448 U.S. at 315 (1980).

41. See *Maher v. Roe,* 432 U.S. 472, 474 (1977).

42. A. Davis, *Women, Race & Class,* Random House, 1983, pp. 202-221. See Davis' essay in this volume.

43. See *Abortion and Women's Choice, op. cit.*

44. See Law, "Homosexuality and the Social Meaning of Gender," 1988 *Wisc. L. Rev.* 187 (1988).

45. See *Powers of Desire, op. cit.;* C. Vance, ed. *Pleasure and Danger: Exploring Female Sexuality* (Boston: Routledge & Kegan Paul, 1984).

46. D'Emilio, "Capitalism and Gay Identity," in *Powers of Desire, op. cit.,* pp. 100-116.

47. See Schneider, "The Dialectics of Rights and Politics: Perspectives From the Women's Movement," 61 *NYU L. Rev.* 589 (1986).

48. *Webster,* 109 S.Ct. at 3067.

Key United States Supreme Court Abortion and Privacy Cases

1965—*Griswold v. Connecticut*

The Court struck down a Connecticut statute forbidding the use of contraceptive devices by married couples. In this decision the Court appealed for the first time to the right to privacy—a right which it said was "fundamental and basic." Although no such right is explicitly recognized by the Constitution, the Court inferred the existence of a "zone of privacy" which protected the sexual relations of married couples.

1972—*Eisenstadt v. Baird*

The Court declared unconstitutional a Massachusetts statute which prohibited the distribution of contraceptives to unmarried persons. The Court asserted the "right of the individual, married or single, to be free from unwarranted government intrusion into matters so fundamentally affecting a person as the decision to bear or beget a child."

1973—*Roe v. Wade*

This decision invalidated nearly all the existing laws restricting abortion. The Court ruled unconstitutional any restriction on abortions during the first trimester of pregnancy. During this period, the decision to have an abortion is left to the pregnant woman and her physician. In the second trimester, the state may protect its interest in the pregnant woman's health by regulating the abortion procedure in ways reasonably related to her health. In the third trimester, the state may restrict and even prohibit abortion because the state has an interest in protecting the fetus after it has become viable.

This ruling was based on the right to privacy: state intrusion into the doctor—patient relationship and into a woman's decisions concerning procreation were seen as violations of that right.

1973—*Doe v. Bolton*

The Court struck down other restrictive abortion laws such as residency requirements; the need to obtain the approval of two physi-

45

cians and/or hospital committees. Such requirements were seen as obstacles to women and physicians and thus as infringements on their rights.

1976—Planned Parenthood of Central Missouri v. Danforth

The Court overturned a law requiring a married woman to obtain her husband's consent for an abortion, stating that a woman's right to choose abortion is not subject to the veto of her spouse. The Court also invalidated a requirement that all minors, no matter how mature or under what circumstances, had to obtain at least one parent's consent. Here, too, the Court stressed that minors have a right to privacy.

At the same time, stepping back from the language of Roe, the Court ruled that a state could attach certain requirements to abortion, such as record keeping and informed consent.

1979—Bellotti v. Baird

The Court re-examined the circumstances under which a minor may choose an abortion. It upheld a Massachusetts law requiring minors to notify both their parents or obtain their consent for an abortion. The Court held that parental consent or notification does not infringe on a minor's rights if the minor can bypass the parents by obtaining judicial consent. A minor may seek this judicial permission from a judge, who will determine if the minor is "mature" and whether abortion is in the minor's best interest.

1980—Harris v. McRae and Williams v. Zbaraz

The Court upheld the right of Congress and state legislatures to refuse to pay for medically necessary abortions for poor women. The Court held that abortion restrictions in the funding context are different from other regulations and that it is legitimate for a state to prefer childbirth over abortion by funding one and not the other.

This decision upheld the Hyde Amendment prohibiting the use of federal Medicaid funds for abortions.

1983—Akron Center for Reproductive Health v. City of Akron

The Court invalidated a variety of restrictions on abortion: state imposed waiting periods; "informed consent" requiring that women seeking abortions be told that a fetus is a "human life," its precise gestational age, and that abortion is a major surgical procedure; that physicians personally give women the required information before the woman consents to the abortion; that physicians perform second-trimester abortions in hospitals; and that physicians performing abortions ensure the "humane and sanitary" disposal of the fetuses. In *Ashcroft* however, the Court upheld a law requiring physicians to submit fetal tissue to pathologists, who are in turn required to report their findings to the health department. (*Planned Parenthood of Kansas City v. Ashcroft* was a companion case)

1986—*Thornburgh v. American College of Obstetricians and Gynecologists of Pennsylvania*

This case dealt with a series of restrictions on abortion of the sort which had been enacted in the Akron ordinance. It was also an effort to overturn *Roe*. The Justice Department under President Reagan had submitted a supplementary brief in the case to argue for overruling *Roe*.

The Court held all of the information-dispensing requirements to be unconstitutional, arguing that they seemed to be overt attempts to discourage abortion.

This decision contains the most forceful assertion of the right to abortion.

1986—*Bowers v. Hardwick*

The Court upheld a Georgia anti-sodomy law. In its decision, the Court said that the right to privacy did not give homosexuals a fundamental right to engage in sodomy. It distinguished the claims at issue in this case from earlier privacy decisions by saying that other private rights were related to family, marriage, or procreation. The Court also endorsed arguments about the validity of prevailing moral standards in determining fundamental rights.

1989—*Webster v. Reproductive Health Services*

The Court upheld various provisions of a Missouri law restricting abortion: its preamble containing the "finding" that "the life of each human being begins at conception"; a state may prohibit "public facilities" and "public employees" from being used to perform or assist abortions not necessary to save the life of the pregnant woman; and a requirement that whenever a woman seeking an abortion appears to be at least twenty weeks pregnant, the physician must conduct tests to determine fetal viability.

In addition, several justices indicated a willingness to reconsider— and some are now ready to overturn—*Roe v. Wade* and to consider further restrictions on abortion.

1990—*Hodgson v. Minnesota* and *Ohio v. Akron Center for Reproductive Health*

The Court again addressed the question of parental notification. In the Minnesota case the Justices said a state could require that a pregnant girl inform both her parents before having an abortion, so long as the law provides the alternative of a judicial hearing. This law requires notification of both parents even if they have never lived with the teen-ager or do not have legal custody. In the Ohio case, the Court upheld the state's law requiring notification of one parent while also allowing the judicial alternative. The Court did not rule on whether the Constitution compels the availability of a "judicial bypass" when notice to only one parent is required.

The Court also upheld the constitutionality of imposing waiting periods after notification of both parents, before the abortion can be performed.

Mobilizing against the State and International "Aid" Agencies: "Third World" Women Define Reproductive Freedom[1]

Jacqui Alexander

The last two decades of feminist political organizing in the United States have highlighted the pitfalls and limits of exclusionary politics and the setbacks that ensue when our movements are co-opted or when we, as feminists, continue to construct definitions and fashion political strategies that draw on the same norms that white masculinist thinking has institutionalized. When women's struggles for reproductive freedoms get narrowly defined as an individual's right to control her body or "choice," we ignore what is fundamentally at stake: a major struggle to redefine women's sexuality by all the institutions (the state, culture, law, the economy, and religion, among others) that historically have had an interest in defining and enforcing ideologies of womanhood.

Ironically, it is not only feminists who assert the centrality of reproductive choice. Gena Corea has shown, for instance, that medical engineers and entrepreneurs (the "technodocs," as she calls them) who have developed and proliferated new reproductive technologies have co-opted the language of choice at the same time that they develop aggressive technologies that are harmful to women.[2] They too claim that choice is inseparable from the struggle for reproductive freedom: an unfortunate scenario aligning science and its entrepreneurs, a multinational billion-dollar drug industry, and feminists in a singular frame of individual rights and choice, albeit for different reasons. Reproductive freedom is not the same as corporate choice, built as it is on the politics of profit and exploitation! And as feminists, we must distance ourselves from this attempted "alliance" of convenience!

Yet, it is still the case that while some white middle-class feminists have fashioned a language to understand how these institutions mutually

49

depend upon and reinforce one another, their practice has sometimes lagged far behind those understandings. And it is also the case that the grounded insights and experiences of women of color, impoverished and working-class women, women with AIDS, disabled women, and lesbians are still marginalized in a feminist movement which largely resists our analyses and leadership. The recognition has been slow in coming that these analyses and experiences should be the touchstone of collective struggle if we are to actively and effectively confront the current challenges of the next decade. As Barbara Smith has argued so poignantly, "It does not dilute our rage to extend [an integrated politics] to every manifestation of a dysfunctional and people-hating system…it strengthens it. We have got to make these connections if we are ever going to make the vision of feminism real."[3] Making the connections and understanding the *specific* contexts within which women's struggles emerge are even more crucial as we come to terms with the meanings of reproductive freedom for "third world" women.

Political struggles are never waged in a vacuum; they emerge and are fought out in a broader arena marked, in this instance, by global and local politics (specifically colonization, imperialism, and nationalist movements) and sustained levels of economic and sexual violence that are often accompanied by domestic repression and militarization. As women bear the disproportionate brunt of ever worsening economic conditions, the strategies that individual governments pursue rely increasingly upon different modes of violence aimed at keeping women "in their place." Militarized economies are devoting significantly less of their national incomes to health services, and that translates into a scarcity of services including preventive and primary care for women and children. The colonial legacy that continues to criminalize abortion forces women to seek clandestine abortions. The death rate from such abortions, already the highest in "third world" countries, will steadily increase in the current economic crisis. Reproductive freedom must be situated *within* this broader arena if it is to be a truly transformative politics.

Movements for sexual autonomy and the legalization of abortion do provide some common ground for solidarity between "first world" and "third world" women. They cannot, however, be plucked from the collective visions through which they have emerged and taken shape solely because they have achieved a certain degree of urgency at this historical conjuncture in the west. Nor can white women afford to build a movement shaped solely on their own sensibilities. Confronting racism at home is one step toward resisting racist moves abroad. Clearly, we are facing a dilemma of a particular kind. Insisting on a "third world"/"first world" geo-political divide reinforces the same boundaries that multinational capital has established to control markets and cheapen women's labor. These are the very relationships that should prompt white feminists in the west to exercise caution as we chart the *political* bases for alliances. The ground on which they are forged cannot be based, therefore, on colonial gestures, but upon the alliances that "third world" women choose to make and the strategies they devise from their particular contexts.

It will be useful before proceeding further, however, to define what I mean by "third world." The "third world" encompasses the peoples and political geography of Africa, South and Southeast Asia, China, the Caribbean, Latin America, and the Middle East. I use the term not to suggest a set of monolithic practices and behaviors, for that would contradict the divergent ways in which women construct their daily lives. Nor do I wish to suggest that the effects of colonial and imperial domination are identical. There is no reason to believe that the form of political struggle in the Philippines will assume the same shape in Mexico, for instance, although they were both colonized by Spain, for that too will erase the importance of historical specificity. What happens at any historical moment arises from the *peculiar* and *specific* conjuncture of indigenous and cross-national relationships at play at that moment. There is, however, what Chandra Talpade Mohanty has called a "common context of struggle" and this is what I want to invoke here as a mode of understanding that will allow us to talk about the "third world" not as a coherent entity but as peoples inhabiting diverse geographies with some shared histories.[4] If what links these countries together is a common history of European and later U.S. imperial domination, then it is also the case that they are linked through political opposition to those very structures. "Third world" women are linked through these very histories of colonial domination and through individual and collective efforts to forge and re-forge communities of resistance.[5] This is what provides the political link between women of color in the United States, Black women in Britain, and "third world" women in their countries of origin.[6] And it is in this very context of political opposition that feminism has emerged.

But even to talk about feminism in the "third world" is to challenge the originary status that western feminism has taken for itself and to subvert prevailing criticisms that nationalist governments have launched against these struggles. Kumari Jayawardena in her work *Feminism and Nationalism in the Third World* has observed the contradiction:

> The concept of feminism has also been the cause of much confusion in Third World countries. It has variously been alleged by traditionalists, political conservatives and even certain leftists, that feminism is a product of "decadent" western capitalism;

that it is based on a foreign culture of no relevance to women of the local bourgeoisie; and that it alienates or diverts women, from their culture, religion and family responsibilities, on the one hand, and from the revolutionary struggles for nationalism and socialism on the other. In the west, too, there is a Eurocentric view that the movement for women's liberation is not indigenous to Asia or Africa, but has been a purely West European and North American phenomenon, and that where movements for women's emancipation or feminist struggles have arisen in the Third World, they have been merely imitative of Western models.[7]

This tendency to see "third world" women's struggles as mere appendages or secondary to those of the "first world" has produced major conflicts, especially at the two conferences in Mexico City and Copenhagen in 1975 and 1980 that marked the beginning and mid-point of the "Decade for Women."[8] As we continue to cross these geo-political boundaries in the decade to come, it is important that we place ourselves, as feminists, squarely within the histories and politics that inform "third world" women's lives and not on any received notions of what those lives ought to be. Colonialism, imperialism, and the polarization, or perhaps the sexualization, of geography into "high fertility" areas ("third world") and "low fertility" areas ("first world") are significant elements of those histories.

In what follows, I sketch some broad trajectories of those histories, focusing primarily on the processes of colonization and imperialism that have helped to legitimate western intervention in "third world" women's lives. This can only be a sketch, for it is not possible to present a comprehensive picture here. Yet, mapping those broad contours will enable us to understand the importance of struggling on several fronts simultaneously to understand, for instance, why struggles against violence and economic injustice are among the most crucial for "third world" women, or why motherhood is often fatal. These struggles are not waged in the terms defined by "development" agencies or a narrowly conceived politics of "choice." I argue that both struggles are intimately linked because the institutions that generate violence are the very ones that engender economic inequality and have consistently structured policies that are detrimental to women.[9] Understanding these connections will help make possible the necessary political alliances among "third world" and "first world" women.

Imperialism at Work:
"Development" and the Politics of Sexuality

The histories of "third world" women have been marked by colonialism and imperialism, both by the superimposition of European political and economic interests as well as by the ideology which colonizers produced to justify and legitimate their rule. Additionally, there continues to be colonization of a different kind which women of color in the United States, Black women in Britain and women in "third world" countries have identified and struggled against. They have identified racism and a lack of political self consciousness on the part of white western feminists who continue to colonize the experiences of "third world" women by using political and analytic strategies that emerge from their *specific* experiences of domination and resistance to characterize the experiences of *all* women in other parts of the world. The location of western feminists within an existing hierarchy of power between "first world" and "third world" countries, with differential/preferential access to funding, publishing houses, organizing international conferences, and so on, help to subordinate and often erase the political struggles of "third world" women. For instance, in its haste to establish a universal sisterhood, a certain brand of feminist theorizing saw *all* women as victims of male sexual violence. When it reached the African continent, however, sexual violence assumed the nomenclature of "genital *mutilation*."[10] In the absence of any broader discussion abut racism, colonialism, and culture, the focus on *mutilation* helped to conjure up and reinforce imagery of the barbaric "other" and also muted "third world" women's understandings of this practice.[11] The caution against reserving for feminism a set of practices which wear the mask of universalism, but which below the surface are quite particular in scope, is crucial as we map strategies and alliances that cross geography.

Other imperialist gestures have been enacted through population control programs of the Rockefeller and Ford foundations and later the U.S. government (US AID) with pernicious effects on women. Together, these institutions promoted the ideology that it was the wild, unruly fertility of "third world" women that was responsible for "overpopulation" and which therefore needed to be curbed because it stood in the way of modernization and progress. Nationalist governments, for their part, either defined women as guardians of culture, arguing that it was women's cultural, even national responsibility to bear and raise children, and/or saw women as appropriate targets to be controlled and ended up installing population control programs. In this scenario, women's wombs became the conduit of "development." Sterilization abuse became the norm, accounting in the case of Bangladesh for example, for about 43 percent of "contraceptive" use.[12] Here, too, coercive programs (euphemistically called incentives) link food subsidy to sterilization, forcing impoverished women to be sterilized. In other instances, there is the widespread use of the pill, IUDs, and other aggressive contraceptive devices that were either banned or were in the experimental phases in countries like the United States.[13] The sterilization of Puerto Rican women (La Operación), Black women in South Africa and the United States, and indigenous women in the United States, Australia, and Aotearoa (New Zealand) reveals that colonialism provides the rationale for intervention while racism works to ensure that it is the lives of "third world" women that are deemed most expendable![14]

Imperialism has also provided an easy entré for the Right to promote procreation while at the same time controlling its material base. Religious fundamentalists and the secular Right from the United States (the same forces behind *Webster* and institutionalization of "the family") have seized upon "third world" feminists' critiques of population control programs, forged alliances with the U.S. government, and worked to tie support for "development" aid to strategies which curtail women's sexual autonomy. Enacted in 1984, the "Mexico City Policy" of the U.S. government prohibited international agencies and voluntary organizations, such as International Planned Parenthood Federation, from supporting private, "third world" organizations that provide abortion services, counseling, and referral.[15] Approximately a decade earlier, the very year that abortion was legalized in the United States, the Helms Amendment to the U.S. Foreign Assistance Act prevented the use of government funds for abortion services overseas.[16] Not surprisingly, women are already feeling the ill effects of this policy in increasing numbers. Hospitals in Lusaka, Zambia have reported increases in the numbers of women who come for medical treatment for complications deriving from incomplete, induced abortions. Most women wait for at least 12 hours, often overnight because abortion cases are assigned to the end of the day. Even in the United States, where abortion is legal, bureaucracy and class operate to push women's concerns at the end of the list, further endangering their lives.[17] In most of Latin America and the Caribbean, where abortion remains illegal, the "electronic church" (as Lucille Mathurin Mair calls it) has circumvented governments and installed its own satellites for proselytizing, equating morality with motherhood; only "bad women" get abortions.[18] What is muted in this analysis by the Right is that "morality is material when it is forged on the smithy of practice into a weapon of ideology."[19]

The ideology of intervention, premised on regulating discrete social indicators, has substituted for these histories the narrow concern with fertility. Not coincidentally, fertility has been the most researched dimension of "third world" women's lives.[20] Appropriated within the "basic needs" approach to development, it is targeted like any other basic need (nutrition, health, water, housing, or education) as a single problem to be solved if "third world" peoples are to move themselves from "tradition" to modernity—the western categories of progress. In this approach, sexuality is not a basic need; instead, regulating fertility (sex and procreation) is seen as the conduit to ensure that the basic needs (food, clothing, and shelter) of a reduced population can be met. In contrast, however, when "third world" women construct understandings of their own sexualities filtered through prisms of their own experiences, they do so through political organizing that shifts the terms away from "fertility" (the definition of nationalist governments and international "aid" agencies) or abortion and "choice" (the narrowly defined agenda of certain feminist politics in the west) to a politics of sexuality. When, in 1984, a group of working-class women in Sao Paulo, Brazil, met to talk about the most urgent problems they were confronting, they demanded sex education and moved to build "collective knowledge about sexuality in a non-authoritarian way."[21] Those meetings have culminated in the publication and wide dissemination of five booklets that deal with women's individual experiences with their bodies and the material conditions affecting their sexualities.[22] Similarly, working-class women in Jamaica used the experiences of "violence" against women to form a group that has worked since 1977 to politicize culture through theater.[23]

"Courageous Women
Hand Us the Banner of Struggle by Surviving"[24]

Political struggles against violence are among the most visible of women's organized movements. Contemporary contexts are ones in which the enthusiasm which greeted the announcement of the "Decade for Women" in 1985 has now given way to some harsh economic realities for the majority of women. Neither "development," "population control," nor the "decade" has proven itself capable of alleviating the poverty of either rural-based peasant women or their urban-based working-class counterparts whose ties to land have been severed. At the moment, economies are being held hostage by agencies like the International Monetary Fund and the World Bank. These institutions build into the conditions of their loans cutbacks in social services and health programs by the borrowing countries that exact a disproportionate toll on women. Many examples like the following can be found. In Mexico, Jamaica, South Korea, Taiwan, Singapore, Indonesia, Malaysia, and Thailand (and in the U.S. Silicon Valley), multinational corporations that remain largely hostile to trade union organizing and collective bargaining are attempting to manage successive waves of capitalist crises by conglomerating "third world" women's labor into Export Processing Zones (EPZs).[25] As the name suggests, the electronics, toys, and textiles which these women produce are consumed not by them, but by consumers in the "first world," who can afford the terms of purchase primarily because of the devalued conditions under which these young women work. Together with nationalist governments, these corporations pursue the twin strategy of simultaneous exploitation of female labor and the female body.[26] They generate and deploy ideologies that continue to naturalize women's subordination, portraying women as "docile bodies" ostensibly providing a rationalization for disciplining the workforce and keeping wages low.[27]

Structural economic violence is in fact one of the conditions women consistently identify as being responsible for increased male sexual violence—a problem which women have put on the political agenda in India, Latin America, the Caribbean, and the Philippines. Sistren, a political, cultural women's collective in Jamaica, has argued, for instance, that persistent economic crises have helped to puncture the ideology of the male breadwinner, resulting in increased incidence of sexual violence in those households where women are economically dependent upon men.[28] Politicizing eroticized domination is difficult indeed in contexts where notions of "privacy," "tradition," and "family," "law," and "culture" conspire to uphold the sanctity of domesticity and marriage, even where heterosexual conjugal relationships are not the predominant form of family. For almost two years women in Trinidad and Tobago mobilized to criminalize rape within marriage—a fact which neither nationalist governments nor their colonial predecessors acknowledged. Rape within marriage is now recognized as a criminal offense!!! (albeit under very circumscribed situations).[29] The same law that has criminalized rape in marriage has moved, however, to criminalize lesbian sex, pointing ultimately to the real limits of viewing the state as the protector of *all* women's freedoms and to the importance of organizing on several fronts simultaneously.[30] In spite of certain victories and reforms which women have wrested from the state, it remains a major force in the defense of patriarchal norms.

When patriarchy, religion, caste, and economic arrangements collude, the conditions for sexual and physical violence are sharpened. Indian feminists writing in "Manushi" have maintained that when women's claims for land threaten existing caste relationships, the landed aristocracy, their goons, and the police move in to keep women in their place (and by extension reinforce patriarchal norms) through violence.[31] It was these conditions that propelled the urban women's protest movements of the 1970s and continue to shape contemporary struggles at present.[32]

But any understanding of structural economic violence is incomplete without also understanding women's sexuality under systemic militarized conditions. This involves not only the meteoric increases in military expenditures and the proliferation of the multinational arms industry but also the militarization of the society—the tendency on the part of "third world" governments to define the most urgent problems confronting their societies in terms of "national security."[33] Health and education never assume the importance of "national security." In 1980, South Korea directed $2 billion toward military expenditures, $904 million toward education, and a mere $97 million toward health.[34] Militarized countries are also the ones that have invited EPZs to "develop" and modernize their economies. As Cynthia Enloe has argued, "patriarchy alone—without police and military reinforcement—is seen by elites as inadequate to sustain the discipline they need in order to reassure foreign investors that their societies are good bets for profitable investments."[35]

Women who have been politically active in Chile and other parts of Latin America have exposed "political terror as daily terror," where the militarized state has refined the means of torture on women. Ximena Bunster-Burotto has unveiled the many faces of torture and violence: brutal, sexual violence and rape of women who have been involved politically; physical and psychic violence to force women into identifying men (husbands, lovers, brothers) whom the state sees as threatening; torturing pregnant women, ostensibly to remind them that their place is in the private sphere of the home and not the public sphere of politics.[36]

These women have implicated the state in repression, economic instability, militarization, eroticized domination, and violence and continually risk their lives in the process. Similarly, in the Philippines, women have politicized the continued presence of U.S. bases and the continuing reliance of U.S. military men (individuals as well as the entire military apparatus) on prostitutes: some 20,000 women (about 9,000 of whom are registered and licensed in Olongapo City near the Subic Bay Naval Air Base) and approximately 8,000 children, who are contributing to the national income, especially in the Subic area.[37]

Women from Micronesia have organized around the defense of land and livelihood and against the nuclear colonization in the Pacific that resulted in birth defects and an increase in uterine cancers. When "Women Working for a Nuclear Free and Independent Pacific" organizes to stop the mining of uranium on sacred lands in South Australia or oppose the U.S. plan to incinerate chemical weapons on Johnston Island, they are organizing for respect for their sacred beliefs, for the recovery of their lands as a source of their livelihood, and for freedom of self-determination.[38] As Haunani-Kay Trask, has stated: "What is the basis of [our] survival? Land—the earth mother, Papa. Land—'aina, source of food and shelter. Land—keeper of our ancestors' bones…The land is all."[39] When women in the Philippines place prostitution back within the economic changes that displace them from the land, they, too, see militarization as anathema to their survival.[40]

The struggle against violence is intimately linked to the struggle for economic justice primarily because violence is enacted most systematically against the most impoverished in the society. Peace and equality cannot be separated from "development." The institutions that generate violence are the very ones that engender inequality, having deployed "development" strategies that have been harmful to or irrelevant for women. In the absence of economic justice, the material character of women's lives is seriously jeopardized. The conditions and experiences of motherhood provide vivid reminders of the political intransigence of state managers in solving the most pressing economic problems in their societies. It is to a discussion of the politics of motherhood that I now turn.

Politicizing Motherhood and the Economics of Abortion

Even as the Right continues to link motherhood to morality and to materiality, available evidence indicates that it is unsafe to consider motherhood or be a mother for the majority of "third world" women, particularly those who are not middle-class. Existing data, subject as it is to underreporting and more often to political manipulation, might well underestimate the true scope of the problem. Nothing is said of the ideological conditions of compulsory motherhood and reproduction or of the enforced silences around open expressions of sexuality, particularly lesbian sexuality. Nor is much attention given to the social conditions of inadequate housing and the disproportionate toll infants suffer in deaths prior to reaching the age of five. There is silence on the numbers of women whom the state has "disappeared" in Latin America, Palestine, and South Africa. Finally, the data does not reflect those women who die annually from clandestine abortions. The laws criminalizing abortion stand as vivid reminders of colonialism. They threaten to impose penalties of from two to 20 years' imprisonment upon women using homeopathic methods or their medical practitioners.[41]

Sometimes abortion presents a complicated picture. In specific instances, it might be used to strengthen patriarchal norms that privilege men over women, male fetuses over female fetuses. Feminists in India who have organized to ban sex determination tests do so in the midst of intense pressure placed on women to abort the female fetus. Gains around legalized abortion might be rolled back as happened in Iran after 1979, or as in Zambia, where cumbersome bureaucratic procedures around medical consent work to keep women from getting abortions to which they are entitled by law.[42] As in the United States, the insidious divisions of class conspire to place impoverished women at greater risk of death and sterility. Doctors benefit from a huge underground practice in a context where medicine assumes the status of religion and the physician assumes the status of God with close material links to the judicial system. Doctors continue to gain the support from a secular cultural consensus that labels women who seek abortions as bad or immoral.

The contradiction of compulsory motherhood, on the one hand, and criminalizing or infantilizing womanhood, on the other, sharpens the politics of resistance and creates greater urgency for women to organize on multiple fronts simultaneously. These contradictions provide some of the bases for political alliances for women across geography based on unity that has to be continually and self consciously forged. It suggests that to come to consciousness of one's individual oppression is to open one's sensibilities to all other communities of resistance, to local and global struggles, and to understand the ways in which they are linked. This means that we must learn to act out of these sensibilities, "making an individual/local case into an issue, turning issues into causes and causes into movements," and building into the process the capacity to make other women's struggles one's own.[43] A politics of feminism must be firmly rooted in these visions.

Notes

1. I wish to thank Virginia Chalmers, Ketu Katrak, and Marlene Gerber Fried for their generosity and patience. And, in the words of Ximena Bunster-Burotto, "I also wish to acknowledge the women who have survived and found the strength to bear witness, and the women who did not survive but who did contribute and are contributing toward change for all of us" (from "Surviving Beyond Fear: Women and Torture in Latin America," in June Nash and Helen Safa, eds., *Women and Change in Latin America*, Granby, MA: Bergin and Garvey Publishers, 1985: 297-325).

2. Noted in Maria Mies, "Sexist and Racist Implications of the New Reproductive Technologies," *Alternatives*, Vol. XII (1987): 333.

3. Barbara Smith, "Making the Connections," *Gay Community News*, Vol. 17, No. 24 (December 24, 1989-January 6, 1990): 5.

4. Chandra Talpade Mohanty, "Cartographies of Struggle: Third World Women and the Politics of Feminism," forthcoming in Mohanty, Ann Russo, and Lordes Torres (eds.), *Third World Women and the Politics of Feminism*, Bloomington, Indiana: Indiana University Press. The caution against the use of monolithic prescriptions applies equally to the categories "first world" and "third world." I have employed quotation marks throughout to suggest that they must be problematized. In spite of their inadequacy, these categories do summarize certain historical practices and cannot, therefore, be discarded at will.

5. A. Sivanandan, "All That Melts Into Air Is Solid, The Hokum of New Times," *Race and Class*, Vol. 31, No. 3 (January-March 1990): 25. This discussion pertained to Broadwater Farm, a community in London. For a discussion of feminist and Black communities of resistance in the U.S., see bell hooks, *Talking Back: Thinking Feminist, Thinking Black*, Boston: South End Press, 1989.

6. Cherríe Moraga and Gloria Anzaldúa, *This Bridge Called My Back: Writings by Radical Women of Color*, New York: Kitchen Table, Women of Color Press,

1983. For a similar treatment of the British context, see Shabnam Grewal et al., *Charting the Journey: Writings By Black and Third World Women,* London: Sheba Feminist Publishers, 1988.

7. Kumari Jayawardena, *Feminism and Nationalism in the Third World,* London: Zed Press, 1986: 2.

8. There are several conferences and alliances that have attempted to move beyond these distortions of historical power. For instance, in 1985 in Nairobi, "third world" women from 26 countries and women from 17 western countries banded together in the face of the internationalized Right and issued the following statement: "Women in the Third World demand access to all methods of family planning, including abortion as a back-up method, and assert our right to choose for ourselves what is best for us in our situation. By protecting our lives, we protect the lives of children that we genuinely want and can care for. This is our conception of 'Pro Life.'" Fred T. Sai and Janet Nassi, "The Need for a Reproductive Health Approach," *International Journal of Gynaecology and Obstetrics,* Special Issue: Women's Health in the Third World: The Impact of Unwanted Pregnancy (Supplement 3, 1989): 111. A similar kind of political strategy was adopted at the Fifth International Women and Health Conference that took place in San Jose, Costa Rica, in 1987. Other networks of note in this regard include: the Bangladesh International Action Group (BIAG), the Boston Women's Health Book Collective, ISIS International with a regional desk in Santiago, Chile, and the Women's Global Network for Reproductive Rights. For a useful discussion of the International Tribunal and Meeting on Reproductive Rights that took place in Amsterdam in 1984, see *Divided in Culture: United in Struggle,* Netherlands: Women's Global Network for Reproductive Rights, 1986.

9. This argument is similar to the general thesis of the DAWN (Development Alternatives with Women for a New Era) group. See Gita Sen and Caren Grown, *Development, Crises, and Alternative Visions: Third World Women's Perspectives,* New York: Monthly Review Press, 1987.

10. Chandra Talpade Mohanty has provided a lucid and pathbreaking analysis of the political and analytical effects of western feminist theorizing that has homogenized the divergent experiences of "third world" women. See Chandra Talpade Mohanty, "Under Western Eyes: Feminist Scholarship and Colonial Discourses, *Boundary 2,* Vol. XII, No. 3/Vol. 13, No. 1 (Spring/Fall, 1983/84): 332-358.

11. *Ibid.:* 338-339. For a discussion of the ways in which racism and Eurocentrism have shaped the discourse on AIDS and promote a similar displacement linking the occurrence of AIDS to "exotic" or "barbaric" practices on the African continent, see Margaret Cerullo and Evelynn Hammonds, "AIDS in Africa: The Western Imagination and the Dark Continent," *Radical America,* Vol. 21, Nos. 2-3 (March/April 1987): 17-23. Some of the impetus for writing this article came from a discussion by Fran Hoskens, entitled "Female Genital Mutilation and AIDS," that appeared in *Sojourner* (February 1988) in which Hoskens makes some spurious and inaccurate correlations between female "*genital* mutilation" and the incidence and prevalence of AIDS. Mohanty, in her analysis, also challenges the "Women as Victims of Sexual Violence" ideology of Hoskens and others. See note above. For a careful and thorough analysis of political organizing by women in the Sudan, Somalia, and other African and Arab countries, as well as groups in Britain, see Liliane Landor, *The Amputation of Desire,* London (unpublished manuscript), 1989.

12. Mies, *op. cit.:* 323-342.

13. The work of Betsy Hartmann is invaluable here. See Betsy Hartmann, *Reproductive Rights and Wrongs: The Global Politics of Population Control and Contraceptive Choice,* New York: Harper and Row, 1987; See also, Hartmann and Hilary Standing, *The Poverty of Population Control: Family Planning and Health Policy in Bangladesh,* London: Bangladesh International Action Group, 1989. For

a discussion of the Indian context, see Gabrielle Ross, "Lured into Sterilization," *Connexions,* No. 31 (1989): 20. For a discussion of the South African context, see "Women's Health in South Africa," *WiserLinks,* Issue No. 11 (May/June 1987): 23-26.

14. For a discussion of the indigenous situation in Australia, see "Claiming my Mothers, Exposing Aboriginal Consciousness to the World: An Interview with Aboriginal Black Lesbian playwright, Eva Johnson," *Black/Out,* Vol. 2, No. 2 (Summer, 1989): 48-53.

15. Adrienne Germain, "The Christopher Tietz International Symposium: An Overview," in *International Journal of Gynaecology and Obstetrics, op. cit.* Adrienne Germaine and Jane Ordway, *Population Control and Women's Health,* New York: International Women's Health Coalition, June 1989: 8.

16. This was the dress rehearsal for the Hyde Amendment, which in 1977 prohibited the use of Medicaid funds for abortion in the United States.

17 Mary Ann Castle, "Abortion in the Third World," *Zeta* (June 1989): 21-22.

18. Lucille Mathurin Mair, "Commentary on the Ethics of Induced Abortion from a Feminist Perspective," *International Journal of Gynaecology and Obstetrics, op. cit.:* 57-60.

19. Sivanandan, *op. cit.:* 29.

20. Janet Henshall Momsen and Janet Townsend, *Geography of Gender in the Third World,* Hutchinson: State University of New York Press, 1987: 36.

21. Carmen Barroso and Cristina Bruschini, "Discussions on Sexuality Among Poor Women in Brazil," forthcoming in Mohanty et al., *op. cit.*

22. *Ibid.*

23. Honor Ford Smith with Sistren, *Lionheart Gal: Life Stories of Jamaican Women,* London: The Women's Press, 1986: xiii-xxxi.

24. Bunster-Burotto, *op. cit.*

25. June Nash and Maria Patricia Fernandez-Kelly, *Women, Men and the International Division of Labor,* Albany: State University of New York Press, 1983.

26. Honor Ford Smith, "Development and the Cultural Worker's Dilemma," paper presented at Women's Studies Seminar, Massachusetts Institute of Technology, October, 1989.

27. Aihwa Ong, *Spirits of Resistance and Capitalist Discipline: Factory Women in Malaysia,* Albany: State University of New York Press, 1987: xiv. Important ethnic and cultural differences are not meant to be conflated here.

28. Ford Smith, *Lionheart Gal, op. cit.*

29. I have developed this argument more fully in an essay, "Recasting Morality: The Post-Colonial State and Sexual Offences Bill of Trinidad and Tobago," forthcoming in Mohanty et al., *op. cit.*

30. *The Sexual Offences Act of Trinidad and Tobago,* Port-of-Spain: Government Printing Office, 1986, clauses 5 and 16.

31. Madhu Kishwar and Ruth Vanita, *In Search of Answers: Indian Women's Voices from Manushi,* London: Zed Press, 1984: 177-200.

32. Kum Kum Sangari and Sudesh Vaid, *Recasting Women: Essays in Colonial History,* New Delhi: Kali for Women, 1989: 2.

33. Cynthia Enloe, "Women Textile Workers in the Militarization of Southeast Asia," in Nash and Kelly, *op. cit.:* 407-425.

34. *Ibid.:* 419.

35. *Ibid.:* 408.

36. Barroso and Bruschini, *op. cit..*

37. Cynthia Enloe, *Bananas, Beaches and Bases: Making Feminist Sense of International Politics,* Berkeley: University of California Press, 1990: 81-91.

38. Micronesia consists of four groupings of islands: Belau, Federated States of Micronesia, Marshall Islands, and the Commonwealth of the Northern Mariana Islands. Women Working for a Nuclear Free and Independent Pacific first formed

in 1984 "to support indigenous people's struggles to be independent and nuclear free." *Pacific Women Speak Out: Why Haven't You Known,* London: Green Line, 1987.

39. Haunani-Kay Trask, "Self Determination for Pacific Island Women: The Case of Hawai'i," paper delivered at Stanford University, 1987.

40. Enloe, *Bananas, op. cit.*

41. It is instructive to note, for instance, that the early colonial laws were designed to criminalize abortion practices among women. Here is an example of a British colonial law of 1925 that is in effect in Trinidad and Tobago: "Every woman, being with child, who, with intent to procure her own miscarriage, unlawfully administers to herself any poison or other noxious thing, or unlawfully uses any instrument or other means whatsoever with the like intent, and any person who, with intent to procure the miscarriage of any woman, whether she is or is not with child, unlawfully administers to her or causes to be taken by her any poison or other noxious thing, or unlawfully uses any instrument or other means whatsoever with the like intent is liable to imprisonment for four years." *Laws of Trinidad and Tobago, Offences Against the Person,* 56 of Chapter 11:08. Port-of-Spain: Government Printing Office, 1986. In the case of the Philippines, the law prohibiting abortion was contained in the 1930 penal code which originated in the Spanish penal code of 1870. Alfredo Flores Tadiar notes that while Spain has been forced to liberalize its own laws, the Philippines retains a restriction that was imposed 120 years ago. (The same can be argued for the United States and Britain and the criminal penalties for abortion in their former colonies.) In 1989, the Catholic Church and conservative forces in the Philippines introduced a bill into Congress advocating the death penalty for abortion! Alfredo Flores Tadiar, "Commentary on the Law and Abortion in the Philippines," *International Journal of Gynaecology and Obstetrics, op. cit.:* 89-92.

42. Haleh Afshar, "Women, State and Ideology in Iran," in *Connexions,* 31, 1989: 9.

43. I have borrowed liberally from Sivanandan's argument to make this point. *Op. cit.:* 29.

Abortion and Sterilization
in the Third World

- Worldwide, 500,000 women die annually of pregnancy complications. 200,000 die from illegal abortions—one woman every three minutes.

- Illegal abortion is the leading cause of maternal mortality, ectopic pregnancies, hysterectomies, and poor health.

- 38 million abortions are performed annually in the third world; 17.6 million are legal, 20.4 million are illegal.

- Of third world women aged 15-44, 252 million live in countries where abortion is illegal or severely restricted; 107 million live in countries that allow abortion only on medical grounds. Most of the 460 million women who live in countries that allow abortion on social grounds live in either China or India.

- Worldwide, sterilization is the most widespread form of birth control. Legal abortion and barrier methods of contraception are largely unavailable in third world countries. In the United States the federal government continues to pay 90% of the cost of sterilization.

- Female sterilization is more common than male sterilization even though it is a more complicated and riskier operation.

- Economic incentives and physical coercion for sterilization are used in many countries. In El Salvador food aid is offered to poor women who get sterilized. In India brute force was used to round up "eligible men" for forcible sterilization.

- 35% of Puerto Rican women have been sterilized.

- Until 1979, when HEW was pressured to release sterilzation guidelines, 100,000 women were sterilized annually in the United States under Medicaid and family planning agency auspices.

- Between 1973 and 1976, 3,406 indigenous women were sterilized at one Indian Health Services Hospital in Oklahoma—one-fourth of the Native American women admitted to the hospital.

SOURCES: *Connexions,* 31, 1989; "The Christopher Tietz International Symposium: An Overview" in *International Journal of Gynaecology and Obstetrics,* Special Issue: *Women's Health in the Third World: The Impact of Unwanted Pregnancy,* Supplement 3, 1989:111; *Reproductive Rights and Wrongs,* Betsy Hartmann, New York, Harper and Row, 1987; *Population Control and Women's Health,* International Women's Health Coalition, June, 1989; *Of Woman Born: Motherhood as Experience and Institution,* Adrienne Rich, New York: W.W. Norton, 1986; *Population Control Politics: Women, Sterilization and Reproductive Choice,* Thomas Shapiro, Philadelphia: Temple University Press, 1985; "Safe Motherhood: An International Conference to Prevent the Deaths of 500,000 Annually," *Women's Health Journal,* Isis International, Latin American and Caribbean Women's Health Network, Santiago, Chile, May/June 1987: 3; World Health Organization, Population Institute.

Right to Life:
What Can the White Man Say
to the Black Woman?[1]

Alice Walker

*What is of use in these words I offer in memory and recognition
of our common mother. And to my daughter.*

What can the white man say to the black woman?

For four hundred years he ruled over the black woman's womb.

Let us be clear. In the barracoons and along the slave shipping coasts of Africa, for more than twenty generations, it was he who dashed our babies' brains out against the rocks.

What can the white man say to the black woman?

For four hundred years he determined which black woman's children would live or die.

Let it be remembered. It was he who placed our children on the auction block in cities all across the eastern half of what is now the United States, and listened to and watched them beg for their mothers' arms, before being sold to the highest bidder and dragged away.

What can the white man say to the black woman?

We remember that Fannie Lou Hamer, a poor sharecropper on a Mississippi plantation, was one of twenty-one children; and that on plantations across the South black women often had twelve, fifteen, twenty children. Like their enslaved mothers and grandmothers before them, these black women were sacrificed to the profit the white man could make from harnessing their bodies and their children's bodies to the cotton gin.

What can the white man say to the black woman?

We see him lined up on Saturday nights, century after century, to make the black mother, who must sell her body to feed her children, go down on her knees to him.

Let us take note:

He has not cared for a single one of the dark children in his midst, over hundreds of years.

Where are the children of the Cherokee, my great grandmother's people?

Gone.

Where are the children of the Blackfoot?

Gone.

Where are the children of the Lakota?

Gone.

Of the Cheyenne?

Of the Chippewa?

Of the Iroquois?

Of the Sioux?

Of the Mandinka?

Of the Ibo?

Of the Ashanti?

Where are the children of the "Slave Coast" and Wounded Knee?

We do not forget the forced sterilization and forced starvations on the reservations, here as in South Africa. Nor do we forget the smallpox-infested blankets Indian children were given by the Great White Fathers of the United States government.

What has the white man to say to the black woman?

When we have children you do everything in your power to make them feel unwanted from the moment they are born. You send them to fight and kill other dark mothers' children around the world. You shove them onto public highways into the path of oncoming cars. You shove their heads through plate glass windows. You string them up and you string them out.

What has the white man to say to the black woman?

From the beginning, you have treated all dark children with absolute hatred.

Thirty million African children died on the way to the Americas, where nothing awaited them but endless toil and the crack of a bullwhip. They died of a lack of food, of lack of movement in the holds of ships. Of lack of friends and relatives. They died of depression, bewilderment and fear.

What has the white man to say to the black woman?

Let us look around us: Let us look at the world the white man has made for the black woman and her children.

It is a world in which the black woman is still forced to provide cheap labor, in the form of children, for the factories and on the assembly lines of the white man.

It is a world into which the white man dumps every foul, person-annulling drug he smuggles into creation.

It is a world where many of our babies die at birth, or later of malnutrition, and where many more grow up to live lives of such misery they are forced to choose death by their own hands.

What has the white man to say to the black woman, and to all women and children everywhere?

Let us consider the depletion of the ozone; let us consider homelessness and the nuclear peril; let us consider the destruction of the rain forests—in the name of the almighty hamburger. Let us consider the poisoned apples and the poisoned water and the poisoned air and the poisoned earth.

And that all of our children, because of the white man's assault on the planet, have a possibility of death by cancer in their almost immediate future.

What has the white, male lawgiver to say to any of us? To those of us who love life too much to willingly bring more children into a world saturated with death?

Abortion, for many women, is more than an experience of suffering beyond anything most men will ever know; it is an act of mercy, and an act of self-defense.

To make abortion illegal again is to sentence millions of women and children to miserable lives and even more miserable deaths.

Given his history, in relation to us, I think the white man should be ashamed to attempt to speak for the unborn children of the black woman. To force us to have children for him to ridicule, drug and turn into killers and homeless wanderers is a testament to his hypocrisy.

What can the white man say to the black woman?

Only one thing that the black woman might hear.

Yes, indeed, the white man can say, Your children have a right to life. Therefore I will call back from the dead those 30 million who were tossed overboard during the centuries of the slave trade. And the other millions who died in my cotton fields and hanging from my trees.

I will recall all those who died of broken hearts and broken spirits, under the insult of segregation.

I will raise up all the mothers who died exhausted after birthing twenty-one children to work sunup to sundown on my plantation. I will restore to full health all those who perished for lack of food, shelter, sunlight, and love; and from my inability to see them as human beings.

But I will go even further.

I will tell you, black woman, that I wish to be forgiven the sins I commit daily against you and your children. For I know that until I treat your children with love, I can never be trusted by my own. Nor can I respect myself.

And I will free your children from insultingly high infant mortality rates, short life spans, horrible housing, lack of food, rampant ill health. I will liberate them from the ghetto. I will open wide the doors of all the schools and hospitals and businesses of society to your children. I will look at your children and see not a threat but a joy.

I will remove myself as an obstacle in the path that your children, against all odds, are making toward the light. I will not assassinate them for dreaming dreams and offering new visions of how to live. I will cease trying to lead your children, for I can see I have never understood where I was going. I will agree to sit quietly for a century or so, and meditate on this.

This is what the white man can say to the black woman.

We are listening.

Notes

1. This article originally appeared in © *The Nation,* May 22, 1989. Reprinted by permission.

SPEAKING OUT FOR WOMEN:
CHOOSING OURSELVES

Before Roe v. Wade

Sharon Cox

Behind the couch I sit
at nine I am always an uninvited guest—
at these women's gatherings
but today I just have to attend—
so many of them at one time is
different and too exciting for me not to listen from
my invisible spot

Behind the couch I can feel the tension like smoke that hangs in
the air—as they speak in whispers about some un-named she
She had to do it—she couldn't have another one—
because if she had it—some also un-named they would
take her kids away—or they might put her in jail
The women agree that this is a real possibility

Behind the couch I sit still and alert—
Like in church I know I must be quiet or risk disgrace
The women are silent between sentences like
some kind of ritual is taking place or a sacred
vigil. They speak of her being in pain, lots of blood
fever, and maybe dying. The women say things like—
I did what I could—put cold compresses on her
head, she didn't look good. I went to you know who's this morning
and she is going to get some medicine from the place she works
maybe it will help fight the infection
One woman says—maybe she should go to the
hospital, no the others say all at once she'll
go to jail for sure and anyway we already
suggested that, she won't go.

Behind the couch my heart is pounding and a new terror
fills me—I know this thing they speak of is a woman's
thing! Over and over the voice in my head asks what is it,
what is it? My mother says this un-named she must

have waited too long or couldn't get the money sooner
to have the A.B.O.R.T.I.O.N. as if to say it
out-right is dangerous.

Behind the couch I sound out these letters—a-bort-ion
I can't wait to get a dictionary, I'm too frightened.
I say loudly what's an abortion? My mother's eyes lock
on me from over the back of the couch—The other women
are silent—mama's eyes tell me I've committed some sacrilege
she is ashamed. Of me? Of herself? I don't know.
Unasked I leave the room. But, the A.B.O.R.T.I.O.N.
word is now associated with had to do it, pain, fever, blood,
death, and women.

Exits and Entrances[1]

Joan Fishbein

College girls I know jumped rope,
gulped castor oil, took hot baths;
Park Avenue doctors scraped
and dilated in locked rooms—
and there was always the hanger.
But in Santurce in 1960, Emilio Lopez,
who drove a black Lincoln Continental and ran
a free neighborhood clinic, did the job
fast and clean on mainland women,
no questions asked, for $550.
Any taxi at San Juan airport could take you
there, a villa of many exits and entrances
where chickens cawed across the street,
the scent of jasmine caught in your throat.
While the ice pack on your belly slowed the bleeding,
numbed the pain, you heard mothers who
crooned in Spanish to babies
waiting for check-ups in the cloister below.
You contemplated palm fronds and coconuts
through arched windows, counted tiles in the wall
to pass time. Tourists gambled in casinos
a few miles away. On the beach
bound by luxury hotels, bodies changed color,
the salt sticking to their limbs.

Notes

1. This poem appeared in a slightly different version in the Fall 1988 issue of *The Kennesaw Review*. Reprinted by permission.

A Question of Survival/A Conspiracy of Silence: Abortion and Black Women's Health[1]

Byllye Avery

Getting Involved

I got involved in women's health around the issue of abortion. My first experience with abortion was in 1973 in Gainesville, Florida. Three of us were identified as women who could help other women get abortions. I didn't know anything about abortions. In my life that word couldn't even be mentioned without having somebody look at you crazy. Then someone's talking to me about how to get an abortion. It seemed unreal. But as more women came to us wanting abortions (and at first they were mostly white middle-class women), we gave them a phone number in New York. They could catch a plane and go there for an abortion. But then a Black woman came. We gave her the phone number, and she looked at us in awe: "I can't go to New York..." Most Black women didn't know they could get an abortion anywhere, and those who did know certainly did not have money to fly to New York. We had no means of helping financially because we were just working women ourselves. We realized we needed a different plan of action, so in May 1974, after abortion had become legal, we opened up the Gainesville Women's Health Center.

What was striking to me was the large number of Black women who came in to get abortions. We also had a well-women gynecology clinic, and that's where the educational work went on about getting in control of your body.

But then the decision was made in Washington to cut off the Medicaid abortion money: I remember when the threat of it started coming down. I interviewed a woman for our newspaper who was a Medicaid patient. She was having her second abortion, and I asked her if she knew that Medicaid funding for abortions was being cut off.

She answered me with a question. Why does the government want hungry children in the world? It was very poignant to me. She continued: we live in this society, where you have to have a place to stay, everyone needs a house. They say you have to have your body covered, which means you need clothing. Nobody gives you anything to eat. You have to have food. "I got a television," she said, "that I bought from Goodwill for $5 and it doesn't half-play but when it plays, I see people eating steak on television, and my children are eating chicken backs and chicken necks."

When you think of it, when access to abortion is taken away from poor people, it doesn't mean that poor women will stop having babies. What it means is that the poor will be poorer.

"Choice" and Medicaid Cuts

When Medicaid was paying for abortion, that mere fact stated to the women that it is all right to have an abortion if you want to. Taking away Medicaid funding says to poor women, "you can't have this—you don't deserve to have this."

All women are oppressed, but poor women have another layer of oppression, and poor Black women have another layer beyond that. Poor people don't feel powerful; they don't feel they have any power or control in their lives. There is a constant experience of things being done to them. If Medicaid pays for abortion, poor women have a little bit of control they can exercise, but remove that funding and that control, and choice is just a silly word.

We have to look at the fact that many women feel powerless. We have to broaden how we look at reproduction. To say to a person who feels beaten down and powerless and who does not have the means, "you can make a choice," is nonsense. We need financing so, if I am poor, I can have this baby any way I want to, or I can have an abortion.

I think that the abortion struggle, if it is to include all women and not just middle-class women, needs to be broadened. I emphasize class, not necessarily race, because I think middle-class women feel and see what the choices are and have enough money to make a choice. Our struggle has to be the struggle of the women who live on lower incomes.

For poor women abortion is a matter of survival: if I have this one more child, it etches away my margin of survival. People always seem not to understand what poor women have to do just to survive, let alone to live. What are you going to do if you're getting just a little bit of money on welfare or if you're working a low-paying job? Many working poor are getting a minimum wage. Who can live on that?

When I started working in the birthing movement I found the same variables that there are for abortion, the same kind of barriers. We have a medical system in which care is given in terms of money, so that poor women don't have options. If they want to have Lamaze, if they want a birthing center, if they want to have it at home but can't afford to, they don't have any options.

Seeing that the same lack of options exists no matter what choices a poor woman makes, frames the struggle for me in a different way. As we learned more about abortions and gynecological care, we realized that we are women with a total reproductive cycle. We might have to make different decisions about our lives, but whatever the decision, we deserve the best services available. So in 1978, we opened up Birthplace, an alternative birthing center. It was exhilarating work; I assisted in probably around 200 births. I understood life and I understood death too. I learned what is missing in prenatal care and why so many of our babies die.

Through my work at Birthplace, I learned the importance of women being involved in our own health. We have to create environments that say "yes." Birthplace was a wonderful space and we fixed it up so that women would want to be there. That's how prenatal care needs to be given—so that women are excited to participate. This is the time to start affecting their lives so that they can start making meaningful lifestyle changes. Health offers all sorts of opportunities for empowerment.

Through Birthplace, I came to understand how important our attitude around birthing is. Many women don't get the exquisite care they deserve. Through the work of Birthplace we have created a prenatal caring program that provides each woman who comes for care with a support group. She enters the group when she arrives, leaves the group to go for her physical checkup, and then returns to the group when she is finished. She doesn't sit in a waiting room for two hours. Most of these women have nobody else to talk to. No one listens to them; no one helps them plan. They're asking: "Who's going to get me to the hospital if I go into labor in the middle of the night, or the middle of the day, for that matter? Who's going to help me get out of this abusive relationship? Who's going to make sure I have the food I need to eat?" Infant mortality is not a medical problem; it's a social problem.

Conspiracy of Silence

Through this work an important thing happened to me. I began looking at myself as a Black woman. Before that I had been looking at myself as a woman. I went to work in a CETA program at a community college, and it brought me face-to-face with my sisters and face-to-face with myself. Just by the nature of the program and the population that I worked with, I had, for the first time in my life, a chance to ask a

19-year-old: why do you have four babies and you're only 19 years old? And I was able to listen, and bring these sisters together to talk about their lives. It was there that I started to understand the lives of Black women and to realize that we live in a conspiracy of silence. We have not been brought up to discuss our health problems. It is only now that women are opening up. Many young Black women, young girls, don't really have the information that would enable them to make informed decisions.

Empowerment, Breaking Silences:
The National Black Women's Health Project

One of the biggest obstacles to having power and control is isolation—not sharing information and not feeling comfortable enough to open up and talk. For example, people are not aware of how many Black women do get abortions. Because women are scared of what other people will say, they keep quiet.

What we have to do as organizers is to bring women together, to get them to sit and to talk openly and to start sharing what things have worked for them. What has your life been like? What has it been like for you growing up as a Black woman? What did your parents talk to you about in terms of sex and sexuality and feelings of being in charge? These discussions allow women to do their own analysis of what is happening to them right now.

It is only after she has done that analysis that she can start moving toward empowerment, toward self-validation. I don't know of any other way to short-circuit that. The main thing that's working against us are these walls of isolation.

This is what the National Black Women's Health Project is all about, groups of Black women getting together and talking to one another about health, about what our issues are, building on what has come out of the women's health movement. The First National Conference on Black Women's Health Issues brought together more than 1,500 women from the United States and the Caribbean. Responding to the rallying cry, "We're sick and tired of being sick and tired," they came with Ph.D.s, M.D.s, welfare cards, in Mercedes and on crutches, from seven days old to 80 years old—urban, rural, gay, straight—to find something.

From the beginning of our organizing we were clear that people needed to be able to work together individually and on a daily basis. This gave us the idea of self-help groups. The first group we formed was in a rural area outside of Gainesville, with 21 women who were severely obese. I thought, "Oh, this is a piece of cake. Obviously these sisters don't have any information. I'll go in here and talk to them about losing weight, talk to them about high blood pressure, talk to them about diabetes—it'll be easy." Little did I know that they would be able to tell me everything that went into a 1,200-calorie-a-day diet. They all had been to Weight Watchers at least five or six times; they all had blood-pressure reading machines as well as medications. And when we sat down to talk, they all said, "We know all that information, but what we also know is that living in the world that we are in, we feel like we are absolutely nothing." One woman said to me, "I work for General Electric making batteries, and from the stuff they suit me up in, I know it's killing me. My home life is not working. My old man is an alcoholic. My kid's got babies. The one thing I know I can do when I come home is cook me a pot of food and sit down in front of the TV and eat it. And you can't take that away from me until you're ready to give me something in its place."

So that made me start to think there was something else to this health piece that had been really missing, that it's not just about giving information; people need something else. We just spent a lot of time talking and planning for our conference. Lillie Allen brought the understanding that we are dying inside. Unless we are able to go inside of ourselves and touch and breathe fire, breathe life into ourselves, then of course we can't be healthy. Lillie started a workshop called "Black and Female: What Is the Reality?" This was a workshop that all of us were terrified of. And we were also terrified not to have it because the conspiracy of silence is killing us.

Violence in Our Lives

When sisters take their shoes off and start talking about what's happening, the first thing we cry about is the violence in our lives. If you look at statistics books, they mention violence in one paragraph. They don't even give numbers, because they can't count it—it's too pervasive.

The number one issue for most of our sisters is violence—battering, sexual abuse. The same thing for their daughters, whether they are 12 or four.

We have to look at how violence is used, how violence and sexism go hand in hand.

When you talk to young people about being pregnant, you find out that most of these girls did not get pregnant by teenage boys. Most of them got pregnant by their mothers' boyfriends or their brothers or their daddies. We've been sitting on that. We can't just tell our daughters, "Just say no." We need to talk to our brothers. We need to tell them the incest makes us crazy. The men need to know that when they hurt us, they hurt themselves because we are their mothers, their sisters, their wives; we are their allies on this planet.

They can't just damage one part of it without damaging themselves. We need men to stop giving consent, by their silence, to rape, to sexual abuse, to violence. You need to talk to your boyfriends, your husbands, your sons, whatever males you have around you—talk to them about talking to other men.

When they are sitting around womanizing, talking bad about women, make sure you have somebody stand up and be your ally and help stop this. For future generations, this has got to stop.

If violence is the number one thing women talk about, the next thing is being mothers too early and too long. For some women who were mothers as teenagers, the very last thing they want is for their daughters to become pregnant as teenagers. Their lives have whipped them totally. They are tired and cannot wait until these kids are grown so that they can have a little freedom, and they don't want to be a grandmother at 38. We are finding that a lot of 38-year-old grandmothers are very angry. They are angry at the world, they are angry at their daughters who got pregnant, they are angry at their lives. And they have a right to be. We need to look at how information about sex and sexuality gets transmitted from generation to generation. It has to start with the individual, and people need to open up and talk honestly with one another.

Part of the problem is that programs on adolescent sexuality deal with the kids, and I maintain that they are not the ones you ought to be dealing with. You need to deal with the mamas and the daddies. It's not a course you can take; it is a life course where you get a little bit of knowledge every day.

We deal with all of these issues at the National Black Women's Health Project and in our self-help groups. Our approach is to broaden the definition of reproductive health. We look at all reproductive choices. We look at infant mortality and other aspects of having children, as well as birth control and abortion. We support women in whatever decisions they make and we are working to empower women to take control of their lives.

Notes

1. Based on an interview by Gail Hovey. Copyright July 14, 1986, "A Question of Silence," *Christianity and Crisis,* 537 West 121st St., New York, New York 10027, and on an interview in *Sojourner: The Women's Forum,* January, 1989, 1050 Commonwealth Ave, Boston, MA 02215. Excerpted by permission of *Christianity and Crisis, Sojourner* and Byllye Avery.

Infant Mortality in the United States

Neonatal mortality (deaths in first 28 days of life) among Black infants increased in 1985 for the first time in 20 years.

The ratio of Black infant deaths to white infant deaths is 1.98:1, the largest gap since 1950.

The rate of low birthweight babies rose in 1985 and has not improved since 1979. Low birthweight is the cause of most neonatal deaths.

14 out of the 15 leading causes of infant deaths are probably preventable by early, continuous, and high-quality health care for women before conception and during pregnancy and for mothers and their babies during delivery and infancy. 25-30% of inner city Black women receive little or no prenatal care. Overall, in 1987, 79% of white mothers and 61% of Black mothers received early care. 5% of white women received no prenatal care; 11% of Black women received none.

The rate of death due to Sudden Infant Death Syndrome (SIDS) is 1.7 times higher for Blacks than for whites.

SOURCE: CDF, (Children's Defense Fund) Reports, January 1988, September 1989.

Choosing Ourselves:
Black Women and Abortion[1]

Beverly Smith

I was asked to try and reflect on what this issue of abortion means for Black women and how we can get Black women involved in organizing. I'm not casting any aspersions at all, but I'd like to take the opportunity to speak not just as a Black woman, but as all the things that I am, which is definitely a feminist, and a health activist who's been involved in this struggle for many, many years.

So, one of the things I want to talk about is what it was like before abortion was legal, because I think there may be some people here who don't have a clue about that. For example, last night I was having dinner with some friends, two men in fact, and my sister and I were recounting the history of the development of battered women's shelters in Boston and we were talking about the time when there was no shelter. I was doing family planning counseling at Boston City Hospital and when a battered woman who was Spanish-speaking came in with cigarette burns, I had nowhere to send her. Nowhere, because there was no shelter. And my friends said they thought there were always things like shelters. So I want to return to the days of yesteryear for a moment because I think that's where the passion comes from for many of us.

This story is about my first day at college. I had a roommate who was another Black woman. And I remember, here we were, nervous and anxious out of our minds. We went down to the basement to look for our trunks, and my new roommate, whom I had just met hours before, started throwing up. She claimed that she was nervous and later told me that she wasn't going to be able to finish out the year. I couldn't quite figure it out. Let me assure you, in 1965 I was quite an innocent. So I don't know how this popped into my mind but I said, the girl is pregnant. A few weeks later, she stayed out all night in violation of the rules that we had at that time. Then she came back and said she would be finishing out the year. So I believe she had an illegal abortion. This was in Chicago. I could have lost a roommate.

Now, of course, she never, ever told me what was going on. She never said that she was pregnant, she never said that she'd had an abortion. One of the most telling things she said—and this gets to the shame of all of this, both as a woman and as a Black woman—was, "You can take the girl out of the ghetto, but you can't take the ghetto out of the girl." That was a pretty intense way to start college, and we never, ever talked about it. When I was thinking of this story, I was thinking about the horrible secrecy that surrounded abortion at that time and how bad that is for the self-esteem and well-being of women.

Related to that secrecy and women's self-esteem is the fact that the reproductive rights movement has never been successful in putting forth certain arguments. Namely, we have never been willing to say clearly that we support abortion because being able to control our reproduction directly affects the quality of our lives, and, in some instances, affects whether we have any lives at all. I'm talking, of course, about death from illegal abortion. There are lots of reasons why we've never asserted this argument. One is that it goes directly against our sexist role conditioning. It's very hard for women to say that when the deal goes down, we choose ourselves. This may mean choosing not to have a baby.

When I wrote that phrase—choosing ourselves, rather than choosing to have a baby—it gave me some insight into the question of why there's been such strong lesbian involvement in the reproductive rights movement. I think it may be because this struggle has to do with giving our love to women. I think so many lesbians work on abortion because we deeply value women's lives, all women's lives, and know in our guts and in our hearts that women need access to abortion in order to have any kind of life at all.

I want to make some comments about the semantics of the abortion struggle and then I want to say a few things about Black women and abortion. It occurred to me this morning that what the anti-abortion people mean by life and what I mean by life are two very different things. Life for them is mostly a biological phenomenon. They don't care about the quality of life for those babies and their mothers, who for many valid reasons don't want a child or feel that they can't have a child, no matter how much they might want to have one. What I think we're fighting for is decent standards of life, including the potential for growth, for all people, including women.

We're fighting for that throughout the lifespan, not just at certain "sacred moments," as the so-called pro-life people would say. And I think there really needs to be an examination of and a commitment to honest terminology about what we're really fighting for. Because I think the truth is very powerful. If we were able to sit down with women and say, "Look, this is the deal, it's not some highfalutin' Constitutional issue, and we're not going to cloak it in those terms," we might actually involve more of the kinds of people that we would like in this movement.

On that note, I would like to talk about some of the issues around Black women in the struggle for abortion. This is problematic, although there certainly have been many of us who have been involved. One thing I feel is that the feminist connection to abortion sometimes turns Black women off, particularly because feminism is so closely associated with white women. That's the immediate image.

Somewhat connected with that is religious fundamentalism. Because as I often say, you people haven't seen fundamentalism—all those TV evangelists to the contrary—until you have seen Black people be fundamentalists. That's not the only tradition of the Black church, at all, but some of us have been fundamentalists since the 19th century and "born again"; I heard that phrase long before it was picked up by the media. I think religious fundamentalism is something we have to grapple with because when you're talking about people who are still very involved in the church, abortion is a very difficult issue to raise.

Now we get to the fear of genocide. Last year I finally came to the conclusion that genocide is a real possibility. Now, of course, there has been a genocidal way of life in this country since we got here as slaves, but there's something about doing AIDS work and my sense that Black people's numbers are actually going to go down in the next decade or so that make me think about genocide in a whole different way. But Black people have always feared genocide, particularly around contraception and abortion.

I have always said that what's genocidal is not being able to control what happens to you. And as people have mentioned, forced sterilization is something that still goes on. The fact that sterilization is paid for or can be paid for through public funding, whereas abortion cannot, is itself a type of force—it's not even so subtle a force. There have been other even more blatant instances. I think with the specter of AIDS what we have to look at is Black women. Black women are 50 percent of the cases of women with AIDS, perhaps more at this point, closely followed by Latinas. When you're talking about women and AIDS, think women of color. Whenever you hear women and AIDS, think women of color. That should be your first image, because that gets lost. I have seen it get lost repeatedly on the part of people who are making policy for us.

We have to be very concerned about women of color being forced to be sterilized or have abortions because they are at high risk for AIDS or because they are HIV positive. And every woman, even a woman who is HIV positive, has the right to make the decision about whether she is going to have children or not.

Here are a couple of things in conclusion. One is that when we're talking about involving Black women in this movement or any movement, we have to look at where abortion and other health concerns fall in the priorities of Black women, particularly poor Black women. It takes space in your life and control of your life to be able to think about working on preserving a right which you might want to exercise in the future. Do you see how speculative that is? You know, maybe in the future or maybe my daughter... You see, that's not immediate and what people living on the edge are dealing with are immediate concerns. When obtaining food and shelter are your most pressing needs, fighting for abortion or doing political work around any issue is unlikely.

Health in general is not high up on the priority list of communities of color at this point. Because you can't really think about going to the doctor, let alone all the stuff that has been mashed on us in the last decade or so around wellness, if food and shelter are literally your priorities.

Another very important thing is that movements end up close to where they start in terms of who is involved in them. Let me give you an example. In 1988, I was one of a few women of color involved in working on the Women and AIDS conference in Boston. There was a fair representation of women of color at that conference: I would say about 10 percent. But, if 70-80 percent of women with AIDS are women of color, that's really skewed. Where were the numbers? Well, there are a lot of explanations, but I think that because the conference really started in the white community, it wasn't able to go that much farther. Later on in the year, we started an organization called the Black Women's Council on AIDS, an all women of color group. And because of where it started, we had a predominantly Black group come out for a forum we planned.

So I think if there was such a thing as a Black women's group in the Black community or in some Black community somewhere that was working on reproductive rights issues, that's where I think you might see some of the participation that you want. I don't know how to bring that about exactly—how can women of color be empowered to work on this issue in their communities? I want to quote from the Third World Women's Committee of the Abortion Action Coalition that formed in 1977. "The right to abortion can be a woman's right to life." I always thought that was a very profound statement.

Notes

1. This article originally was presented on January 22, 1989, at a forum organized by the Reproductive Rights Network of Boston and the Boston Women's Health Book Collective. Reprinted by permission of Beverly Smith from *Gay Community News*, February 19-25, 1989.

Hidden History:
An Illegal Abortion in 1968[1]

Margaret Cerullo

My story is not unusual. Like many women of my generation, women now in their late thirties and forties, my commitment to abortion rights drew its initial passion from my own illegal abortion, 21 years ago. I have come to think of my story most recently as part of the hidden history of 1968-1969, as an emblem for a period of profound social upheaval in this country, indeed throughout the world. To me, one of the striking things about the recounting of that period today is how much the story is being told from the standpoint of straight white men. The story I have to tell is far less audible, less frequently heard. But the escalating attack on abortion requires that it come to light.

In 1968 I was 20 years old and I was a student, a junior in college at the University of Pennsylvania. In 1968 I was a revolutionary and, in 1968, against my will, and much to my dismay, I was pregnant, a fact I discovered the Saturday before my final exams were going to begin. Not only was abortion illegal in 1968, so was birth control. In Philadelphia where I lived (not a backwater) you could only get the pill (the only form of birth control I thought of) if you were married, had your parents' permission, or were 21 years of age. I was too young, I wasn't married, and my parents were practicing Catholics. Women students at Penn had just discovered a doctor in Philadelphia—one doctor—who would accept a letter of permission not only from your parents, but also from your aunt. So, we sat around the dorms granting our "nieces" permission to use birth control. I participated in these letter-writing sessions, knowing that by the time I got the pill it might already be "too late."

I was about nine or ten weeks pregnant by the time I figured out where I could get a pregnancy test, had one, and waited for the results. I really had very little idea how I was going to go about getting an abortion, but I was absolutely clear that I did not want to have a child. Like so many young women who get pregnant, I had not been sexually active for long. I felt I was only beginning to know the possibilities of my body, as I was only beginning to dream the possibilities of my life.

I really cannot remember exactly how I found the phone numbers, but I suppose I got them through the various means of the underground student/political/counter-cultural scene. I began making calls all over the East Coast, very coded telephone calls. "Hello, this is Mary; I'm calling because I just saw John; well, actually, I saw John about nine and a half weeks ago." You coded the relevant information about what you wanted and how serious the situation was. I made three or four of these calls from pay phones in between taking exams, and the person on the other end of each one of them hung up abruptly after I blurted out the critical information. Eventually, I found out there was a major crackdown in process, just a chance regular kind of repressive crackdown on illegal abortionists on the East Coast. The weeks were ticking away and I was starting for the first time to feel nervous. I knew after twelve weeks I would really be in trouble and I had to go home to see my family after exams were over. I was worried about how I would disguise nausea and morning sickness.

Finally, I got the number of the "Clergymen's [sic] Council on Problem Pregnancies" and I went to visit a clergyman in the Philadelphia suburbs. The Council tried to match you with clergymen of your own faith, but there were none of my faith participating. It was explained to me that there was one place they thought it would be possible to have an illegal abortion very quickly, a place called Towson, Maryland, outside of Baltimore. I would have to appear with $600 in small bills.

It seemed an enormous amount of money then (I was living on $5 a week spending money) and not simple to find. (I have recently calculated that $600 in 1968 is equivalent to approximately $2,100 in 1989 dollars.) The money was what made me decide to tell the guy I had gotten pregnant with. He agreed to dress up in a suit and go to the bank and apply for a loan. He got it and that's how I came up with $600 in small bills. I was to appear in Towson at 2:00 in the afternoon outside the movie theater and wait until a man carrying a bag of groceries appeared at the theater and follow him. The clergyman with whom I spoke suggested that I think about the experience I was going to have as an act of civil disobedience against an unjust law. To call up righteous anger at a moment of terror was a great help to me.

I was a philosophy student then, and another student had recently suggested that I read a book by John Barth in which the lead character was a philosophy professor. The book was called *The End of the Road* and I can't remember much about the philosophy professor. What I do remember is the story of a woman who had an illegal abortion in Towson, Maryland. The procedure was botched and she died: that was the "end of the road." So I went to Towson with that vivid image fresh in my mind. I encountered the man carrying a bag of groceries. He gestured and I went off with him to his car. There was another woman already there, another college student. She told me later she got pregnant the first time she slept with her boyfriend. We stopped by the mall and picked up a third woman, then drove for about 45 minutes. The third woman, who was from near Towson, said that we had taken an amazingly circuitous route to arrive at a little cottage in the woods where the grocery bag man lived with his wife. On an end table in the living room was a gold-leaf-framed picture of their son in his military uniform, a formal portrait taken before he left for Vietnam. In his absence, his bedroom had been turned into an "operating room."

The "doctor" eventually came, carrying a black bag (the sign he was a doctor) and wearing a mask that made me think of the Lone Ranger. We tossed coins to determine who would go first and proceeded to have our abortions in turn. Mine was a straightforward procedure, an old-fashioned "D&C" with no complications, and not more pain than I expected or was stoically prepared to endure. One of the other women, however, the other student, bled for a very long time, so instead of turning up back at the movie theater in Towson at 6:00 p.m. as I had been told, we didn't return until about 10:00 p.m. At about 7:00, I was allowed to call my friends in Baltimore to say I would be late, so those waiting in Towson had only about an hour and a half of anxiety that something had gone wrong or, almost unspeakable, that I would not return.

As I rode in the back seat of the car through Maryland countryside on my way to have an illegal abortion that day in May 1968, I came to a shocking realization. For the first time in my life, I understood that I was a woman, not a "human being," but a woman. For the first time, I understood something about what it meant to be a woman in this society—that the lives of women were not of value. And I realized, in an inchoate rage that is with me today as I recall this story, that in this society, *because I had sex, someone thought I deserved to die.*

Today, I believe we must draw on our experiences to clarify what the stakes are in the current public confrontation over abortion. I had certain and powerful perceptions when I had an illegal abortion that often don't find expression or are sidelined in much of the current debate on abortion. Even as more of us are mobilized and are speaking out, our opponents define the terms of the public debate whenever we hear, for example, that no woman ever *wants* to have an abortion, that abortion is always traumatic, but sometimes women are *forced* by economic *necessity* or psychological *desperation* to have them. When I was young and unwillingly pregnant and afraid I wouldn't find an illegal abortion in time, *that* was traumatic. Finally arranging for an abortion and having one produced a great relief, the end of my trauma. My desperation consisted of not wanting to be a mother in 1968. I did want to be sexually active. That was and is sufficient reason.

We have lost ground whenever we hear that the main issue in the abortion debate is whether the fetus is a person—not whether women's lives have value. Our experiences are discounted when we accept the rhetoric of "pro-life" vs. "pro-choice." When I had an illegal abortion 21 years ago, hidden away, out of sight, unaccountable, I knew a life was at stake—that life was my own. Nor do I think the issue is whether you believe in more or fewer choices; the issue is whether you *trust women* to make choices of life and death significance.

I have felt both much braver and more vulnerable speaking recently about my illegal abortion, in these years of steady erosion since we won the right to abortion in 1973. While those who oppose women's right to abortion have not hesitated to proclaim their positions publicly, those of us who support abortion rights, and perhaps especially those of us who have had abortions, legal and illegal, have until recently been more reluctant to speak out about them. When we concede the public space of discussion to our opponents, we forget that what we are struggling for in the fight over abortion is not only safe and available procedures, though that is a crucial part of our struggle. We are also struggling for space, the public space for women to have the experience of abortion and to talk to one another about what our experiences have meant. We want procedures, but we also want to transform the meaning of those procedures, most particularly for the women who have them. If we accept that the abortion issue is about whether or not you're in favor of "privacy," we diminish our fight and obscure the stakes in women's refusal to be punished for our sexuality, either by public law or private shame. It is up to us to remember and remind everyone else what our experiences have taught us: our fight is not just "*pro-choice*," but "*pro-sex, pro-woman, pro-choice.*"

Notes

1. This was originally presented at a Speakout at Hampshire College, April 1989. A videotape of the Speakout entitled "Silent No More" is available by writing to the Civil Liberties and Public Policy Program, Hampshire College, Amherst, MA 01002.

The Abortion

Susan Tracy

I.
The respectable school doctor was stunned,
When I confirmed that
The stomachaches and vomit and pain
was not an ulcer.

Finally, he assured me in his understanding way
That the college
Was very good about
Girls like me.
They would not expel me.
And the Catholic relief charities
In Northampton
Would see that The Baby
Was placed.

"There will be no baby."
I told the doctor blankly
"There will be no baby
To be placed."

II.
The abortion was arranged
In a faraway city
Quite illegally of course.
Because unlike today
Those were the days
When men owned women's bodies.
That good doctor was calming.
He said I would be dancing
That evening.
But he was wrong.
It was not at all
"Like having a tooth pulled."

III.

The ride home was too long.
We were very quiet and
I didn't feel like dancing.
But when the pain started creeping up my legs
Strangling all conscious thought
And the blood started pouring out from deep inside me,
And I crossed over into that cold, blank darkness
I finally felt the rage
Of a woman betrayed.

IV.

I am still not sure
How I got into that white room.
But there I was,
Back in the stirrups again.
And a kind doctor was there.
He said I had been very foolish
To have had an illegal abortion.
And didn't I know
That I almost died.
And what would my parents think.
And why didn't I use contraceptives
In the first place.
And he would see me in the morning
To discuss "my case".

V.

My head was spinning
And I felt cold with nausea and fright.
It was not the time for a debate.
So I could not remind him
That contraceptives were illegal
For single girls like me.
And although abortions were illegal, too,
My parents could better live
With an unknown abortion
Than with a "bastard" who shared their name.

This story is true.
It happened long ago
In those days
When men owned women's bodies.

Just Call "Jane"

"Jane"

Faced with a choice between the law and our lives, we will choose our lives. This can be a terrible choice, filled with guilt and self-blame. For years before legalized abortion, millions of women made that choice. Sometimes they paid for that choice with their lives. For women with money, at least the physical dangers could be minimized. Pricey doctors or trips abroad were always available. Poor women, working women, and women with no money of their own were caught. Their desperation led them down back alleys, into the hands of practitioners whose competence and motivation were, at best, questionable. Cook County Hospital in Chicago had a whole ward for women suffering from septic abortions. That ward was often full.

In the 1960s women began to break their isolation and speak publicly about their abortions. With the growth of the women's liberation movement, early feminists saw the right to abortion, to control reproduction, as a touchstone for women's ability to participate on an equal footing in the world. Everywhere groups organized to find competent practitioners, provide emotional support and counseling, and refer women for abortions. Many of these women and men had heard the desperation, listened to the suffering, and experienced, first-hand, the nightmares encountered outside the law. These committed people were determined to provide a safer passage for women who choose abortion.

In Chicago, if you were poor and needed an abortion, you called Jane. Jane began as a counseling and referral service like all the others around the country. But Jane was different. Within two years, we had acquired all the skills necessary to perform safe, supportive, low-cost, first- and second-trimester abortions. Jane had become an illegal, floating, feminist, underground abortion service, run by women for women. By the time Jane ended in the spring of 1973, we had done over 11,000 abortions. But no one from Jane's earliest days in 1969 had any idea, any inkling, of what this group would become.

"The service," as we referred to it, was organized in the late 1960s by one of the founders of the Chicago women's movement. She wanted a group of women to take over the counseling and referrals she had been providing informally on her own. The group knew that women would feel more comfortable calling a person, so they called themselves Jane, an everywoman name.

The way it worked was simple. A woman would call and meet with a counselor who explained the procedure, discussed the cost, and answered any questions. Then the woman's name and number would be given to the doctor, who would take it from there. Only after the abortion, when the woman was back home, was the counselor able to contact her again. The abortions were D&Cs, done in hotel rooms; the cost was $600.

The women in the group realized almost instantly that they needed more control over what was happening to the women we referred—and we needed to get the price down. For a woman with means, in 1969, $600 was a lot of money, but still possible. But for the vast majority of women, $600 might as well have been $6 million. Two women from Jane met with a representative of the doctor and started negotiating. If we could guarantee so many abortions a week, he would lower the price to $500 and, on occasion, do one for free. Since the number of women calling Jane each week was less than the guaranteed number, we had to start publicizing our service.

At the same time that Jane was organizing and growing, so was the Chicago Women's Liberation Union. The union provided a ready forum to spread the word about Jane. There were women speaking out on women's liberation everywhere and, when they did, they talked about abortion and passed along Jane's number.

The doctor who worked with Jane was very secretive about his identity. No one in the group was allowed to meet him, and women having abortions were blindfolded. One day, an irate husband showed up at the hotel room. The doctor fled and called Jane. The women who came to his rescue saw his face and knew his identity. Later, as they sat around one of their living rooms, discussing the close call, they suggested that he begin working in their homes, instead of hotel rooms. Their homes would be safer for him, and more comfortable. And now that they knew who he was, there was no reason why they couldn't be present to assist during the abortions. Almost by chance, women in Jane gained an opportunity to control the abortion process.

Because the few women who had seen him were the only ones he wanted to see him, he agreed to the new arrangement. As these women sat through the abortions, holding hands, talking with women, cleaning up the room and the equipment, they realized that the procedure they were watching was not that complicated. They thought, "This doesn't look so difficult. We can learn to do this and charge a whole lot less too." Gradually they began to do some of the medical/technical work, giving shots, inserting specula, all the preparatory steps to a D&C. Wearing down the doctor's resistance, they brought other women, one at a time, into the work.

Meanwhile, women were still turned away for lack of funds. We asked them to spend a few weeks trying to raise money to pay for their abortions. What can you hock? Who can you borrow money from? How important is this to you? Money became the biggest conflict between the service and the doctor. The battle to lower the price was never-ending. He was badgered unrelentingly. Eventually he became a salaried employee of the group, the price was lowered, and no woman, ever again, was turned away for lack of funds.

In any medical/surgical procedure there is the possibility of complication. In abortions, the most common complications are heavy bleeding or infection. What could we do in case of emergency? We heard reports from women who had been harassed by emergency room staffs, told they would not get treated unless they talked; frequently the police were called in. We started talking to our own doctors obliquely about what we were involved in, feeling them out on the whole subject of abortion. We asked medical students we knew for the names of sympathetic doctors, and, when a doctor referred women to us regularly, we contacted him. We asked these doctors to provide medical back-up for emergencies and we asked them for all kinds of medical information. Some would admit women to the hospital; some would get us the drugs we needed; some would see women for follow-up exams. One taught us how to do pelvic exams.

Back at Jane meetings, women were starting to question whether our doctor was, in fact, a licensed doctor. Finally it was revealed that he was not. For some women, this was a crisis. Women left the group. One woman cried because she felt she had been lying to the women she counseled. By this time, Jane had over a year's experience with this man. He was competent and responsible. The reports from follow-up exams were all very positive. It was clear to us that someone who performed so many D&Cs was probably more competent than a doctor who rarely did one. In the midst of the discussion, one woman said, "If he can do it and he's not a doctor, then we can do it too." She noticed a small smile on the face of the woman across from her. Neither she nor most of the women at that meeting knew that this woman was already learning.

By the late summer of 1971, the blindfolds were gone, and so was the man. We lowered the price to $100 or what you could afford. The average price paid for an abortion was $40. The control we felt was so essential was finally ours. From hands-on experience we learned that the more relaxed a woman was, the easier the abortion would be. And, more significantly, we saw that the more a woman knew and understood about what was happening, and the calmer and more comfortable we were, the more relaxed she would be.

We worked three days a week, doing an average of 20-30 abortions a day. A few women had learned to do complete D&Cs and induced miscarriages. Other women were in the process of being trained, a kind of apprenticeship. An experienced practitioner worked side by side with a woman in training. The apprentice would begin with the first step of the abortion, and, when she was comfortable with that, move on to the next. We worked all over the city, in our own apartments, our friends' homes, any safe place we could find. Occasionally we rented an apartment. These apartments were also used by women we induced in their second trimester to complete their labors and miscarriages.

When a woman called Jane she got a tape recording saying, "This is Jane from women's liberation; please leave your name and number and someone will call you back." A Jane member would return each call and ask for the woman's name, address, phone number, date of her last period, pregnancy history, and any medical problems. The information was written on 3x5 cards. At meetings, the stack of cards was passed around and everyone selected cards of women they could counsel that week.

Each counselor would arrange to meet with the women whose cards she had picked. The woman was encouraged to bring anyone she wanted with her. What we called counseling sessions were really information sharing sessions. Over cups of tea, we explained the procedure: where she would go, who would be there, exactly what would happen, what instruments would be used, what it would feel like, and what to watch for afterwards. We shared everything we knew about birth control and handed out newsprint copies of *Our Bodies Ourselves, The Birth Control Handbook,* and *The VD Handbook.*

On the day her abortion was scheduled, the woman would go to an apartment we called the Front. She was encouraged to bring someone with her. The Front was one of our homes or our friends' homes. At the Front there would be lots of other people—women waiting, their friends, husbands, boyfriends, mothers, and children. A counselor worked at the Front answering questions, calming jittery nerves, making sure there was plenty to eat.

We drove women in small groups from the Front to the place where the abortions were performed, another apartment or house belonging to one of us or our friends. The abortions were performed in the bedrooms on regular beds. There was always someone from the service sitting with the woman, holding her hand, and talking with her. We talked about the procedure, her job, her kids, school, whatever. We did pap smears for every woman, and showed her her cervix with a mirror.

When the abortion was complete, we reviewed the dos and don'ts for the next few weeks, and gave her little boxes of pills for bleeding and infection. Each counselor tried to keep in touch with the woman she counseled for up to two weeks to monitor her recovery.

The women who sought Jane's services were from every racial, ethnic, and religious group. Once New York State legalized abortion in 1970, and we were able to lower our price, Jane became a service for poor women, women who couldn't leave the Chicago area even for a day, and, more and more, women of color. The women who came to Jane were between the ages of 13 and 52. There were young, frightened women who had never had a gynecological exam. There were older women who had several children. Women came who had gotten pregnant while using every method of birth control. Women came who had never used birth control. Many were working at subsistence level pay, barely able to provide for their families. Some women came with support from friends and family, while others came in secret, terrified that someone would find out. They had gotten Jane's number from their doctor, a clinic, the cop in their neighborhood, a friend, passed around by word of mouth. It was, in fact, the best known secret in Chicago.

From 1969 to 1973 between 100 and 120 women were members of Jane at one time or another. In the early days, members were mostly housewives and mothers; husbands' incomes provided the freedom to organize the fledgling group. There were always college students involved. Later on, when the volume of calls had increased dramatically, a group of young, single, radical feminists, who were able to support themselves on very little, joined Jane. The housewives' energy enabled the group to organize and establish itself; the young feminists enabled the group to continue and thrive. Although there were always a few women of color in the service, the group was mainly white. Many of us were uncomfortable with the racial composition of the group; we talked about it constantly. Members ranged in age from 19 to our late forties. There were suburban schoolteachers and "hippie" feminists, women active in NOW, and women who had no use for NOW's middle-class politics. There were members who, to this day, do not consider themselves feminists. Our styles varied; our personalities were sometimes in conflict. But the work was more important than anything that divided us. For most of us, this was our first work in the women's movement; for many of us, our first real political work of any kind.

By May 1972, 250 women each week depended on us for abortions. Then we were busted. Acting on a complaint from a relative of a woman scheduled, the police raided our work place, arresting seven women, including many of our trained abortionists. During the next few weeks everything was chaos. What would we do for all those women waiting? The clinics in New York and Washington, D.C. were extremely helpful. At least one offered free abortions for women referred from Jane. We had counselors at the airport to get women on planes, and counselors to meet them when they got back. Meanwhile, the women who were busted met with lawyers, made court appearances, and waited for the Supreme Court to announce their pending decision in *Roe v. Wade.*

Within two weeks Jane was back at work, operating more clandestinely. In less than two months, we were back to business as usual. By the fall of 1972, 300 women each week counted on us for abortions.

In January 1973, the Supreme Court legalized abortion. We continued our work until the first legal clinics opened in Chicago in the spring of 1973, making legal abortions accessible. Then, without fanfare, Jane went out of business. The case against the busted practitioners, "the Abortion 7," was dismissed. Jane women breathed a collective sigh of relief. No longer would we be forced to break the law to choose ourselves, to choose survival. But our relief was tinged with concern. We knew from experience that abortion in the hands of medical professionals, even legalized, would be a different experience than abortion controlled by women. The medical model, with its powerful mystique which had made us ignorant of our own bodies, would be unlikely to offer women the information, control, and support we so desperately needed.

Because we operated outside the law and, indeed, outside the bounds of accepted behavior, we were free to base our service on our own values and on the need we were meeting. From our own experiences with the medical profession we knew that the difference between a good experience and a bad one was in the amount of information and control we had and respect we received. We believed in each woman's right to self-determination. We treated the women we saw the way we wanted to be treated ourselves. With these values as our foundation, we focused on our commonalities as women, without disregarding differences in background, experience, and personality. Gaining control of the abortion process had given us a sense of our own power in the world. We did what we could to ensure that every woman we saw went away with that same sense of control, with a positive feeling about the experience, a feeling that this experience belonged to her. We wanted every woman to walk away from us with more of a sense of herself, and the power of her decisions. We tried to create an opportunity for women to take back their bodies and, by taking back their bodies, take back their lives.

The women who came to us were included in the experience as much as possible. Rather than being acted upon, they acted with Jane members. It was imperative that every woman who came understand that Jane's safety lay in her hands just as her safety lay in ours. From their first contact with the service, women were told: "This makes you complicitous. We don't do this to you, but with you." We believed that information was power, so we shared everything we knew and hid nothing. Women were expected to participate and encouraged to help one another. Any woman could do what we were doing, and, in fact, she did. Many of the women in Jane joined after having abortions with Jane.

Yet in many ways, the values that we worked hard to communicate to the women who came to us were lacking in our own internal dealings. Under the guise of a "leaderless democracy," a handful of women controlled the group. Illegality created real pressures; we operated on a need-to-know basis. Each of us knew what our work required us to know and no more, so the more work a member did, the more she knew. Since we operated ostensibly as a collective, there was no formal, stated structure. Rather than hierarchy, power evolved through a series of concentric circles, with the outer circle composed of service members whose involvement was tangential. Smaller circles led to the inner circle, the women who had all the information because they had the greatest involvement, who could and did make the major decisions. These women often met informally, over cups of coffee in the afternoon, to do the business of the group. Decisions were presented to the group as *faits accomplis*. There were jokes about the "kitchen cabinet" meeting separately, in the kitchen, to plan the meetings. Whenever issues of power and decision making were raised, the response would be the same, "We don't have time for this stuff. We have hundreds of women waiting. Their lives are at stake." That fact could never be denied. Although there were the inevitable back-biting alliances and power struggles, and the classic inability to confront each other directly, the bottom line was always the work. And the work itself was so consuming and never-ending that many of us were content to leave well enough alone—as long as the work got done.

By taking the abortion tools—curettes, forceps, dilators—in our own hands, we had effectively demystified medical practice. No longer would we see doctors as gods but rather as skilled practitioners, just like us. But that act of self-reliance left us vulnerable. Even though a D&C is a fairly simple surgical procedure, there are always risks, as with any surgery. Unlike medical professionals, we were operating without societal sanctions. No one had given us permission. In the event of a serious problem, we knew there would be no institution to protect us. Aside from breaking the law, we were breaking a very potent taboo, and eventually we would suffer the consequences.

We were ordinary women, living in extraordinary times, who seized an opportunity to act and, despite all of our failings, accomplished something extraordinary. The need for our service, which grew rapidly as word of the service spread, pushed us to be as competent as possible. A woman came to us with a problem—she was pregnant and didn't want to be—and, when she left, that problem was solved. That daily experience of success gave us a feeling of incredible power and satisfaction. And the work itself was so life-affirming.

Through these tangible experiences, we learned the real truth of some basic ideas. We learned that ordinary people can make things happen, that individuals, working together, can make a difference. We learned that no one has to wait for permission to act, nor is it necessary to wait until the project has been perfected or the process completed. We learned that if a thing needs to be done and it can be done, then you can do it, figure it out, piece by piece. When Jane began, there was no grand plan; we had no idea where we were heading. Each step moved us beyond what we thought we were capable of and on to the next step. We wanted each woman we saw to have the opportunity, through her decisions, to choose herself and her life. With Jane, we learned to choose our own.

The Politics of Menstrual Extraction[1]

Laura Punnett

That the medical profession is neither aware of, nor accountable to, women's needs and interests has been well demonstrated by feminists in recent years. Mary Daly has written: "Under patriarchy, 'method' has wiped out women's questions so totally that even women have not been able to hear and formulate our own questions to meet our own experiences."[2] For, frequently, women's concerns about our health and well-being—what are lesbians' health needs; what is the difference between menopause and normal aging of the human (female) body— are "nonquestions" in the medical system of knowledge. Other problems, such as menstrual cramps and irregular periods, are either dismissed as psychosomatic or used as the reason for experimentation on us without our knowledge or consent.

Feminists are recognizing that physicians cannot or will not correct these faults simply in response to our good faith requests, and that we must struggle for active control over the information and technology that pertain to our ability to care for our bodies. The self-help movement is one way in which women have begun to take direct and immediate control over some of these basic skills.

Through self-help, we develop our abilities in two directions. We increase our concrete "medical" skills and information, and we gain in self-confidence. When we are not limited by dependence on external (male/professional) authority, we are able to use our resources better and in more creative ways. In contrast to patriarchal medicine, self-help is a positive experience for women, affirming our experiences, our bodies, and our ability to act concretely to fulfill our own needs. Self-help creates a situation in which women can thrive by incorporating values of self-determination and respect for all women.

Menstrual extraction is a self-help technique and, therefore, is based on and develops the technical and psychological resources of the women who practice it. Menstrual extraction is done most commonly to eliminate the general nuisance of menstrual flow and to relieve menstrual pain, including such symptoms as cramps and lower back ache. It can also be used to reduce the need for abortion. As a form of woman-controlled medical research, menstrual extraction is a means of gaining, and sharing with other women, information about our bodies and our periods; for example, it can be used to control some of the many variables of a normal menstrual cycle in order to test certain hypotheses concerning the cause(s) of cramps. The experience of learning and practicing the menstrual extraction procedure also helps us to break down the mystique of medical practices.

The medical profession's predictable response to self-help ranges from extreme hostility to a refusal to acknowledge self-help at all. This is consistent with the patriarchal response to feminism in general. Menstrual extraction has elicited resistance, co-optation, and redefinition to deprive it of its original, feminist meaning. To read editorials in medical journals would be to learn that menstrual extraction is performed by doctors on women as a paid service, when in fact the term correctly refers to a technique developed seven years ago in which lay women in small, advanced self-help groups extract each other's normal menstrual flow.

Menstrual extraction is not done by a woman on herself, which would be difficult and dangerous; this common misconception implies an individualistic solution which entirely misses the importance in the self-help movement of the group as a source of information-sharing and support. All the women in a menstrual extraction group have done self-help together over a length of time and are familiar with their bodies and the normal health status of each woman. Every woman has her own period extracted *and* learns to extract other women's periods; there is no distinction between practitioner and patient, since each woman takes all roles in turn and literally cares for her sisters' bodies as she does for her own.

The fact that menstrual extraction is still an experimental method must be clearly understood. This is true, not so much because of the known side-effects, which are negligible so far, but because of those, as yet unknown, which might occur within a large group of women over a long period of time. The indication is that these are minimal. Women involved in self-help research would not perform a procedure on ourselves that we did not feel to be safe. On the other hand, the lack of long-term data on the procedure's side-effects must be made clear to all women considering it.[3] Its experimental status requires that we work in skilled groups with careful observations and evaluations of our bodies' functioning. This should be well understood by all participants, so that each woman can formulate her own criteria for deciding whether she wishes to experiment on her own body in this manner. However, unlike the population control experiments to be discussed later, research within a self-help model insures that a woman at risk is also a woman in control of the project.

Menstrual Extraction as Birth Control

Menstrual extraction used as a birth control method is not the same thing as endometrial aspiration, pre-emptive abortion, menstrual induction, minisuction, or early uterine evacuation, all terms for a very early abortion-type procedure. This procedure is a single aspiration to remove a possible pregnancy, performed by a physician on a woman in the role of passive patient. Menstrual extraction, on the other hand, is done in the context of a self-help group where the "patient" is, in fact, the active and controlling subject of the procedure. The extraction is also probably one in a series of regular monthly extractions and would have been done whether or not there was a chance of pregnancy. Many women see menstrual extraction as an ideal contraceptive technique or back-up method. In contrast to other birth control methods, it does not interfere with sexual intercourse, does not change the body chemistry and does not require the continuous use of a device or substance which can cause continuous side-effects. Moreover, it is easily accessible, highly effective, and under the control of the woman herself, rather than a physician.

The use of menstrual extraction for birth control is important politically. Many women, including some who are not in need of birth control themselves, wish to develop their skill in using the technique in order to make this an abortion option available to more women. Given the always-tentative legal status of abortion in this country and others, it becomes preferable to develop our own technology and health systems as an alternative to dependence on men (law-makers, doctors, priests, etc.) for access to abortion.

The cut-off of federal funds for abortion, effectively prohibiting poor women from freely choosing whether or not to bear children, requires that we respond on many levels simultaneously. Prior to the legalization of abortion in 1973, some feminists were establishing underground, women-controlled abortion services (such as "Jane"[4] in Chicago). Rather than waiting for the abortion crisis to reappear in full force before we act, the interim period of legal access to abortion has been used by some women as a time of greater access to resources, to develop our skills in preparation for the next crunch. Menstrual extraction represents one possibility for expansion of our options.

The Medical Backlash and Co-optation

There is actually very little mention of menstrual extraction in medical or gynecological literature. This is not because physicians are unaware of, or uninterested in, menstrual extraction. In fact, they are quite aware of its growing appeal to women, and their resistance grows at a similar pace. With one or two exceptions, they prefer not to acknowledge the technique in their own journals, while their professional disapproval is reflected in virtually every article on the subject in lay journals, newspapers, and books. Medical opposition is supposedly based on safety concerns: the use of lay women and "inadequate" equipment to perform the procedure; a supposed greater danger resulting from this practice, especially an increased risk of infection, perforation, or both; the hazards of frequently repeated extractions; and the risk of using aspiration as birth control before a positive test confirms pregnancy.

These objections rarely proceed from any solid evidence or clear understanding of the menstrual extraction procedures. In fact, the very utilization of lay women, using a method that is slower than standard abortion techniques, is largely responsible for the safety of menstrual extraction. Excluding possible long-term effects which have not yet been documented (the indication is that these are minimal), menstrual extraction is an almost inherently safe procedure. This claim can be backed up by data compiled by self-help groups which have performed several hundred menstrual extractions to date with no major or minor complications other than rare infections. Uterine perforation from menstrual extraction is virtually impossible. Physicians have widely exaggerated the possibility of complications and have used this as a basis for arguments against the practice of menstrual extraction. The motivation for this becomes clear when we examine the real impact of menstrual extraction on women and on the medical profession. Doctors "were more upset at the independence that period extraction in particular and self-help in general gave women rather than at the dangers of either for...they say, quite correctly, that period extraction was developed precisely to give women autonomy over their own bodies and that it was inseparable from the concept of self-help."[5] This reaction on the part of physicians to defend their monopoly against self-help is very similar to their campaign against midwives at the turn of the century.[6] Midwives were blamed for high rates of maternal and child deaths, while there is evidence that generally doctors were more responsible for mothers' complications and infants' deaths.

Obviously, the practice of menstrual extraction by *lay women only* is the key issue here. Paramedical personnel have been endorsed by a variety of sources, when they are certified and regulated by the medical profession. In other words, the reaction to non-professional health workers depends greatly on the context and the amount of real power or autonomy the workers have. When they are strictly controlled, or working to further the interests of the male medical/population control establishment, they are seen to pose little threat. However, the conceptual basis of the independent self-help movement is that women with skills and information are qualified, simply by having those skills, to use them with other women; formal credentials then become irrelevant to controlling the quality of primary care procedures ranging from pelvic exams and Pap smears to menstrual extraction. (This is true whether or not one also believes that there is a need for feminists within medicine, nursing, or other health-related fields.) The 1972 National Self-Help Convention agreed that the movement should continue independent of academic credentialing to enable the participation of large numbers of women on a peer level, and to maintain independence from the male profession's oppression of women.

To understand the importance of a women's self-help movement which remains autonomous of the medical profession, it is helpful to remember that an attempt to convince or enlist the sympathy of physicians (as with other male groups) often opens the door to drastic co-optation. For example, the types of arguments which doctors raise against menstrual extraction are completely reversed when the profession transforms the menstrual extraction concept into menstrual regulation.

Menstrual Regulation and Population Control

"Menstrual regulation" is a term used sometimes to refer to a clinical endometrial aspiration or similar procedure, and sometimes for a practice more like menstrual extraction in that it uses a syringe or other non-electric vacuum source. The main distinction here is that these menstrual regulation procedures are being exported internationally for purposes of population control, rather than to increase individual women's options to decide about their own childbearing. Menstrual regulation will be used here to refer to this assortment of procedures and techniques which have in common, at minimum, that they are promoted by the medical establishment rather than by the women's self-help movement.

Unlike menstrual extraction, menstrual regulation has received a steady share of attention in medical publications, both as an early abortion method and as a population control technique (these two uses are not necessarily easily distinguished from each other). Where it is discussed favorably, its backing generally comes from the international population control establishment.

Population control is "a large-scale social policy of limiting births throughout a whole society or in certain social groups for the purpose of changing economic, political and/or ecological conditions."[7] The population control establishment referred to in this essay is a group consisting of men, both medical and non-medical, with various interests in controlling the size of poor and third world populations in order to maintain a racist and imperialist status quo. In this scheme women are merely pawns, our individual lives used to achieve imposed goals— whether those are positive ones, such as reducing the consumption of our natural resources, or questionable ones, such as protecting a multi-national corporation's profits.

By treating women as expendable, these men continue in their historical tradition of colluding through their religious, medical, and legal institutions to control the accessibility of birth control and abortion.

> From the persecution of the socialist nurse, Margaret Sanger, in the second decade of this century for her agitation about birth control, to the pushy endorsement of birth control by an aggressive United States government and the big profits in the worldwide sale of pills, intrauterine devices, foams, gels, and what have you, has been fascinating change. The women who fought valiantly and effectively for birth control information could not have imagined the control that the medical and pharmaceutical concerns would establish over their daughters, granddaughters, and above all, over women of other cultures that they in their respectable middle-class worlds did not take cognizance of.[8]

These policies have resulted in exploitative birth control experimentation and systematic sterilization abuse in Puerto Rico and other economically colonialized third world countries, and among Black, Native American, and Latina women in this country.[9] Sometimes direct coercion is used, as when women are denied abortions unless they "consent" to sterilization at the same time, or are forced to sign consent forms while in labor. Many women are threatened (illegally) with loss of welfare benefits unless they undergo abortion, sterilization, or both. Native American women are beginning to refuse, *en masse,* to give birth in hospitals, because once under anesthesia they are sterilized and not told of this fact before *or* after the operation. It is also common for women to be only partially informed, or completely misinformed, as to the nature of a sterilization operation. Spanish-speaking women, for example, are often given explanations and consent forms only in English, or are told that the procedure is easily reversible.

***

As the medical profession and the population control establishment spend enormous amounts of money, time, and energy to find and develop a single "ideal" technique for controlling births through controlling women, menstrual regulation is one procedure that has been offered as a potential "solution." One pair of researchers wrote: "Because of the great increase in legal abortion throughout the world and the urgent need to slow population growth, new techniques of pregnancy termination are currently being studied. There is considerable interest in very early abortion (i.e., menstrual regulation) because of its greater acceptability from an emotional and philosophical viewpoint, and its potential simplicity. The safety, efficacy, and economy of very early aspiration abortion can serve as standards against which prostaglandins and other new chemical, steroidal, and physical abortifacients can be compared."[10]

In December 1973, an International Menstrual Regulation Conference was held in Honolulu, Hawaii, organized by the Battelle Population Study Center, with assistance from the International Planned Parenthood Foundation, the U.S. Agency for International Development (AID), the Population Council, and the Rockefeller Foundation. The purpose of the conference was ostensibly to assess the state of the art, although women from the Feminist Women's Health Centers of California, who had developed the menstrual extraction technique, were specifically denied admission. The organizers used the opportunity to enlist native doctors, many of them women, from third world countries (India, Pakistan, Taiwan, Indonesia, Korea, Fiji) in plans to use menstrual regulation to limit population growth.

All the advantages for which feminists advocate menstrual extraction (such as safety, lack of discomfort, economy, simplicity, and accessibility to lay women) were used to promote schemes such as that which would require a woman to "turn in" her monthly menstrual period in order to pick up her monthly welfare check! In addition, physicians were encouraged to think of this as a procedure which could be handled adequately by "midwives" (not birth attendants, but rather women paramedics similar to China's barefoot doctors). This route was seen as preferable because midwives have greater trust and credibility with local women, who often (and rightly) fear male doctors and gynecological procedures.

In summarizing the Hawaii conference, a report from the Population Information Program, supported by AID, explained that the procedure could be used in different ways depending on the geographical area. In Asia the technique would be an early abortion method "as a back-up for contraceptive failures"; in Latin America, where abortion is illegal in many countries, it was suggested instead that the procedure be used to handle the incomplete and septic abortions that result from those rigid laws. In either case, participants were encouraged to consider means for introducing menstrual regulation into their own countries so as to give it an image of respectability and safety that did not "generate rumors" or "embarrass politicians."[11]

In most instances, the economic domination of imperialism is furthered by the use of complex technology, so that a dependency on the more industrialized nation is maintained, even at the expense of economy or accessibility for the colonized people. Population controllers' concern for facilitating the use of this simple technology in the third world might therefore seem contradictory to the usual corporate imperialist practice. It is more directly in the interest of this establishment, however, to increase access to abortion technology than it is to create technological dependence in this particular sphere. In other words, controlling the size and growth of third world populations is crucial to the maintenance of economic domination in any other form.

The idea of lay women performing abortion-type procedures in this country is wholeheartedly opposed by the patriarchal establishment because (at least at the moment) it would be an indication of and a furthering of women's self-determination and autonomy. However, in the third world, at the present time, menstrual regulation could be a means to achieve greater control and manipulation of women's options, to further the goals dictated by male supremacy, and so this usage of women against other women is just as wholeheartedly endorsed in that context.

Where Do We Go From Here?

It is important to publicize and to stop individual instances of exploitation of women through population control experimentation, of which menstrual regulation is only one example. However, even if that were entirely possible, it still would not be a complete solution in itself; longer range goals are required.

The self-help movement has offered some suggestions for challenging the professional monopoly on "health care." Feminists are redefining "health" to mean the status of our total functioning: physical, psychological, social, economic, spiritual. We do not subscribe to the idea that all our health concerns must be dealt with by a doctor; in fact, the extension of the medical profession's authority over those areas of our lives, "cooptive control,"[12] has many negative consequences for us. It is essential that we ourselves maintain power over all aspects of our being in the world. Self-help can serve as a framework in which women can heal ourselves while affirming a positive self-image. Through self-help, women can conduct medical research based in the philosophy of women's choice and women's control. Menstrual extraction can be an alternative to abortion. While not free from legal constraints imposed by the patriarchy, it offers us an alternative to negotiating for favors and is a way to involve lay women in political work around health care and the control of women by the medical system. "As we assert control over ourselves, we confront the society that has determined many of [the objective conditions of our lives]…As we struggle for such societal change, that very struggle alters how we see ourselves, thus creating a continuous process of change and growth."[13]

As feminists we must also recognize that imperialism is an enemy of people's self-determination and thus of women's struggles. Because of economic dependence within the U.S. "sphere of influence," U.S. money through AID or other channels can be used to directly or indirectly pressure nations to set up population control programs. Donor nations also have the power to substitute population aid for other types of development assistance and to support specific policies of racism, such as was the case of Rhodesian family planning programs for blacks only. And, as I have already pointed out, population control almost always uses women as its pawns, as in Puerto Rico, where one-third of all women of childbearing age have been sterilized.[14] The U.S. Office of Population Control has set as its goal the "voluntary" sterilization of one-fourth of the women of the world, listing as one of its reasons the protection of U.S. international economic interests. Local or national autonomy is not sufficient as a solution for women; we must also struggle within each ethnic or political grouping, under each government, for our rights and for our political power.

Feminist organizing against coercive population control must take various forms. Women in self-help groups learn to rely on our own skills and each other instead of on male providers for primary health care, and to increase all women's access to complete information on health-related matters ranging from birth control techniques to alternative insemination. Feminist health centers provide access to medical services for women which are supportive and empowering rather than exploitative. They also work to protect women's right to safe, inexpensive abortions as an option which population controllers would deny us. Groups such as CESA (the Committee to End Sterilization Abuse) publicize this widespread form of population control and genocide. They fight for passage and enforcement of laws and regulations that would make institutional sterilization abuse more difficult, and they pursue precedent-setting court cases.

Population control is only one aspect of the intersection of patriarchy and imperialism. Without political power, women in the third world or in the United States have little long-term defense against medical exploitation and the continued denial of self-determination. Feminism requires that we organize to build that power as well as to confront the individual institutions that oppress us.

Notes

1. This is an edited version of an article which originally appeared in *Quest,* Vol. IV, No. 3, Summer 1978. Reprinted with permission of author.

2. Mary Daly, *Beyond God the Father: Toward a Philosophy of Women's Liberation* (Boston: Beacon Press, 1973), pp. 11-12.

3. In attempting to help sponsor such a study, the self-help movement is faced with major constraints. Menstrual extraction is extralegal (not against the law) but it has been subject to legal harassment, and menstrual extraction groups are forced to do their work underground. Consequently, not only are security precautions a barrier to public recognition, but the likelihood of a self-help group ever being founded to conduct a study in line with our priorities and without a physician is very low.

4. A description of "Jane" can be found in "Seizing the Means of Reproduction: An Illegal Feminist Abortion Collective—How and Why It Worked" by Pauline B. Bart, in *Women, Health and Reproduction,* Helen Roberts, ed., (New York: Routledge and Kegan, Paul, 1981). See also, "Just Call Jane," in this volume.

5. Ellen Frankfort, *Vaginal Politics* (New York: Bantam Books, 1973), pp. 203, 197.

6. Midwives had been the target of male physicians' attacks in other countries and at earlier times. By the early twentieth century, medical opposition to midwives, especially in the large cities of the eastern United States, had expanded its political and economic resources enough to actually force midwives out of practice in most states. See Francis E. Korbin, "The American Midwife Controversy: A Crisis of Professionalization," *Bulletin of the History of Medicine,* July-August 1966, pp. 350-363; Barbara Ehrenreich and Deirdre English, *Witches, Midwives and Nurses* (New York: The Feminist Press, 1973).

7. Linda Gordon, "The Politics of Population, Birth Control and the Eugenics Movement," *Radical America,* VIII:4, p. 62. See also: Bonnie Mass, *Population Target: The Political Economy of Population Control in Latin America* (Brampton, Ontario: Chartres Publishing Co., 1976).

8. Helen Rodriguez-Trias, "A Young Woman's Death: Would Health Rights Have Prevented It?" APHA 102nd Annual Meeting, Oct. 20-24, 1974, New Orleans.

9. Barbara Caress with Nikki Heideprien, "Sterilization: Women Fit To Be Tied," *Health-PAC Bulletin,* #62, Jan/Feb. 1975, pp. 1-6, 10-13. See also: Maritza Arrastia, "New Regulations for Sterilization," *Seven Days,* II:2, 2/24/78, pp. 13-14.

10. Alan J. Margolis et al., "Early Abortion Without Cervical Dilation: Pump or Syringe Aspiration," *Journal of Reproductive Medicine,* IX (Nov. 1972), p. 240.

11. Theresa van der Vlugt et al., "Menstrual Regulation Update," *Population Report,* Series #4, Population Information Program, George Washington University Medical Center, Washington, DC, May 1974.

12. Barbara and John Ehrenreich, "Health Care and Social Control," *Social Policy,* May-June 1974, pp. 29-30.

13. Charlotte Bunch, "Self Definition and Political Survival," *Quest: a feminist quarterly,* I:3, pp. 2-3.

14. Harriet Presser, *Sterilization and Fertility Decline in Puerto Rico,* Population Monograph Series (Berkeley, California: California Institute of International Studies, Series 13, 1973).

THE FEDERATION OF FEMINIST WOMEN'S HEALTH CENTERS

The Federation of Feminist Women's Health Centers is a non-profit, tax—exempt association of women's health projects and their supporters who provide health services to women, including abortion, well—women care and birth control. Our goals are to secure reproductive rights for women and men, to educate women about the healthy functioning of our bodies, and to improve the quality of women's health care.

A common vision of empowering women to take a larger role in their health care led groups of women to open a number of women's health projects in the early 1970s. Feminist Women's Health Centers, in particular, developed a new model of health education for women, the Self—Help clinic, in which women are taught self-examination with a plastic vaginal speculum.

The Federation distributes a video, "No Going back" which introduces the concept and the technique of menstrual extraction.

For more information contact the Federation at: 6221 Wilshire Boulevard, Suite 419—A, Los Angeles, CA. 90048.

Abortion without Apology[1]

Lynn S. Chancer

In 1974, when I was 18, I had an abortion. I had become pregnant, as do untold numbers of teens, accidentally. I certainly wasn't looking to have an abortion, but neither did I have any moral qualms about it. Wanting or having a child was so out of the question that I did not wish to, nor felt I ought to be forced to, even entertain the idea. In my own personal and genuinely felt belief system, abortion was not in the least bit unethical: I didn't think then, and I don't now, that it was "murder" or "killing."

What I do recall feeling about the abortion was severe squeamishness: a sense of alienation from a medical procedure long shrouded in patriarchal shame and treated with delicacy; and some odd cosmic thoughts, not so much of a fetus in the present, but the baby it might become when it left my body, fathered by a guy I had become convinced was a creep. For me, abortion was and is a perfectly moral and valid decision—one that doesn't even have to be all that traumatic if people don't make it so.

But that was in 1974, when it was easier to emerge with those beliefs intact or at least relatively unscathed, when no one had yet managed to accost me in front of the clinic or shove printed literature from *The Silent Scream* in front of my eyes. In 1989, declaring that abortion has nothing to do with killing or immorality has been made to sound like a confession. Conviction has been watered down with cautiousness. During a conversation about our plans to march in Washington on April 9, 1989 in support of *Roe v. Wade,* a friend of mine mentioned her fear of women losing the right to abortion even though, she went on confidentially, abortion is really very "unpleasant." After we parted, I found myself wondering whether she or I or most feminists would have thought it necessary to add that rather apologetic and defensive qualification—that "but"—back in 1973, immediately after the Court's decision. Certainly we wouldn't have in 1970 or 1971, when the struggle for sexual freedom and control of our bodies was being waged full force and the words of de Beauvoir and *Sisterhood is Powerful* still resounded in our ears, bolstering confidence that *ours* was a battle in favor of life, of the mental and physical well-being of women who were injured or dying in back rooms and alleys. Abortion then was clearly a *sine qua non* of feminist politics.

What has happened in the 16-year interim? Perhaps legalization facilitated the transformation of anger and indignation into a greater degree of ambivalence and self-doubt (even as the majority of both Americans and certainly women still agree with *Roe v. Wade*). But it is far more likely that the anti-abortion perspective has been drummed into us so persistently, so invasively, throughout the culturally conservative 1980s, that it may have crept subtly into pro-choice thinking and ways of speaking about abortion. The terms of the anti-abortion movement have come to dominate the debate, and that has given us little choice but to respond, reactively.

No, countered another friend (also a feminist) vehemently, you can't create ambivalence and self-doubt unless abortion itself is an intrinsically unsettling matter. Destroying a fetus simply can't be equated with going to the dentist and having a tooth removed: it has to be weird, she said, for one is always conscious of the potentiality the fetus represents.

Perhaps it is precisely this issue of presentation that is at stake, rather than abortions and fetuses *per se*. Perhaps abortions and fetuses are merely floating signifiers, an occasion for projecting and displacing a host of cultural contradictions onto a symbolic terrain. The word *intrinsically* bothers me, threatening to abstract abortion from the social realities and pressures that continue to define its meaning for us, whether we like it or not. For women, feelings about abortion would seem to be inseparable from the profound conditioning that has told us we are supposed to have babies and feel guilty for sex that bears no consequences, that we are supposed to prioritize others over ourselves whatever their ontological status or lack thereof. And for the Right, abortion may be an opportunity to play that already-engendered guilt for all it's worth, undermining the moral legitimacy of both abortion and the larger issue of women's sexual freedom it signifies.

Anti-abortionists leave no doubt about what they want us to believe. The stories abound, like that described to me by a family planning counselor in suburban New Jersey, of an 18-year-old woman who was surrounded by a mob screaming "You killed your baby!" as she left a clinic parking lot with her boyfriend after a recent abortion. It is hard to imagine this charged atmosphere *not* affecting teenage women, *not* exacerbating or creating guilt that might not have been there "intrinsically."

Based on her current discussions with young women in different parts of the country, sociologist Ruth Sidel describes the guilt-inducing anti-abortion efforts of both government officials and private groups as one of several factors influencing teens to carry pregnancies to term. According to Alice Radosh, formerly head of New York City's Adolescent Pregnancy and Parenting Services office, for many teens abortion has become shrouded in secrecy and stigma, something they're not comfortable telling their friends about, even when they've chosen to do it nonetheless.

Today, an 18-year-old experiences a cultural atmosphere still inconsistent in its commitment to abortion long before she ever walks through a screaming crowd in a parking lot. That schizophrenia and the strength of right wing backlash that feeds it may slyly touch even the attitudes of those who believe in the right to abortion. According to Wendy Simonds, another sociologist who worked in a city abortion clinic for several years, even the attitudes of many abortion counselors have shifted radically from the feminist advocacy which motivated them in the 1970s to a much more judgmental "distaste" about abortions and the women seeking them in the late 1980s. She recounts her experience with clinic workers who had come to presume that clients *must* be feeling something negative about abortion (particularly if they returned for more than one) and the clinic workers' expectation that something must be wrong with the woman if she did not express "grief and/or guilt." In those cases, a counselor might begin by inquiring in a non-threatening tone how the woman felt about being there *again.*

Not simply the tone but the content of language itself compounds the social pressure, that compulsory imposition of meaning that casts an aura of moral illegitimacy around abortion. Not only does loaded terminology continue to flood media reportage; it filters into numerous scholarly accounts written from an apparently feminist perspective. A good example is Kristin Luker's oft-referred-to *Abortion and the Politics of Motherhood,* in which Luker uses "pro-life" in an attempt to give an "objectively" balanced account of the debate. Yet she examines the bias of words themselves. The moment the "life" terminology is granted, so is a particular construction (conception, so to speak) of reality foisted upon us. Immediately, pro-choicers have lost some ground, and anti-abortionists gain: both the fact that not everyone equates a fetus with life in the rhetorical sense the latter intend, and the anti-abortionists' disregard for *women's* lives vanish from the debate. This is a swift linguistic disappearing act.

Nor do I doubt there are subliminal effects of having lived through then-father-figure President Reagan's endorsement of fetal memorial services in 1982 and the publication of his *Abortion and the Conscience of the Nation* in 1984. The cultural innuendo communicated by many "pro-choice" figures (Ferraro, Cuomo, and most recently, the embattled Health and Human Services-nominee Louis Sullivan at one of his supposedly more daring and politically suicidal moments), when they say they support the right to abortion even though they *personally* oppose it, reinforces the impression that there's something terribly wrong about abortion after all.

Even a supposedly liberal journalist like Murray Kempton writes disparagingly, blithely, of women who "choose an abortion for no reason more pressing than [their] own convenience." (To this October 21, 1988, *Newsday* absurdity, Ellen Willis, in an unpublished letter, wonderfully and patiently responded that pregnancy was a little more "inconvenient" than a long line at the bank or a runny nose and pointed out the normative concept of motherhood he had so unconsciously imbibed.) In this sense, abortion, from the historic 1973 decision until now, is an instance of new rights "officially" created, but not without a backlash of old attitudes so severe they haunt, mockingly, the real meaning of the new. (For women who need federal funds in order to afford abortions, of course, the Hyde Amendment [and now *Webster*] saw to it that even the "official" part was negated in some states.)

As Alice Radosh also reminded me, the critical fact remains—amid the sexual guilt, ambivalence, Operation Rescue, the powers of language and innuendo, and the incumbency of office—that over half of the approximately 60,000 pregnant teens in New York City yearly choose to have abortions anyway, whether they are white, Black, or Hispanic (in the latter category, slightly under 50 percent). Even if some women undergo abortions with greater qualms and difficulties than they might have 10 years ago, even if for others social intimidation from family, friends, priests, or medical personnel is and always would have been present—the fact remains that they have abortions nonetheless. And, if an outpouring of responses to a recent Hers column in the *New York Times* by Barbara Ehrenreich is at all symptomatic, many women still manage to experience abortion as I did at 18—as neither immoral nor intrinsically traumatic.

Here is where my temperature begins to rise at even the thought of a revoked or modified *Roe v. Wade*, where I begin again to feel as though the solid old pro-choice arguments have been rendered virtually invisible by the dominant terms of the present debate. For the moment, it is acknowledged that a good number of people feel abortion to be not immoral but moral and valid for them—how can the state, with the New Right as its appointed midwife, force us to act as though we believe otherwise? (We all know—right-to-"lifers" included—that women wouldn't act otherwise. We'd do just what we did pre-1973: endanger ourselves physically and psychologically, even die, as minority women did 12 times more frequently than white women in the years immediately preceding *Roe*.)

If a church/state dichotomy has any basic meaning, it is in pointing toward a "hands-off" category of issues that must be left to individual choice because they reach so far toward the hazy nether regions of life/death problems that they are practically religious questions, controversial and impossible to define. The impossibility of consensus on these questions is what *Roe v. Wade* held about first- and second-trimester abortions, when over 90 percent of all abortions occur. And, interestingly enough, according to the 1987 book *Women, Society, the State and Abortion* by Patrick Sheeran, anti-abortionists *consciously* tone down or totally deny the religious or quasi-religious elements of their campaign. It is in their interest to do so, Sheeran comments, especially when at the same time they speak elsewhere about the importance of religion in modern life and advocate mandatory prayer and pledges of allegiance. Sheeran's point about the desire to downplay religion is borne out by a March 26, 1989 *New York Times* op-ed piece, in which University of Chicago public policy professor Laurence E. Lynn Jr. confesses to finally having come "out of a closet" in opposition to abortion, despite his otherwise liberal *weltanschauung*. Lynn swears his opinion has nothing to do with "sectarian religious conviction," and that he still respects the separation between church and state. However, by skirting this church versus state infringement, with all its civil libertarian implications, the fact that *they* are the ones who are aggressively denying people's rights is cleverly obfuscated in the case of abortion.

The pro-choice position is inclusive; that of the anti-abortionists exclusive, undemocratic, and ultimately, I would argue, theocratic, by threatening to undermine that (ironically) traditional division between church and state in so many areas of American life. Is this inclusiveness argument boring, obvious, old hat? Possibly—but badly in need of restatement. It is extremely difficult to keep remembering that *our* rights are under blatantly undemocratic assault when the anti-abortion campaign *looks* like it is about something else, namely fetal rights. It's as though present reality has been banished not to the after-life but to the before-life, as we confusedly watch demonstrators adopt the civil disobedience and political protest tactics with which we used to associate ourselves. Yet what the New Right and anti-abortion forces manage to camouflage ideologically is that which seems so evident and inalienable: that is, that anyone with the slightest bit of discomfiture, doubt, distaste, moral or ethical misgivings, or worse, can act on *their* legitimate beliefs by not having an abortion.

Contrary to anti-abortionist criticisms, abortion and family planning counseling has always placed the burden of proof on the *abortion,* not the *pregnancy.* (I remember being rudely, momentarily, jolted from my stalwart, trying-to-be-superteen determination to get an abortion when a counselor insisted I think about how I'd manage a baby—the still standard "exploring of options.") How often we hear about the depression women feel after an abortion, when they may think about the baby they could have had. But what about the depression of women who go ahead and have babies, only later to regret not having had an *abortion?* And perhaps it's abortion, rather than the problematic lack of social support for her pregnancy, that comes to be blamed when a woman feels unable to have a child she may actually have wanted desperately. Even a highly intelligent and provocative book like *Not an Easy Choice,* by Canadian pro-choice feminist Kathleen McDonnell, or Linda Bird Francke's *The Ambivalence of Abortion* seem to faintly mirror the anti-abortionists' focus on which feelings and beliefs *we* rather than *they* have excluded. Feminists, meanwhile, remain on the political defensive—unless, that is, we become appropriately infuriated at the thought of exactly whom and what anti-abortionists are trying to exclude, whom *they* are trying to control.

Clearly, control is aimed at women as a whole. The anger of anti-abortionists seems to rise in direct proportion to the degree to which women can in good faith have abortions guilt-free. It could not be otherwise. If it were, women would have reached a point of sexual freedom already, freedom from one's life being mired in unwanted mothering, liberation from long-lasting and potentially punishing repercussions of pleasure—all of which are still extraordinarily radical and threatening to most of us who have tasted of it briefly or even not at all. The ire of the anti-abortionists cannot be understood outside the context of a larger sexual and cultural reaction to feminist gains, terrifying precisely because they have opened a Pandora's box with the promise that the traditionally gendered world may never be the same again. Nor can such panic be separated from reactive wishes to resuscitate family morality and values, from fear of gay and lesbian challenges to heterosexual exclusivity, from fear of change in general.

The abortion debate is full of ironies. The irony of moral and existential terms being used fervently about forms not everyone agrees are "alive" anyhow, while all around us real human beings rot in homelessness and poverty, racism and sexism. The irony that the same modern abortion technology anti-abortionists condemn is glorified when used to provide the latest scientific view of magnified fetuses. And, irony of ironies, the final blow to essentialist complacency about male and female *natures* is that the Justice who cast the decisively limiting vote was Sandra Day O'Connor, the first woman on the U.S. Supreme Court.

When my anger cools, it starts to mix with sadness and sobriety about what feminism means or doesn't mean for the many women who identify themselves strongly with the anti-abortion movement, who, these days, often wear the same guise of passionate political protest with which I identify myself—though now reversed, worn inside-out. I start to wonder at how easy it is to begin slipping into another linguistic pitfall, to begin referring to other women as "they," the enemy, the political "other." Perhaps emerging from defensiveness requires not only reviving our ability to argue cogently on behalf of abortion, thereby re-stimulating our historical memory, but also reflecting on broader theoretical and political questions.

Ultimately, the "moral righteousness" of the case against abortion is less troubling to me than what abortion represents to many women at the level of the floating signifier. I worry whether it is possible to assuage the threat many women must feel feminism poses to the older gendered universe in which they have a stake, the one that offers the comfort and security of the familiar—how it is possible to talk to those women in suburbs, rural areas, households, across the differences of class and race. Women for whom feminism does not seem useful or relevant to everyday life? Finally, I wonder if the desire to make abortion morally illegitimate does not reflect a deeper feeling of anxiety on the part of many women that one's *own* life—not that of the *fetus*—is what is really in jeopardy. If so, then it's those more complex experiences of powerlessness and alienation that somehow have to be addressed. In the meantime, it is essential that abortion not take the bum rap, and that the right of women to decide whether or not we want them not be eroded further.

Notes

1. This article originally appeared in the *Village Voice*, April 11, 1989. Reprinted with permission.

Breaking Silences:
A Post-Abortion Support Model

Sarah Buttenweiser and Reva Levine

Having control over her own reproduction determines whether a woman has control over her own life. The question of whether women should have that control is the root of the current abortion rights battle. The anti-choice movement declares that abortion is a sin and that women who make this choice are murderers. Their propaganda is pervasive both in the media and throughout the culture. The infiltration of these messages affects the ways people view the abortion issue. The intensified political turmoil surrounding abortion has made abortion increasingly difficult for women.

Along with the stresses which accompany any major decision, women must exercise this choice in a social climate that has become increasingly shrouded with messages of guilt and shame. Although the majority of the population, according to virtually all polls, is pro-choice, the imagery of the anti-choice movement has insured that a climate of virtual hysteria prevails. Appropriating the rhetoric, methods, and symbols of the civil rights movement, anti-choice activists have attempted to win converts and to intimidate women even if they do not gain active supporters. The societal stigma of abortion overwhelms many women. As the anti-choice movement blares its messages of immorality, death, and cruelty, its imagery has an impact on society in general and women in particular. The furor of this movement robs many women of the chance for social acceptance of their choice to abort. Others are unable to speak out about the reality of their situations and decisions.

The anti-choice offensive dovetails only too well with other cultural phenomena—the current fascination with parenting and babies, and traditional sex roles which equate being a woman with having children. All of this contributes to the impact of the anti-abortion movement and the pressures women feel in making childbearing decisions. We are very far physically and emotionally from being able to make choices about abortion freely. Abortion is still portrayed as a necessary evil, and the idea of "good" and "bad" abortions prevails. A "good" or acceptable abortion is the result of circumstances outside of the pregnant woman's control: her health, rape, or incest. A "bad" or unacceptable abortion is one which results from her trying to take control of her life, expressing a preference. Women who are victims deserve our sympathy. But the majority of women seeking abortions fall into the "abortion on demand" category, one which has taken on increasingly pejorative connotations.

This way of thinking about and of portraying abortion shapes the abortion experience and has a profound impact on the way that some women experience abortion. While women have had abortions at about the same rate for the past decade, direct talk about the actual abortion experience has been progressively silenced, as it was before legalization.

There is no single way in which women experience abortion. The way the experience affects them is contingent on a myriad of circumstances, including: the strength of their support systems, their relationships, their moral or religious beliefs, their desire for children, their feelings about themselves. For women who are struggling over their abortion decisions and experiences, the stigmatization and silencing of abortion, and thus of their own experience, are both painful and damaging.

At the Everywoman's Center at the University of Massachusetts, we have designed a post-abortion support group in order to facilitate emotional healing. Our group is based on a strong pro-choice/pro-woman vision. It is also based on our perception of an emotional vacuum. While the pro-choice movement has been on the defensive, it has felt the need to minimize the emotional aspects of abortion for women while emphasizing the incredible importance of legal abortion for women's lives and health. Legal abortion has meant safe medical procedures, and the significance of this cannot be overstated. At the same time, there has been little room for addressing the pain that may accompany the experience. Many clinics offer abortion as a minor outpatient surgical service with little or no counseling available. One woman said to us, "The nurses and doctors were asking me about school, small-talk, while I was going through the worst crisis in my entire life." When both the medical profession and the pro-choice movement treat abortion as if it is devoid of any emotional cost, they minimize its impact on women. The same social stigma that contributes to the turmoil women may feel about their abortion experiences has forced abortion care providers and pro-choice activists to avoid dealing with any emotional distress.

Although our movement has been critical of the opposition for taking women out of the picture, in a way it has done the same by denying the emotional struggle that many women experience in making and living with abortion decisions. While we are convinced that the distress is an effect of a conscious strategy employed by the anti-abortion movement, this does not make it any less real, painful, or debilitating for women. Ignoring this dimension of abortion has enabled the anti-choice forces to capture the emotional turf. We aim to take it back.

The only prevalent model for post-abortion distress, known as "Post-Abortion Stress Syndrome," has been created by the anti-choice movement. Despite efforts by the Reagan/Bush administrations to present "scientific evidence" showing the harmful effects on women, the medical community has discredited these claims. This has not stopped the anti-abortion movement, but it does make clear that politics, not women's well-being, is their motive. The anti-choice movement frames the issue as one of losing a baby. Women in their groups are told that they have murdered their babies, although they are also viewed as having been forced into doing so by pressures from partners, society, abortion providers, etc. In this model, women are both criminals and victims. Regret and guilt are the only appropriate feelings.

Our post-abortion group was inspired by the women's self-help health movement and the consciousness-raising groups of the 1960s. This model encourages women to become aware that their problems result not from personal failures but from the effects of living in a sexist society. Consciousness-raising groups brought women together on the premise that talking about their oppression together would enable them to see the societal basis of it and relieve them of individual paralyzing guilt and shame. These groups were envisioned as a step toward individual and collective empowerment. Self-help groups brought the message that women could act, could solve their own problems, could provide the knowledge, expertise, and care that were absent in the male-dominated health care system.

Similarly, we think that public recognition by the pro-choice movement of the emotions a woman may experience after an abortion and of the silence that surrounds her experience could lead to the creation of safe, woman-affirming spaces which would enable women to confront anti-abortion taboos. Creating a model for post-abortion emotional work that deals with individual women's experiences without isolating them from other women or from societal conditions is politically as well as therapeutically important.

A conceptual basis for our post-abortion group is drawn from Joanna Macy's Despair and Empowerment work, which she developed in the context of the peace movement.[1] The premise of Despair and Empowerment is that people function in a state of "psychic numbness" due to their terror over the nuclear threat, and that by experiencing and then working through their own despair about this terror, they can become empowered to be more aware of and actively address these issues. Similarly, our treatment combines emotional and spiritual support and political activism. For women who are in pain over their abortion experiences but unable to find a safe space to discuss their feelings, a comparable phenomenon of numbing occurs. Many women who are in distress over their abortions deny their feelings. These women report being unable to discuss the issue of abortion; they cannot tolerate being close to pregnant women or babies; they will not return to the abortion provider for follow-up medical care; they are terrified of becoming pregnant again. In our post-abortion model, participants are guided through grieving and encouraged to place their own abortion experiences in context, so that they can better live with their experiences and become empowered to be active agents for abortion rights. Our work shares with Macy's the fundamental assumption that commitment to social change comes from personal discovery.

Using elements of consciousness raising and psychotherapy, we offer women a new lens to view their abortion experiences, emphasizing that societal factors significantly influence how women interpret their personal conflicts with abortion. As women share their life experiences with one another, their personal stories take on greater meaning. The accumulation of these stories invites each woman who participates in the group to view herself in a larger context. She is given the opportunity to validate her own experience and to make it part of the collective experience of all women. Through this process her individual experience becomes politically significant.

We have three main goals: to enable women to break their own silences about their abortion experiences; to teach women how to grieve; and to help each woman re-frame her own experience so that she can accept her decision. Our hope is that women will translate personal distress into a broader understanding of the need for social change and political action. In order to achieve these goals, we have outlined a series of issues which we believe to be integral to the abortion experience, including: isolation, loss, anger, resentment, relationships, family, sexuality, fear, sadness, control, self-esteem, future, politicization, birth control, sexually transmitted diseases, religion, morals, and responsibility. We determined these to be key issues for women in large part through the work we have done as abortion counselors, paying special attention to women with whom we did post-abortion counseling or who had come to the clinic for repeat abortions.

We have offered three cycles of these groups using this model. The groups have met weekly in 8- to 12-week cycles, for 2-hour sessions. We recruit participants through flyers at local clinics, women's centers, and on local campuses. Many women also find the group by word of mouth, including the recommendations of past participants. Trust builds quickly within these groups. During the first meeting, we brainstorm to list issues women want to cover, and women share anecdotes of their own experiences. This kind of sharing begins to normalize the experiences and emotions each woman has felt in isolation. Up to this point, each woman's abortion experience has been fundamentally silent. Significant people in the woman's life have not been told, and this secrecy has resulted in eminently painful consequences. Once the group is underway, the first major task is the sharing of each woman's abortion story. The group provides a place where secrets which women had been carrying for months or years are divulged, and shame is lifted. Women validate one another's experiences and act as gauges for one another by revealing the normalcy of each individual's experience.

Almost all women in the group have been unable to discuss their abortion experiences with significant women in their lives, such as mothers, sisters, and close friends. Keeping this event hidden from other women is especially difficult to resolve: women embody potential empathy, since they share the physical immediacy of being able to experience pregnancy. Feeling unable to share the experience with women shakes not only the foundations of specific relationships, but the general promise of shared trust and empathy between women. It is as if the club one imagined was open to all begins to have segregated and conditional memberships. A participant in our first group was raised in a Catholic household consisting of her mother, her twin sister, and a sister who was two years younger than she. Because of her mother's strong anti-choice sentiment, this woman felt unable to share her abortion experience with her family. Not only did she feel removed from them, but she worried that her younger sister was sexually active and not using birth control. This woman wanted her sister to benefit from learning about her experience.

The inability to tell a partner about abortion is also difficult, but for different reasons. The inability to share this experience with a partner contributes to a sense of failure about the relationship itself. The silence can also build a wall of anger into the relationship.

The invisibility of the abortion experience causes painful isolation in a time of need. Because the experience is often cloaked in secrecy, family, friends, co-workers, and even partners may be unaware that a woman is in crisis. Most crises are more easily shared with those close to us than is an abortion experience, more easily shared even with strangers. If we are sick, for instance, our personal networks know, as well as others, such as medical personnel, the pharmacist, the mail carrier, etc. While some people inevitably must share the abortion experience, the lack of recognition of crisis is detrimental to the trust women feel in these close relationships. If a woman feels unable to safely share her abortion with people she counts on for support, she internalizes a sense of shame about the event and feels culpable for its occurrence. This was the difficulty for a woman whose own abortion was followed by her sister's pregnancy and birth of a baby. She wanted to be supportive or to share why she was unable to show enthusiasm, but because no one knew, she ended up feeling isolated. In perhaps a more commonplace example, one participant had an abortion during sports season and missed practice for a week. She had to hide the physical cause of her absence from the coach and team, and was unable to explain her bad mood, which caused anxiety on her part and annoyance on the team's part.

The issues of grieving and loss are complex and multifaceted, raising questions for each woman about the personal nature of her loss. We believe that women mourn a variety of losses, many of them seemingly intangible, within their abortion experiences. This notion contradicts the anti-choice movement's narrow definition of women's experience of post-abortion loss as the loss of a child. Each woman must define for herself what losses she may or may not feel. She may feel the loss of the opportunity to become a parent. One woman had an abortion weeks before her mother died, so that the loss of that chance to become a mother was emotionally tied to the loss of her own mother and to the inability to share the experience with her.

After her abortion, a woman may experience a loss of sexual freedom because she fears becoming pregnant again. In a society where the media glamorize the thrills of sexual risk-taking, the reality of unplanned pregnancy is particularly divergent from these images, and women often feel they have failed. For one woman, the fear of getting pregnant was so great that she felt the need to be on the pill, and to use a diaphragm and condom as well, so that for months, sexual relations were like braving out with all possible armor on, often a frightening experience rather than a pleasant one. In time, she began to trust the pill, and stopped using the diaphragm in tandem.

A woman may experience a loss of youth, since becoming pregnant and deciding how to handle a pregnancy are an adult situation, responsibility, and choice. Having an abortion may be one of the first "adult" experiences adolescents or young adults have had to handle, and often for the first time without parental support. For one woman who had an abortion at 14, with the support of her aunt, going back to junior high school the day after her procedure was difficult. She felt she had experienced something which didn't fit into the framework of her peers' world.

Many women have difficulty acknowledging or processing feelings of loss, believing that since they chose to abort, they no longer have a right to grieve. These attitudes are reinforced by anti-choice propaganda that portrays women who have abortions as willful killers. Often women who have repeat abortions are left feeling more guilt and shame than they experienced with first abortions. One abortion can be seen as an accident; more than one is often assigned stronger negative connotations—such as stupidity, self-destructiveness, or a sign of the woman's "looseness." Rarely is the woman having repeat abortions seen as exercising control over her own life.

The inherent "femaleness" of pregnancy and abortion often makes women feel great distance from men. Women describe feeling angry that they are solely responsible for the consequences of pregnancy. Men and women have different reactions to abortion, especially in terms of its impact on sexuality and in terms of the long-term process of grieving. Some women feel pressured by their partners to have intercourse, and report that their partners act as if the pregnancy and abortion had never occurred. This pressure alienates them from their partners and from the gradual process of rediscovering their sexual lives.

Making the connection between pregnancy and sexuality is of fundamental importance. The crisis aspect of having an abortion seems to be heightened when a woman has not considered what she would do if she faced an unplanned pregnancy or has not discussed this with her partner. One goal of our groups is to help women take control of their choices around sexuality—including the use of birth control, employment of safer sex practices, and learning to find sexual pleasure. Taking responsibility for one's sexual behavior is especially important in the age of AIDS, since the possible consequences of unprotected sex are far more grave than unplanned pregnancy.

Our post-abortion support groups give women the opportunity to place their abortion experiences in the context of their lives and of the broader society—looking at issues like family, sexuality, self-esteem, and relationships. In this model, as women build personal frameworks for their abortion experiences, the process of politicization occurs. They begin to develop a feminist awareness about the societal conditioning of women to become mothers, the pressure to consent to sex, and the inequality of burden when women are physically responsible for birth control and at risk of pregnancy. All these realities give sexual intercourse a different context for them than for their partners. They begin to acknowledge the political urgency of reproductive rights issues, and often become pro-choice advocates.

These women speak with passionate voices in the struggle for abortion rights because their voices have been previously shamed and silenced. They talk and write about their personal experiences either within their social networks or publicly. They get involved in political activism. They study the issue for classes. Even though they may not become fulltime political activists, they strengthen their own lives and foster their concerns for social change issues. They become outspoken advocates for themselves, recognizing their own needs often for the first time in their lives, and begin to go after what they need and desire.

In the 1960s, when the first speak-outs on abortion and birth control were held, the experience of going public not only challenged social stigmas, but empowered women, both those who participated and those who listened. As societal taboos around abortion and sexuality become increasingly volatile, the act of speaking out has again gained significance. Many group participants have cited the experience of speaking out as a kind of personal breakthrough for themselves after having felt afraid to share their experiences in a room full of supportive listeners. Others have benefitted in hearing other women speak. Speaking out, when one feels ready to do so, reinforces the political nature of hearing personal stories. It allows women to gain more support from others and to acknowledge respect for their own experiences. Publicly speaking out grows naturally out of the initial sharing of stories in the post-abortion group. It breaks silences, normalizes a range of experiences, and puts women's personal stories into a political realm.

These groups offer an opportunity for women to identify their own power and oppression in this society. For the pro-choice movement, our post-abortion model offers a positive method for dealing with the pain and ambivalence some women experience with the abortion decision. The complexity of women's abortion experiences is acknowledged, and a framework is built, both emotionally and politically. Our groups provide a forum for dealing with difficult feelings. This model opens the door of the movement wider by encouraging compassion, empathy, and honest emotions. In the larger political climate of the 1990s, we believe these ideals of compassion, empathy, and honesty are crucial to the continued growth and success of the pro-choice movement. This is part of restoring women and their experiences to the center of the abortion debate.

Notes

1. See *Despair and Empowerment in the Nuclear Age*, Philadelphia, New Society Publishers, 1983.

Who Has Abortions in the United States?

- Each year, almost three out of every 100 women aged 15-44 has an abortion.

- Women under 30, especially those 18-19, have the most abortions.

- Hispanic women are 60% more likely to have abortions than non-Hispanic women (but less likely than Black women).

- Unmarried women are 4-5 times more likely to have abortions than married women.

- Poor women are 3 times more likely to have abortions than those who are not poor.

- Catholic women are more likely to have abortions than Protestant or Jewish women. The abortion rate of Catholic women is 30% higher than that of Protestant women. "Born-again" or Evangelical Christians are half as likely as other women to have abortions.

- Three-fourths of women who have abortions cite three reasons: having a baby would interfere with work, school, or other responsibilities; two-thirds say they could not afford to have a child at this time; half say they do not want to be a single parent or they have problems in the relationship they are in.

- Nearly one-third of all women who choose abortion report a fear of others discovering that they had become pregnant.

- Most women who have abortions after 15 weeks (the first trimester) experienced problems detecting their pregnancy. Half were delayed because of problems arranging the abortion, usually because they needed more time to raise the money.

- 70% of women having abortions say they intend to have children in the future.

- About half of the women having abortions became pregnant even though they were using some form of contraception, either because of inconsistent or incorrect use or because of a method failure.

- 9% of abortion patients studied had never used a contraceptive method.

SOURCE: News Release, The Alan Guttmacher Institute, October 6, 1988, based on two separate national surveys conducted in 1987 and 1988 of women who obtained abortions. The first study surveyed 1,900 women nationwide who obtained abortions in 30 facilities. The second study surveyed nearly 10,000 women who obtained abortions at 103 facilities.

Putting Women
Back into the Abortion Debate[1]

Ellen Willis

Some years ago I attended a New York Institute for the Humanities seminar on the New Right. We were a fairly heterogeneous group of liberals and lefties, feminists and gay activists, but on one point nearly all of us agreed: the right-to-life movement was a dangerous anti-feminist crusade. At one session, I argued that the attack on abortion had significance far beyond itself, that it was the linchpin of the Right's social agenda. I got a lot of supportive comments and approving nods. It was too much for Peter Steinfels, a liberal Catholic, author of *The Neoconservatives,* and executive editor of *Commonweal.* Right-to-lifers were not all right wing fanatics, he protested. "You have to understand," he said plaintively, "that many of us see abortion as a human life issue." What I remember best was his air of frustrated isolation. I don't think he came back to the seminar after that.

Things are different now. I often feel isolated when I insist that abortion is, above all, a feminist issue. Once people took for granted that abortion was an issue of sexual politics and morality. Now, abortion is often discussed as a question of "life" in the abstract. Public concern over abortion centers almost exclusively on fetuses; women and their bodies are merely the stage on which the drama of fetal life and death takes place. Debate over abortion—if not its reality—has become sexlessly scholastic. And the people most responsible for this turn of events are, like Peter Steinfels, on the Left.

The left wing of the right-to-life movement is a small, seemingly eccentric minority in both "progressive" and anti-abortion camps. Yet it has played a critical role in the movement: by arguing that opposition to abortion can be separated from the Right's anti-feminist program, it has given anti-abortion sentiment legitimacy in left wing and (putatively) pro-feminist circles. While Left anti-abortionists are hardly alone in emphasizing fetal life, their innovation has been to claim that a consistent

"pro-life" stand involves opposing capital punishment, supporting disarmament, demanding government programs to end poverty, and so on.
This is of course a leap the Right is neither able nor willing to make. It's
been liberals—Gary Wills to the Catholic bishops—who have supplied
the mass media with the idea that prohibiting abortion is part of a
"seamless garment" of respect for human life.

Having invented this counter-context for the abortion controversy,
Left anti-abortionists are trying to impose it as the only legitimate context
for debate. Those of us who won't accept their terms and persist in seeing
opposition to abortion, anti-feminism, sexual repression, and religious
sectarianism as the real seamless garment have been accused of obscur-
ing the real issue with demagoguery. Last year, *Commonweal*—perhaps
the most important current forum for Left anti-abortion opinion—ran an
editorial demanding that we shape up:

> Those who hold that abortion is immoral believe that the bio-
> logical dividing lines of birth or viability should no more deter-
> mine whether a developing member of the species is denied or
> accorded essential rights than should the biological dividing
> lines of sex or race or disability or old age. This argument is open
> to challenge. Perhaps the dividing lines are sufficiently different.
> Pro-choice advocates should state their reasons for believing so.
> They should meet the argument on its own grounds...

In other words, the only question we're allowed to debate—or the
only one *Commonweal* is willing to entertain—is "Are fetuses the moral
equivalent of born human beings?" And I can't meet the argument on its
own grounds because I don't agree that this is the key question, whose
answer determines whether one supports abortion or opposes it. I don't
doubt that fetuses are alive, or that they're biologically human—what
else could they be? I do consider the life of a fertilized egg less precious
than the well-being of a woman with feelings, self-consciousness, a
history, social ties; and I think fetuses get closer to being human in a
moral sense as they come closer to birth. But to me these propositions
are intuitively self-evident. I wouldn't know how to justify them to a
"non-believer," nor do I see the point of trying.

I believe the debate has to start in a different place—with the
recognition that fertilized eggs develop into infants inside the bodies of
women. Pregnancy and birth are active processes in which a woman's
body shelters, nourishes, and expels a new life; for nine months she is
immersed in the most intimate possible relationship with another being.
The growing fetus makes considerable demands on her physical and
emotional resources, culminating in the cataclysmic experience of birth.
And childbearing has unpredictable consequences; it always entails
some risk of injury or death.

For me all this has a new concreteness. I had a baby last year. My much-desired and relatively easy pregnancy was full of what anti-abortionists like to call "inconveniences." I was always tired, short of breath; my digestion was never right; for three months I endured a state of hormonal siege; later I had pains in my fingers, swelling feet, numb spots on my legs, the dread hemorrhoids. I had to think about everything I ate. I developed borderline glucose intolerance. I gained 50 pounds and am still overweight; my shape has changed in other ways that may well be permanent. Psychologically, my pregnancy consumed me—though I'd happily bought the seat on the roller coaster, I was still terrified to be so out of control of my normally tractable body. It was all bearable, even interesting—even, at times transcendent—because I wanted a baby. Birth was painful, exhausting, and wonderful. If I hadn't wanted a baby it would only have been painful and exhausting—or worse. I can hardly imagine what it's like to have your body and mind taken over in this way when you not only don't look forward to the result, but positively dread it. The thought appalls me. So as I see it, the key question is, "Can it be moral, under any circumstances, to make a woman bear a child against her will?"

From this vantage point, *Commonweal*'s argument is irrelevant, for in a society that respects the individual, no "member of the species" in any stage of development has an "essential right" to make use of someone else's body, let alone in such all-encompassing fashion, without that person's consent. You can't make a case against abortion by applying a general principle about everybody's human rights; you have to show exactly the opposite—that the relationship between fetus and pregnant woman is an exception, one that justifies depriving women of their right to bodily integrity. And in fact all anti-abortion ideology rests on the premise—acknowledged or simply assumed—that women's unique capacity to bring life into the world carries with it a unique obligation: that women cannot be allowed to "play God" and launch only the lives they welcome.

Yet the alternative to allowing women this power is to make them impotent. Criminalizing abortion doesn't just harm individual women with unwanted pregnancies, it affects all women's sense of themselves. Without control of our fertility we can never envision ourselves as free, for our biology makes us constantly vulnerable. Simply because we are female our physical integrity can be violated, our lives disrupted and transformed, at any time. Our ability to act in the world is hopelessly compromised by our sexual being.

Ah, sex—it does have a way of coming up in these discussions, despite all. When pressed, right-to-lifers of whatever political persuasion invariably point out that pregnancy doesn't happen by itself. The leftists often give patronizing lectures on contraception (though some find only "natural birth control" acceptable), but remain unmoved when reminded that contraceptives fail. Openly or implicitly, they argue that people shouldn't have sex unless they're prepared to procreate. (They are quick to profess a single standard—men as well as women should be sexually "responsible." Yes, and the rich as well as the poor should be allowed to sleep under bridges.) Which amounts to saying that if women want to lead heterosexual lives they must give up any claim to self-determination, and that they have no right to sexual pleasure without fear.

Opposition to abortion, then, means accepting that women must suffer sexual disempowerment and a radical loss of autonomy relative to men: if fetal life is sacred, the self-denial basic to women's oppression is also basic to the moral order. Opposing abortion means embracing a conservative sexual morality, one that subordinates pleasure to reproduction: if fetal life is sacred, there is no room for the view that sexual passion—or even sexual love—for its own sake is a human need and a human right. Opposing abortion means tolerating the inevitable double standard by which men may accept or reject restriction in accordance with their beliefs, while women must bow to them out of fear—or defy them at great risk. However much *Commonweal's* editors and those of like mind want to believe their opposition to abortion is simply saving lives, the truth is that in the real world they are shoring up a particular sexual culture, whose rules are stacked against women. I have yet to hear any Left right-to-lifers take full responsibility for that fact or deal seriously with its political implications.

Unfortunately, their fuzziness has not lessened their appeal—if anything it's done the opposite. In increasing numbers liberals and leftists while opposing anti-abortion laws, have come to view abortion as an "agonizing moral issue" with some justice on both sides, rather than an issue—however emotionally complex—of freedom versus repression, or equality versus hierarchy, that affects their political self-definition. This above-the-battle stance is attractive to leftists who want to be feminist good guys but are uneasy or ambivalent about sexual issues, not to mention those who want to ally with "progressive" factions of the Catholic Church on Central America, nuclear disarmament, or populist economics without that sticky abortion issue getting in the way.

Such neutrality is a way of avoiding the painful conflict over cultural issues that continually smolders on the Left. It can also be a way of coping with the contradictions of personal life at a time when liberation is a dream deferred. To me the fight for abortion has always been the cutting edge of feminism, precisely because it denied that anatomy is destiny, that female biology dictates women's subordinate status. Yet recently, I've found it hard to focus on the issue, let alone summon up the militance needed to stop the anti-abortion tanks. In part that has to do with second-round weariness—do we really have to go through all these things twice?—in part with my life now.

Since my daughter's birth, my feelings about abortion—not as a political demand but as a personal choice—have changed. In this society, the difference between the situation of a childless woman and of a mother is immense; the fear that having a child will dislodge one's tenuous hold on a non-traditional life is excruciating. This terror of being forced into the sea-change of motherhood gave a special edge to my convictions about abortion. Since I've made that plunge voluntarily, with consequences still unfolding, the terror is gone; I might not want another child for all sorts of reasons, but I will never again feel that my identity is at stake. Different battles with the culture absorb my energy now. Besides, since I've experienced the primal, sensual passion of caring for an infant, there will always be a part of me that does want another. If I had an abortion today, it would be with conflict and sadness unknown to me when I had an abortion a decade ago. And the anti-abortionists' imagery of dead babies hits me with new force. Do many women—Left, feminist women—have such feelings? Is this the sort of "ambivalence about abortion" that in the present atmosphere slides so easily into self-flagellating guilt?

Some Left anti-abortionists, mainly pacifists—Juli Loesch, Mary Meehan, and other "feminists for life"; Jim Wallis and various writers for Wallis' radical evangelical journal *Sojourners*—have tried to square their position with concern for women. They blame the prevalence of abortion on oppressive conditions—economic injustice, lack of child care and other social supports for mothers, the devaluation of childrearing, men's exploitative sexual behavior and refusal to take equal responsibility for children. They disagree on whether to criminalize abortion now (since murder is intolerable no matter what the cause) or to build a long-term moral consensus (since stopping abortion requires a general social transformation), but they all regard abortion as a desperate solution to desperate problems, and the women who resort to it as more sinned against than sinning.

This analysis grasps an essential feminist truth: that in a male-supremacist society no choice a woman makes is genuinely free or entirely in her interest. Certainly many women have had abortions they didn't want or wouldn't have wanted if they had any plausible means of caring for a child; and countless others wouldn't have gotten pregnant in the first place were it not for inadequate contraception, sexual confusion and guilt, male pressure, and other stigmata of female powerlessness. Yet forcing a woman to bear a child she doesn't want can only add injury to insult, while refusing to go through with such a pregnancy can be a woman's first step toward taking hold of her life. And many women who have abortions are "victims" only of ordinary human miscalculation, technological failure, or the vagaries of passion, all bound to exist in any society, however utopian. There will always be women who, at any given moment, want sex but don't want a child; some of these women will get pregnant; some of them will have abortions. Behind the victim theory of abortions is the implicit belief that women are always ready to be mothers, if only conditions are right, and that sex for pleasure rather than procreation is not only "irresponsible" (i.e. bad) but something men impose on women, never something women actively seek. Ironically, Left right-to-lifers see abortion as always coerced (it's "exploitation" and "violence against women"), yet regard motherhood—which for most women throughout history has been inescapable, and is still our most socially approved role—as a positive choice. The analogy to the feminist anti-pornography movement goes beyond borrowed rhetoric: the anti-porners, too, see active female lust as surrender to male domination and traditionally feminine sexual attitudes as expressions of women's true nature.

This Orwellian version of feminism, which glorifies "female values" and dismisses women's struggles for freedom—particularly sexual freedom—as a male plot, has become all too familiar in recent years. But its use in the abortion debate has been especially muddleheaded. Somehow we're supposed to leap from an oppressive patriarchal society to the egalitarian one that will supposedly make abortion obsolete without ever allowing women to see themselves as people entitled to control their reproductive function rather than be controlled by it. How women who have no power in this most personal of areas can effectively fight for power in the larger society is left to our imagination. A "New Zealand feminist" quoted by Mary Meehan in a 1980 article in *The Progressive* says, "Accepting short-term solutions like abortion only delays the implementation of real reforms like decent maternity and paternity leaves, job protection, high-quality child care, community responsibility for dependent people of all ages, and recognition of the economic contribution of childminders"—as if these causes were progressing nicely before legal abortion came along. On the contrary, the fight for reproductive freedom is the foundation of all the others, which is why anti-feminists resist it so fiercely.

As "pro-life" pacifists have been particularly concerned with refuting charges of misogyny, the liberal Catholics at *Commonweal* are most exercised by the claim that anti-abortion laws violate religious freedom. The editorial noted above hurled another challenge at the pro-abortion forces:

It is time, finally, for the pro-choice advocates and editorial writers to abandon, once and for all, the argument that abortion [sic] is a religious "doctrine" of a single or several churches being imposed on those of other persuasions in violation of the First Amendment...Catholics and their bishops are accused of imposing their "doctrine" on abortion, but not their "doctrine" on the needs of the poor, or their "doctrine" on the arms race, or their "doctrine" on human rights in Central America...

The briefest investigation into Catholic teaching would show that the church's case against abortion is utterly unlike, say, its belief in the Real Presence, known with the eyes of faith alone, or its insistence on a Sunday obligation, applicable only to the faithful. The church's moral teaching on abortion...is for the most part like its teaching on racism, warfare, and capital punishment, based on ordinary reasoning common to believers and unbelievers...

This is one more example of right-to-lifers' tendency to ignore the sexual ideology underlying their stand. Interesting, isn't it, how the editorial neglects to mention that the church's moral teaching on abortion jibes neatly with its teaching on birth control, sex, divorce, and the role of women? The traditional, patriarchal sexual morality common to these teachings is explicitly religious, and its chief defenders in modern times have been the more conservative churches. The Catholic and evangelical Christian churches are the backbone of the organized right-to-life movement and—a few Nathansons and Hentoffs notwithstanding—have provided most of the movement's activists and spokespeople.

Furthermore, the Catholic hierarchy has made abortion a litmus test of loyalty to the church in a way it has done with no other political issue—witness Archbishop O'Connor's harassment of Geraldine Ferraro during her vice-presidential campaign. It's unthinkable that a Catholic bishop would publicly excoriate a Catholic officeholder or candidate for taking a hawkish position on the arms race or Central America or capital punishment. Nor do I notice anyone trying to read William F. Buckley out of the church for his views on welfare. The fact is there is no accepted Catholic "doctrine" on these matters comparable to the church's absolutist condemnation of abortion. While differing attitudes toward war, racism, and poverty cut across religious or secular lines, the sexual values that mandate opposition to abortion are the bedrock of the traditional religious worldview, and the source of the most bitter conflict with secular and religious modernists. When churches devote their considerable political power, organizational resources, and money to translating those values into law, I call that imposing their religious beliefs on me—whether or not they're technically violating the First Amendment.

Statistical studies have repeatedly shown that people's views on abortion are best predicted by their opinions on sex and "family" issues, not on "life" issues like nuclear weapons or the death penalty. That's not because we're inconsistent but because we comprehend what's really at stake in the abortion fight. It's the anti-abortion Left that refuses to face the contradiction in its own position: you can't be wholeheartedly for "life"—or for such progressive aspirations as freedom, democracy, equality—and condone the subjugation of women. The seamless garment is full of holes.

Notes

1. This article originally appeared in the *Village Voice,* July 16, 1985. Reprinted with permission.

Raising Our Voices

Loretta Ross

Conspiracy of Silence

I had an abortion in 1970, yet I find it difficult to write about abortion. I have escorted friends to get abortions, yet I find it difficult to talk with them about abortion. I have tried to talk them into defending the clinics against anti-abortionists. But I couldn't convince them because they felt scared—scared about carrying out a decision that had been right for them.

They felt they needed to be secretive about their experience, and that was hard. It made them feel ashamed. They did not hear voices validating their decision, supporting their experience, so they questioned their choice. They were lucky if they had a girlfriend to escort them to have an abortion. Often they had only an angry parent or lover, or they went alone. It is not easy for Black women to talk about abortion. It is not easy for Black women to have abortions.

Our abortion experiences have been invisible. News cameras do not find us when we speak out for abortion rights. Instead, the few Black anti-choice voices are given prominence and are presumed to speak for all of us. Black women are said to be anti-choice. But we have spoken silently with our actions. Black women get abortions at twice the rate of white women. But we have had to act without community support because of the conspiracy of silence surrounding abortion.

No Black woman should have to go through an abortion alone. The lack of open discussion about abortion in our communities prevents us from building support for abortion rights within our communities. It prevents us from organizing in our own interests. A silent community cannot commit itself to change. A silent community cannot support sisters doing what they need and choose to do.

White women have begun to break their silence about their abortions. But they do not speak for us. We need to start telling our stories about how illegal abortion killed our mothers and how legal abortion saved our lives. We have to talk to each other as Black women, sister to sister. This will allow us to talk to Black women who are anti-choice, and hopefully we will find that we have more in common with these sisters than we have dividing us. We cannot and will not see each other as enemies. We have to respect each other's opinions, while affirming the essence of freedom for all of us. This freedom is the right to control, at all times, our bodies. We can listen to the sisters who are pro-choice but anti-abortion, and we must support the sisters who are actively pro-choice.

We Will Change the Abortion Debate

As we break our silence about abortion, we are creating our vision of "choice." Thus far, the abortion debate has largely been between white men and white women. It has centered on abstract arguments about personhood or fetal rights. Even when the debate has managed to take up women's lives, it has focused on the lives of white women. Black women's voices will push the parameters of the abortion debate further.

We want to talk about life and choices—real life, real choices. Our history as slaves has given us a deep understanding of what it means to choose life for ourselves and our children. We made life and death "choices" in wretched human conditions. We must still do so today when many of our people live in poverty: without work, without homes.

When we choose abortion, we choose life for ourselves and for our families. This is not easy when we do not control the circumstances of our lives. But lack of control is not lack of understanding. We make decisions from the full perspective of our lives. We are capable decision makers and reject any claims to the contrary. We know that only we can control our lives by making the choices we think are right for us, and we resist any efforts to prevent us from having that control.

Black women are now learning to talk about abortion. We are internalizing and understanding what it means to be the "sleeping giant" of the pro-choice movement. Each generation of a movement creates its own vision of what the movement should be. We will push its parameters too. We come to the movement with a low level of confidence in a system which has historically exploited people of color. The health care system has never met our needs. The judicial system has systematically discriminated against us. Institutions of power have never represented our concerns. When women of color enter the post-*Webster* abortion rights movement, we are not, therefore, likely to be focused on legislative or legal strategies. Instead, we are asking how we can begin to take abortion and other aspects of our health and reproduction into our own hands.

Black women bring to the pro-choice struggle a herstory of women controlling their own lives. Black women have always used abortion as a means of childspacing. Herbs and potions were used by women in Africa. My elders told me about the roots their grandmothers used in the 19th century. Early 20th-century douche powders were advertised in Black newspapers for "missed cycles." An African sister was recently featured on the radio speaking about the tradition of women teaching themselves about their own bodies. We have lost that tradition in the United States. We can regain it.

Within our own communities, there are those who do not want us to have that control. We should not be surprised, confused, or intimidated when Black anti-choice activists call abortion genocide. Whites who oppose abortion call it genocide for whites. I imagine that anti-choice Jews, Italians, or Native Americans make the same allegations. We should see this for what it is—an attempt to silence us and through that silence to control us, to prevent us from controlling our own lives.

The contemporary effort to control us through our reproduction is not new. In the 1960s, Black women were told to throw away their birth control pills and "have a baby for the Black Revolution." The men would fight racism and we would produce Black babies (males) to carry on the struggle. But Black women did not do as they were told. They were unwilling to accept a political ideology that made *their* freedom expendable in the fight for racial liberation. We must and will make a revolution, but we will not give up control of our bodies and our right to make our own decisions.

I am not rejecting the genocide argument. We do, however, need to make sure the shoe is on the correct foot. The fervor of the anti-abortion movement comes at a time when the white birth rate is declining. Seventy percent of abortions in the United States are obtained by white women between the ages of 20 and 24. These are the wombs that the anti-choice forces are trying to manipulate. I do not think that the mostly white anti-abortion movement really cares how many Black or Puerto Rican children are born except to feel that there are too many of "them." I do think they are deathly afraid of the demographic prediction that by the year 2012 the majority of people in the United States will not be white.

I am also sensitive to the genocide question from within the pro-choice movement. Too often arguments for abortion have appealed to racist notions about "overpopulation" by third world people. The important message for Black women is that we must refuse to be used and abused by someone else's political agenda for our womb. We reject all efforts to do so, whether by anti-abortion or right wing zealots, international family planning agencies, or those within our own communities.

Implications for Action

Only since the dire *Webster* decision has our Black society realized the threat posed to essential freedoms. Now we must use this new-found consciousness in a different way. We should see it as an incredible gift—the power to save Black women's lives by giving us permission to talk about abortion. Each of us can break the conspiracy of silence about abortion in our own lives. We can continue to model ways for other women to talk to each other and support each other through this decision. We have to end the confusion and lack of validation our sisters experience whether talking about abortion or having one. We may not be able to escort every sister to a clinic in a time of crisis, but if we raise our voices in her community she will know that she is not alone.

We must also raise our voices within the civil rights movement. While most Blacks, 87 percent, are pro-choice, Black civil rights organizations have not been particularly solid or organized to defend their pro-choice positions. The abortion issue has been used by opponents of abortion to divide and weaken the civil rights coalition and to stall progress on civil rights. The effort to pass the Civil Rights Restoration Act in 1988 was a good example of this. The primary barriers to its passage were several anti-abortion amendments; ultimately it was passed with the amendments.

Vacillation by the civil rights movement on the question of birth control and abortion rights is a relatively new phenomenon. We need to publicize the pro-choice activities of Black organizations in the first half of the 20th century. Leading Black groups viewed birth control and abortion, even when illegal, as integral to issues of economics, health, race relations, and racial progress. Major organizations and Black newspapers gave sustained coverage to pro-choice organizing and participated actively in the debate on abortion and birth control.

In the 1960s, the Black Power movement re-opened the genocide debate of the 1920s, and this had a profound influence on the civil rights movement which is still being felt today. Reproductive rights were characterized as "white women's issues." We need to challenge this. Reproductive rights are civil rights, fundamental necessities for Black women (and men) to gain control over their lives.

The civil rights movement needs to become less vulnerable to "abortion baiting" by anti-choice groups. This effort was strengthened by recent electoral campaigns in which Black men who were explicitly pro-choice won over white candidates who were anti-choice. The effort will also be strengthened by expanding the leadership of Black women within the movement and in society. We must also contend for power within the pro-choice movement. We have a long way to go on this, since fewer than 5 percent of Black women work with white women in the pro-choice movement. Those of us who do are usually isolated, pained, and exhausted by having to reinterpret the debate for white women and Black men. And we are demoralized by having to defend these efforts to our Black sisters who support abortion rights yet totally distrust the pro-choice movement. With the notable exception of Faye Wattleton, President of Planned Parenthood, Black women and other women of color are not represented in the leadership or on the boards of mainstream pro-choice organizations. Without the participation of Black women, the movement will continue to flounder and commit the political suicide of not truly representing all women. The changes required are profound. I am not talking about "colorizing" a basically white picture. We have had enough of such tokenism. What I am talking about is building a multi-racial movement where power and resources are equitably distributed.

Although the number of Black and other women of color joining mainstream pro-choice organizations has grown in the past decade, most women of color will continue to join their own political formations. The number of Black women's organizations has more than tripled in the past 10 years. Most Black women believe in inter-racial coalitions, not inter-racial organizations.

I believe that coalition-building is the way to bring together the different perspectives of white women and Black women about abortion and reproductive rights. I also believe that women of color will take the lead in the coalition-building effort in the 1990s because we know this is the only way to win. In order to participate in this effort, predominantly white organizations will have to change their leadership and their agendas. And white women must do intensive anti-racist work. White women and men must understand how to gain positive power from being white, power which does not involve oppressing Black people.

We can build the strong coalitions we need to win our struggles. As Black women and other women of color articulate their agenda, we are creating a new reproductive rights movement, one that will represent all women. I hope white organizations and activists will add their voices to ours and help to create an agenda and a strategy that will get us there.

DEFENDING ABORTION RIGHTS: THREATS TO ACCESS

Emergency Memorandum
to Women of Color

Loretta Ross, Sherrilyn Ifill, and Sabrae Jenkins

TO: CONCERNED PEOPLE OF COLOR AND ALLIES
FROM: COALITION OF WOMEN OF COLOR FOR REPRODUCTIVE
           HEALTH
RE: EFFECT OF PENDING SUPREME COURT CASE ON THE RIGHT
           OF WOMEN OF COLOR TO CHOICE
DATE: FEBRUARY 16, 1989

On January 9, 1989, the Supreme Court of the United States announced that it will hear and decide a case of critical importance to women of color throughout the United States. This case, *Webster v. Reproductive Health Services, Inc.,* implicates the right of poor women to exercise their constitutional right to choose abortion. The Solicitor-General of the Reagan administration, one of the most influential legal figures in the government, submitted a brief to the Supreme Court urging it to use *Webster* to overturn the right to choose safe and legal abortion won by women in the 1973 landmark case, *Roe v. Wade.*

All of the restrictions of the Missouri law in the *Webster* case, if declared constitutional, will have a disproportionate impact on poor Black, Latina, Native American, and Asian-Pacific American women, who often cannot afford private medical care.

This case, like many others, demonstrates that the anti-abortion war is being fought primarily against women of color. We cannot permit our lack of economic clout, nor our limited political clout, to strip us of our right to bodily integrity and self-determination. No matter what our individual views on abortion, we and our daughters must have the right to choose the safest health option. If the Supreme Court uses this case to overturn *Roe v. Wade* and returns to the individual states the power to declare abortion illegal, countless low-income women and teens will be forced to carry unwanted pregnancies to term, even if that pregnancy is the result of rape or incest.

Because the majority of women seeking services from public hospitals are women of color, upholding the Missouri law would severely limit access not only to abortion services, but also to information, counseling, and funding for all related reproductive health care problems. A pregnant patient who has the AIDS virus, for example, could not be counseled about the life-threatening risks if she decides to continue her pregnancy. Pregnant women with severe diabetes, hypertension, or sickle cell anemia also could not be counseled about the health risks involved in continuing their pregnancies. Likewise, women experiencing ectopic pregnancies—a condition that could result in the death of the mother if an abortion is not performed—could not be told that they are in a life-threatening situation that requires immediate action.

Women of color already suffer disproportionately from a variety of serious health conditions which may be exacerbated by pregnancy. For instance, Black women have a higher prevalence of high blood pressure, hypertension, and diabetes than white women. Hispanic and Native Americans also suffer from chronic diabetes to a greater degree than whites. Chronic hypertension may lead to a stroke during pregnancy. In fact, hypertension is associated with up to 30 percent of maternal deaths and up to 22 percent of perinatal deaths. Pregnant diabetics run the risk of aggravating debilitating vascular conditions.

Certain forms of cancer are also more prevalent among women of color than whites. The mortality and incidence rates for cervical cancer, for instance, are approximately 2.5 times higher for Black women than white women. A pregnant woman with sickle cell anemia may go into sickle cell shock and die as a result of pregnancy. Perinatal mortality and spontaneous abortion are also risks to pregnant sickle cell patients. Failure to provide such patients with full medical information and options about terminating pregnancies amounts to complicity in these potential deaths.

AIDS is the newest health crisis for women of color. The incidence of AIDS in Hispanic women is almost 11 times that for white women. Fifty-two percent of all women with AIDS are Black, and nearly 80 percent of all AIDS pediatric cases are either Black or Latino. A pregnant AIDS patient must be told the risks to her health and that of her child, particularly since some theories suggest that pregnancy may accelerate the progression of the AIDS virus.

The *Webster* case represents a critical juncture in history. If abortion is made illegal again, women will *not* stop having abortions; they will stop having *safe* abortions. Before legalization, 49 percent of the pregnancy-related deaths in New York were due to illegal abortions. Of these deaths, 50 percent of the women were Black and 44 percent were Puerto Rican. Prior to legalization, 93 percent of the therapeutic abortions (safe abortions performed by doctors) were performed on white women in private hospitals.

Access to quality health care is determined by one's economic status. Those who rely on federal funds for abortion are already restricted by the 1976 Hyde Amendment prohibiting the use of federal funds for abortions. Currently, this primarily affects poor women, Native Americans who use the Indian Health Service, military dependents, and Peace Corps volunteers. The immediate impact of a negative ruling by the Supreme Court will be that an inadequate health care system for women that is already class-based will get worse. Wealthy women will be able to travel to Canada or Mexico where abortion is legal to obtain safe services. Poor women will be denied access to abortion information, forced to return to the back-alley butchers who will leave them bleeding their reproductive lives away. Or they may try equally dangerous self-abortion procedures with coat hangers and/or toxic chemicals.

Of the 55 million women in the United States between the ages of 15 and 34, the majority, 36 million, are trying to prevent pregnancy. Three million unintended pregnancies occur each year due to either contraceptive failure or the lack of use of contraceptives. Of Black women between 15 and 34, 170.3 per 1,000 become pregnant, and 25.4 percent of these have miscarriages. Black women are 2.5 times more likely to get pregnant than white women. Of teens 15-19, 181.3 per 1,000 become pregnant. Among white teens, 44.7 per thousand become pregnant, and of that number, 60 percent abort. Of Black teens, 94.6 per thousand become pregnant and 21 percent of those have abortions. Of all the abortions performed in the United States, 70 percent are obtained by white women, mostly between the ages of 20 and 24. Thirty percent are obtained by women of color, while 20 percent of all abortions are obtained by Black women.

These statistics portray the grim reality of abortion. No one likes it. No one joyfully chooses it. But as you can see, white women account for 70 percent of the abortions in America. Our Coalition is convinced that the mostly white anti-abortion movement is worried about that statistic. We do not believe that they care about the number of Black or Latino children born or unborn. They are concerned that the white population in America (particularly the male population) is dwindling so that in a few short decades, the majority of people in the United States will be people of color. They are trying to stop white women from having abortions, and women of color are caught in the crossfire.

This new threat will further jeopardize the health of poor women, a disproportionate number of whom are women of color, in a myriad of ways. Besides the inability to obtain safe and legal abortions, many programs that deliver other reproductive services will be forced to close down, as patients turn to illegal providers to obtain abortion services. This may mean that poor women will not come to family planning clinics or health care centers. If a crisis such as hemorrhaging occurs, they will end up in hospital emergency rooms.

Limitations on the types of reproductive information and services provided by publicly funded facilities will disproportionately limit the range of reproductive options available to women of color, including access to contraceptives. This in turn will increase the number of un-wanted pregnancies and promote continuing cycles of infant mortality, maternal morbidity, poverty, and despair, while creating unnecessary medical risks for women of color.

Our communities must become involved in this debate—we must actively defend our lives and the lives of our children. We cannot be caught in the crossfire between opposing groups of white people. We must see beyond the hysterical rhetoric and look at the facts. Adolescents, poor women, and women of color have been and will continue to be the first to experience the negative consequences of the Supreme Court decision. We must make the Supreme Court hear our voices.

Abortion Rights, Poor Women, and Religious Diversity[1]

Sabrae Jenkins

The Religious Coalition for Abortion Rights (RCAR) is an organization of 30 national Christian, Jewish, and other religious bodies. Each of our member faith groups approaches the issue of abortion from the unique perspective of its own theology, yet our member organizations share some common principles. First, that abortion is a moral and theological concern, and that an abortion decision should be the result of thoughtful consideration, based on one's own conscience and religious beliefs. Second, that there are some instances in which abortion may be a moral alternative to a problem pregnancy. Third, that in our pluralistic society, no one religious viewpoint on the beginning of human life should be imposed on all Americans by secular law. Our belief in reproductive freedom is closely tied to our belief in religious freedom.

The Religious Coalition for Abortion Rights holds in high respect the value of potential life; we do not take the question of abortion lightly, and we are not pro-abortion. We are pro-choice and we are pro-life. We do not believe in or support abortion as a means of birth control or sex selection. We believe that abortion should be kept safe, legal, and an available option to *all* women. We also believe that *all* women should be supported in their decision to carry their pregnancies to term.

A decision regarding abortion is not one to be taken lightly, then cast aside. When faced with a problem pregnancy, the decision a woman makes is not clearly right or wrong, black or white—it is finding the peace that lies in the middle, in the gray area. Women must have the ability to find that middle, to choose the option which best reflects their needs.

Over 200 diverse groups in the United States espouse starkly and mutually inconsistent views about abortion. Yet, some of these denominations—including the Presbyterian Church (U.S.A.), the United Methodist Church, the Christian Church (Disciples of Christ), the Episcopal

Church, the United Church of Christ, the Moravian Church, and members of the Reform, Conservative, and Reconstructionist Jewish communities—have come to respect the diversity of theological opinions on this issue.

Some organized religious groups adhere to basic respect for individual conscience about abortion because of the variety of views held by members of those groups. Others support a woman's choice regarding abortion for different reasons: potential risks to the life or physical or mental health of the mother; concerns about the social situation in which the infant might be born; severe fetal deformity. In religions like Judaism, where the fetus is not seen as a person before birth, abortion is not only permissible, but indeed required if the life of the mother is threatened by continuing the pregnancy.

Even the Roman Catholics, who wrote most of the anti-abortion books prior to the *Roe v. Wade* decision legalizing abortion, agree that the Bible is silent on the issue of abortion. Since definitive doctrine on personhood is absent, many Catholic theologians and Church members believe that when there is doubt, there is freedom to make an individual choice, as evidenced by the statistics of the many Catholic women who have abortions.

The anti-choice movement is largely represented by Evangelicals who are attempting to impose their religious doctrine upon everyone in this country. While each Evangelical church is independent and has a loose relationship with the national body, they obviously do not respect the diverse religious beliefs or convictions of other persons of faith and certainly do not believe in the separation of church and state. Generally, they believe that the fetus is a person from the moment of conception and, thus, that abortion is murder. Irrespective of the circumstances, they believe that the existence of the fetus totally outweighs the existence of the mother in most cases.

I personally find that these people's behavior resembles that of the segregationists of not too long ago. When the issue of segregation erupted in the South, it was a moral question, an economic question, and a political question—as is the issue of abortion. Racial segregation was professed as "God's will," no matter what the consequences. Are anti-abortionists doing "God's will" when they bomb clinics or verbally harass women who are seeking health care, or when they try to inaccurately align themselves with the civil rights movement of the 1960s? Where is the righteousness in their actions? And where are the right-to-lifers in battles for programs which save the lives of poor women and their born children?

In 1986, the United States ranked eighteenth in the world in infant mortality rates, with 10.4 deaths per 1,000 live births. Poor children are twice as likely to be born too early or too small and to die in infancy. Low birthweight contributes to two-thirds of the deaths among babies in their first month of life. A large percentage of low birthweight births are preventable with early and adequate prenatal care. Furthermore, there is a consistent correlation between lack of early and sufficient prenatal care and low income. Only 61.6 percent of Black women received prenatal care during the first trimester in 1986 as compared to 79.2 percent of white women. Moreover, 10.6 percent of Black women began prenatal care in the third trimester or not at all, more than twice the 5.0 percent of white women. The rates of both infant mortality and low birthweight for Blacks are more than twice those for whites. According to the Public Health Service of the U.S. Department of Health and Human Services, the infant mortality rates for Hispanics, Asians, and Native Americans are underestimated due to problems in classifying race and origin on birth and death certificates. They believe that infant mortality rates have been underestimated by 26 percent for Native Americans, by 39 percent for Japanese-Americans, by 51 percent for Filipino-Americans, and for other Asian-Americans by 61 percent.

The Women, Infants, and Children program (WIC) is a supplemental food program which is federally financed. WIC provides screening, nutritional counseling, and food supplements for low-income pregnant women and for children up to age five who are diagnosed as nutritionally at risk. WIC is extremely effective; however, it reaches fewer than 40 percent of the seven million women, infants, and children eligible for the program. Although President Bush has proclaimed support for this program, there has been no adjustment for inflation, virtually cutting $47 million from the amount needed to preserve current service levels. A cost-savings analysis shows that $1 invested in the prenatal care component of WIC has saved as much as $3 in short-term hospital costs. In a *Washington Post* editorial, syndicated columnist William Raspberry stated that the United States spends more than $2.5 billion a year on neonatal intensive care alone—more than any other country in the world. Neonatal facilities cost anywhere from $20,000 to $250,000 for a few days' care. Many infants who are physically and mentally impaired as a result of their mothers poor health care never fully overcome their disabilities, which could have been prevented by spending just a few hundred dollars on prenatal care during nine months of gestation. The long-term benefits of prenatal care include reduction in infant mortality and low birthweight births, and improvement of nutritional outcomes for children during the first six years of their life. I ask you, where are the right-to-lifers on this issue?

It is quite interesting that the anti-choice movement argues for adoption. During a recent hearing in the Wisconsin legislature on abortion, a state representative described the Black children in her district that needed to be adopted and asked the anti-choice witness whether or not she supported the adoption of babies of color by white families. The anti-choice woman's response was that she was currently spending $18,000 to adopt a Black baby from Paraguay. I was stunned that she had totally missed the point of the question—that there are numerous Black children *in the United States* who need to be adopted. Also, she seemed to miss the point that her $18,000 could have been used to strengthen an existing family structure, perhaps allowing a mother to keep her child.

In 1985, the U.S. Department of Health and Human Services estimated that there are approximately 36,000 children awaiting adoption in this country at any given point of time, of whom one-half are minority children. They also estimated that 42 percent of the 276,000 children in the foster care system are minority children.

While Black foster care children are less likely than white children to have physical or mental disabilities, they remain in foster care much longer than do white children, according to the National Urban League publication "The Status of Black America 1989." Many Black families who want to adopt are screened out by insensitive criteria that place higher priority on middle-class status, two-parent families, heads of households under 40 years old, and no children of their own. Taking into account the general socio-economic status of many Black families and the fact that over 52 percent of all Black families are female-headed and living below poverty, adoption of Black children by Black families is not a realistic possibility under such criteria. Thus, hundreds of Black foster care children are never adopted; instead they grow up in foster care. According to a 1989 study performed by the National Black Child Development Institute, between 25 percent and 40 percent of children in foster care nationally are Black. It has been estimated that half of all homeless youths in New York were formerly in foster care.

Anti-choice public officials have spent a substantial amount of time attempting to implement their agenda upon those least able to defend themselves by attaching anti-abortion amendments to legislation before Congress, including the Civil Rights Restoration Act, Indian Health Care Bill, Title X, the Fair Housing Act, domestic family planning, and international family planning. Not only is their aim to restrict the rights of individuals in this country, but they also push restrictions in other countries as well. In 1984, the Reagan administration barred grants to foreign family planning groups that provide abortion services, even if these groups provide those services with their own money. Although illegal in every Latin American country except Cuba, abortion is currently Latin America's leading cause of pregnancy-related death. An estimated

200,000 women die each year from the effects of unsafe abortions in developing countries, one-quarter of them in Latin America. Every day, 480 women around the world die from back-alley abortions. If international family planning agencies were able to continue to perform abortions, many of these women would be alive today.

Whether legal or illegal, economics dictates that the "haves" may choose to purchase whatever health services they may need or want. The "have-nots" have very few choices and in many instances must rely on the federal government. An excellent example of this can be found in the Hyde Amendment, which restricts the use of Medicaid funds for abortion services and directly impacts millions of impoverished Americans, of whom 5 out of 10 are women of color.

Currently, there are only 13 states that pay for Medicaid abortions. Poor women and women on Medicaid have limited options available to them. However, the abortion rate of women on Medicaid was approximately three times that of women who were not covered. This means that women without Medicaid coverage either did not pay rent or did not feed themselves or their families in order to obtain abortion services. A study on this subject found that about 20 percent of women who would have obtained a Medicaid-funded abortion, had funding been available, carried their unwanted pregnancies to term in the absence of funding.

The first woman to die as a direct result of the cut-off of Medicaid funds produced by the Hyde Amendment was a young Mexican-American mother in McAllen, Texas. Only a semester away from graduating with her college degree in education, Rosie Jiménez had to choose between having that baby and not finishing her degree, using her $700 scholarship check for a legal abortion and again forfeiting completion of her education, or taking her chances with an illegal abortion in order to realize her dream of a better life for her daughter than her migrant farming parents had been able to provide for her. Unfortunately, Rosie decided on an illegal abortion, hoping to live out her dream. For Rosie and for millions of women of color in this country and around the world, oppression is the absence of choices.

On July 3, 1989, poor women, particularly women of color, lost another fundamental right. The result of the Supreme Court decision in *Webster v. Reproductive Health Services* is that being poor further restricts your reproductive choices and options. What the Court said was simple. *Roe v. Wade*, the historic ruling that recognized a woman's right to choose abortion, is still the law of the land. But if you live in the state of Missouri, and are poor, you must find ways to obtain an abortion without the assistance of any outside agency. The *Webster* decision restricts access to some of the best medical facilities, regardless of your ability to pay. Even private doctors in public hospitals cannot help you.

Some of the best medical facilities are teaching hospitals which receive government monies. And, more important, if your doctor thinks that your fetus is 20 weeks or older, you have to submit to and pay for expensive medical tests on the fetus before an abortion.

This decision places enormous financial and emotional burdens and restrictions on poor women who have to face whether or not to terminate an unwanted pregnancy. Poor women, most of whom are women of color, were told that abortion is still legal, but if you don't have the money, there are really no other choices but to carry the pregnancy to term. Yet the past has shown us that many of these women will choose not to carry their pregnancies to term.

The bottom line is that if you have money, abortion remains an option. If you don't have the money, the federal government will pay 90 percent of the cost of sterilization on demand. Therefore, if a poor woman becomes pregnant she can choose either to have that child or to never have another child. The regulations set forth by the Reagan-Bush administrations, specifically regarding family planning, and the potential for restrictions by individual states opened by the Supreme Court leave no choice for poor women. The door has been nailed shut for young, poor women, most of whom are Black and Hispanic, preventing equal access to necessary medical treatment.

Make no mistake about this. Women will continue to seek abortions, whether they are legal or not. Restrictions on abortion have not and never will halt its use. Women will make life-threatening sacrifices that jeopardize their existing families. Women will die at the hands of butchers. And the first to die, again, will be poor women of color.

RCAR believes that women ultimately make the best decision for themselves in consultation with their families and in accordance with their religious beliefs. While a number of us will never elect to have an abortion, we should never deny that right to other individuals. This is a free country, and we must be forever vigilant to protect our freedoms.

Notes

1. Statement of Sabrae Jenkins, Director, Women of Color Partnership Program, Religious Coalition for Abortion Rights, October 17, 1989, before the Health and Welfare Ministries Program Department, General Board of Global Ministries, United Methodist Church.

The Reproductive Health of Black Women and Other Women of Color

There are many myths about the health of Black women that have been handed down and circulated throughout our communities: from the misconception that Black women don't have abortions to the unreal assumption that teenage women are not having sex to the already age-old lie that AIDS is a disease of gay, white males. These are barriers to our wellness. Below are compiled a few basic facts and realities about the health of Black women and other women of color to put wellness in perspective. The categories selected are those which most affect women in the Black community.

General Health

- Hypertension is 82% higher among women of color than white women.

- In 1983, life expectancy reached a new high of 75.2 years for whites and of 69.6 for Blacks, a gap of 5.6 years. Blacks today have a life expectancy already reached by whites in the 1950s.

- One in 165 Black people is born with sickle cell anemia, while 25% of the Black population have the sickle cell trait. Pregnant women with sickle cell anemia are more prone to miscarriages, aggravated circulatory problems, and depression.

- A diabetic is most likely to be a non-white, retired woman living in the inner city.

- The incidence of cancer for Blacks has risen 34% over the past 25 years, as compared to 9% for whites.

- Prevalence of smoking among Black women is 25.1%.

- Lupus is three times more common in Black women than in white women.

- 71% of female-headed families living below the poverty level are headed by Black women.

Public Funding

- In 1980, 18% of Blacks under the age of 65 lacked any form of health insurance, including Medicaid, while only 9% of whites lacked any form of coverage. In addition, 23% of Black children were uninsured as compared to 8% of white children.

- Women of color constitute over 30% of Title X patients, family planning clinics funded totally or in part by the federal government. Similarly, 32% of Title X patients are adolescents.

Pregnancy and Mortality

- 25% of Black pregnancies end in miscarriage.

- The babies of women of color in this country have nearly twice the neonatal mortality rate of white babies. In 1976, the death rate was 9.7 per 1,000 for white women and 16.3 for women of color.

- In 1981, the Black infant mortality rate was 25.5 per 1,000 while the white infant mortality rate was 14.1.

- Black babies die at a rate of 6,000 more per year than white babies living in the same geographic area, due mainly to low birthweight among Black babies—which is entirely preventable.

- 25-30% of inner city Black women receive little or no prenatal care, one of the contributing factors to low birthweight babies.

- The rate of death due to Sudden Infant Death Syndrome (SIDS) per 1,000 live births for Blacks is 1.7 times that for whites.

- About 20-40% of women who are infected with the AIDS virus and become pregnant pass the virus to their babies during pregnancy.

Teenage Women

- 40% of young Black women become pregnant at least once before the age of 20.

- Of Black teens, 94.6 per 1,000 become pregnant. 21% of these teens have abortions.

- Black teenagers tend to wait an average of one year between initiating sexual intercourse and first using a prescription method of contraception.

- Of all births to teens under the age of 15 in 1982, nearly 60% were born to Black mothers.

Abortion

- Before the legalization of abortion, 50% of women who died from illegal abortions in New York were Black.

- In 1969, 75% of the women who died from illegal abortions were women of color.

- Over 60% of Blacks polled by the *Washington Post* support a woman's right to choose abortion.

- 20% of all abortions in America are obtained by Black women, 10% by other women of color, while the majority, 70%, are obtained by white women.

Reproductive Abuses

- Caesareans performed by court order are disproportionately directed toward low-income women and women of color. 81% of the women were Black, Asian, or Hispanic. 24% did not speak English as their primary language. Of the orders sought, 40% were for Black women, 33% were for African or Asian women, and only 20% were for white women.

- In 1970, 20% of all married Black women had been sterilized. 43% of women sterilized through federally subsidized programs were Black.

- In 1972, the federal government funded nearly 200,000 sterilizations in women. This number in one year nearly equals the number of sterilizations Hitler initiated.

- By 1982, some 15% of white women were sterilized, as compared to 24% of Black women, 35% of Puerto Rican women, and 42% of Native American women.

AIDS

- Nearly 40% of all people with AIDS in the U.S. are people of color; 25% are Black.

- It is estimated that by 1990, over 200,000 Black Americans will be infected with AIDS.

- 52% of all women with AIDS are Black; 75% are women of color.

- 80% of all children with AIDS are born to women of color.

- Of IV-drug-using women, Black women have a 15 times greater chance of contracting AIDS than white women.

CONTRIBUTORS: Dázon Dixon, Loretta Ross, Byllye Avery, Sabrae Jenkins

Kathy's Day in Court[1]

Angela Bonavoglia

On Wednesday, September 23, 1987, at 7:30 a.m., a pregnant 17-year-old we will call "Kathy"[2]—her court-designated name—left her home in a working-class neighborhood of Birmingham, Alabama, and drove alone to the Jefferson County Family Courthouse. Kathy wanted an abortion. But in Alabama, as in 20 other states in the nation, a law exists that forbids a minor (anyone under the age of 18) to give her own consent for an abortion. Alabama's minors must ask one parent for permission, and if they can't do that, they must get a judge's approval before they can have an abortion.

Kathy is a friendly young woman with a big hearty laugh. Her face is round with residues of baby fat, and framed in a mane of blond hair. People tend to describe her as "sensible," which she is, but her sense of competence comes from having had to take care of herself much too early in life. Six years ago her mother remarried, to a man who is an alcoholic. For the last year and a half Kathy has lived mainly on her own, since she doesn't get along with her stepfather. Kathy always wears a delicate antique ring that belonged to her grandmother, and a man's watch, which she says she more or less pilfered from her stepfather, although "I don't wish to claim him as that," she insists.

Normally, on a Wednesday, Kathy would be driving to her $4.75-an-hour job as a sales clerk at a clothing store, a job she loves: "All the people coming through there, all the noise, the music on the sound system. I feel kind of funny if I'm in a quiet place." She works full-time, with two weekdays off. Kathy has been working since school ended in May. She finished the twelfth grade, but didn't graduate because she failed several subjects. By her own admission, she was not "in the upper class of students, the ones that took the notes and knew everything that was going on." She has also been sick most of her senior year. "I had real bad headaches...all the time." Her mother took her to three doctors who believed they were caused by stress, but were unable to help her.

It's difficult for Kathy to talk about Tom, her 19-year-old boyfriend, a factory worker by day and drummer by night. Her answers are tense, whispered, monosyllabic. Yes, she loved him. Yes, they had been in a relationship for five months when she found out she was pregnant. At the time she went to court, he didn't know she was pregnant or that she wanted an abortion. "I knew a girl and she had an abortion," said Kathy. "Her boyfriend didn't like the idea of it too much and they broke up...I'm kind of insecure and I didn't want that to happen."

Waiting for her at the courthouse that September day was the abortion provider Kathy had contacted when she realized she was pregnant. Diane Derzis, the director of Summit Medical Center, is a tough, chain-smoking rail of a woman with dark blond hair and long red fingernails. Besides running the center, she has been taking a full load of law school courses for the past three years. Every January, on the anniversary of *Roe v. Wade*, the 1973 Supreme Court decision that legitimated abortion, Derzis gives her roomfuls of patients—Black, white, teenagers and women in their forties, childless and mothers of many—red roses and notes that tell them they are part of a critical, historical movement to protect a woman's right to choose.

Alabama's new consent law for minors' abortions incenses Derzis; she fought against it for a full seven years. When the state legislature finally passed it in June of 1987, to be put into effect on September 23, Derzis decided that if she was going to have to live with the law, she would challenge it—immediately. The statute requires that if a minor cannot or does not want to ask one parent for consent to have an abortion, she must seek a judge's determination of whether she is, according to the law, "mature and well-informed enough to make the abortion decision," or, if she is found to be immature, whether the "abortion would be in [her] best interest." The law gives no guidance as to how a judge should make these decisions. Diane Derzis wanted to find a teenager willing to go to court and take her chances with this ambiguous law. If a judge turned this test case down, she would help the girl to appeal, going as far as necessary in the court system to show how punitive the statute is.

When Kathy, sounding calm and mature, called Summit Medical Center in mid-September to arrange an abortion, just before the law went into effect, Derzis asked to meet with her. She was struck by Kathy's composure: "She's a 35-year-old, really." Derzis asked Kathy if she would wait five days and become the first girl in Jefferson County required to seek a judge's permission for an abortion because she could not go to her family for consent. (As it turned out, Kathy was the first minor in all of Alabama to have an abortion hearing.) In return, Derzis would arrange for Kathy's abortion to be performed for free; it would have cost Kathy

$260 otherwise, since she could not put it on her mother's health plan without her mother's finding out. Until September 22, Kathy could have had an abortion without parental or judicial involvement. Once she agreed to go to court, the decision of whether or not she would bear a child was up to the discretion of a judge.

"The money was a little bit of why I did it," said Kathy, "but I could have paid." More to the point was that "Diane told me it would be a big help to the people who came after me. Everyone thought I was the perfect person to try this out: seventeen, living on my own. And, I thought, with all I've been through, I'm still here, I *know* I can handle this."

Following the instructions set forth in the Alabama law, Derzis had submitted Kathy's request for a judicial hearing to the Jefferson County Family Court. By law, the court had to provide Kathy with free legal representation for her hearing. Her papers were brought by a court officer to a Legal Aid lawyer, J. Wynell (Wendy) Brooks Crew, on September 21. That gave Crew two days to prepare for Kathy's hearing, which was scheduled for the day the law went into effect. Crew believed herself to be Kathy's lawyer even though Charles Nice, the judge who would be hearing the case, had not signed papers formally appointing her. According to Crew and the officer who gave her the papers, in most cases a formal appointment is not necessary for work to begin on a case, especially when there is a rush, as there would be with Kathy's abortion request. The officer had understood Judge Nice to say that minors' abortion requests should be handled by Legal Aid. Crew went to work on the case, researching the law and talking with Kathy by telephone several times during the two days before her court appearance. According to Kathy, it had been hard to talk to a stranger about her pregnancy and decision to abort, "but not as hard, because it was Wendy," who made her feel very comfortable.

But on the day after Crew believed herself to have been appointed as Kathy's attorney, Judge Nice's bailiff approached her and a private attorney, Marcus Jones. According to Crew, the bailiff told Jones *he* had been appointed to represent the minor, and she was to represent the fetus. Wendy Crew said no. She pointed out that she had already talked to Kathy. She also noted that appointing a lawyer for the fetus would be unconstitutional, since, under *Roe v. Wade,* the fetus cannot be considered a person and does not have a right to representation. The bailiff, Crew recalls, told them to work it out themselves. A 30-year-old dynamo who had left private corporate law three years earlier to join the staff of Legal Aid, Crew has earned a reputation as a fierce defender of children's rights. Once, when she represented a minor charged with murdering her violent stepfather, Crew was beaten up in court by the stepfather's family in a scene the local press referred to as "a 10-minute brawl." She had survived that and was not about to let herself get thrown off Kathy's case. She knew that without signed papers from Judge Nice, her position was precarious, but she felt the court officer had been following established procedure and she told Jones she wanted to continue as Kathy's lawyer.

On the morning of the 23rd she met with Kathy and Diane Derzis in the courthouse. Remembers Kathy: "I was just petrified. Me and Diane went upstairs and met with Wendy in this big conference room with a big humongous table." While they were sitting there, Crew was called out of the room. The same officer who had given her the papers told her she was off the case. He showed her the appointment papers from Judge Nice on which she saw that something had been whited out in the section naming Kathy's counsel—she presumed it was "Legal Aid"—and Marcus Jones' name written in.

Crew and Jones went into the judge's office. Nice, 68, a slightly built, benevolent-looking man, had in his office pamphlets for Lifeline, an adoption agency run by the virulently anti-choice Save-A-Life Christian ministry. Hanging on his wall was a photo of some of Lifeline's adoptive parents at their last reunion. Crew told him she wanted to stay on the case. She asked to be appointed Kathy's guardian or to be co-counsel. Judge Nice refused both requests and dismissed Crew.

Now Marcus Jones went into the conference room to meet Kathy. "I was mad," said Kathy. "I felt like I could pull this through with Wendy. Then they bring some man in fifteen minutes before the trial. Men don't really know about this. How is some man gonna stand up there and fight for me when he doesn't even know what's going on? I thought to myself, 'I'm gonna lose.'"

At approximately 9:45 a.m., Kathy and Diane Derzis walked down the hall from the conference room to Judge Nice's courtroom. Papers covered the window on the door, to guarantee the complete confidentiality of the hearing. Kathy walked to the large, wooden witness stand at the front of the courtroom and sat down. "I was having heart failure," she said. She wanted Derzis to stay, but only court personnel were allowed in the room. That left Kathy in a room with four men—Nice, Jones, the bailiff, and the court officer—whom she had never met before that morning. There was also a young, female court reporter.

Jones began his questioning. What follows is Kathy's recollection of what occurred in that courtroom, since the court records are confidential in abortion hearings. Kathy testified that she would not be 18 until the end of the year, and was therefore still affected by the parental consent law. To establish her maturity, Jones asked her about school. She told him that since she had not graduated, she planned to take the high school equivalency test. She also testified that she had been working full-time and part-time for the last two years and contributed to her own support.

Marcus Jones asked about her family. Kathy testified that her alcoholic stepfather abused her mother and herself. According to Kathy, he beat her so badly one night, she left and moved in with friends. "I told the judge my mother wanted me to come back home and I finally did, but then neither of us could stand it anymore," so both Kathy and her mother moved out. Her mother is back with the stepfather now. Kathy testified that for the last year and a half she had been living mostly by herself. "Mother just stays over there all the time, but when they get into a fight, she comes to our apartment." Kathy said she was 10 weeks pregnant. She didn't want to tell her mother about the pregnancy because her mother told her stepfather everything, and if he found out about this he might get mad and end by beating her mother.

Kathy testified that she had considered adoption as well as abortion and remembers being surprised when Judge Nice continued to question her about this: "He asked whether I had thought about giving it to some adoption agency. He mentioned about three adoption groups and kept asking, 'Have you thought about this?' 'Yes, sir,' I said about two times. Then he asked Marcus if he wanted to ask me more about adoption, but Marcus told the judge I had already answered the question." Kathy had to say whether the pregnancy was the result of incest—a word that had to be explained to her before she could respond—or rape.

After 45 minutes of testimony, Judge Nice left the courtroom to make his decision. Kathy stepped down from the witness stand and sat on a bench, talking nervously with the court reporter. Fifteen minutes later, Judge Nice returned and read his decision: he would not grant Kathy's request for an abortion; she was not mature enough; it was not in her best interest. The judge told Kathy she should talk to her mother about this decision.

Kathy was stunned. "I was about in tears. How can he say this about me? He didn't feel I was mature enough; to make this decision myself? I could feel my eyes pooling up, and I was going, 'Don't cry, don't cry.'"

"Everyone here at the clinic thinks I'm such a hard bitch," said Diane Derzis, "but I came back the day of that hearing and cried to think of what Kathy went through. I called Wendy and said, 'I can't believe we put her through that. Why didn't we just take her to Georgia?'"

But they persevered, filing an appeal of Judge Nice's decision. Meanwhile, said Kathy, "time was runnin' real short." Although she knew Derzis would help her get an abortion one way or another, she became very nervous. "I kept thinking, 'This is gonna take too much time. It's gonna be dangerous.'" Derzis and one of Kathy's friends tried to keep her spirits up. She has never said that she regrets her decision to go to court, but admits that the waiting was terrible. "I kept wishing I had already gotten it over with."

Fourteen days after the hearing, the Alabama Court of Civil Appeals overturned the judge's opinion, rendering a scathing decision:

> The trial judge in this case abused his discretion by denying the minor's request…More importantly, we can neither discern from the trial court's judgment nor from the record any ground upon which the trial court's conclusion could rest. We can safely say, having considered the record, that, should this minor not meet the criteria for "maturity" under the statute, it is difficult to imagine one who would.

Kathy could now have her abortion. But the nearly-three-week delay from the day her petition was brought to the courthouse until the day of the abortion put her in her twelfth week of pregnancy, at the very end of the first trimester. An abortion performed during the second trimester of pregnancy has greater risk for the patient and is considered a more serious medical procedure than an earlier abortion.

After the Appeals Court decision came down, Kathy told her boyfriend, Tom, that she was pregnant. His reaction "was about like mine—afraid and scared." He was supportive about her decision to abort and offered to go with her. "I told him not to, because he might lose his job if he skipped work."

On Friday, October 9, Kathy arrived at Summit Medical Center for her abortion. Summit is housed in a neat red-brick building; its interior, decorated in bold prints and bright colors, strains for cheerfulness. Kathy had been brought by the friend who had consoled her during the long wait for the Appeals decision; then the friend left to go to work. Diane Derzis was there to greet and shepherd her through the procedures, but Kathy felt totally alone that day. "It was the most horrible experience of my life. I had to fill out a bunch more papers…do a little counseling thing. The counselor was talking to us about birth control and told us exactly what they were going to do. I couldn't really tell you what she said 'cause I didn't pay attention, 'cause I didn't want to know.

"After we got out of there, she took us down a hall to a little dressing room thing, and they had gowns in there. We had to change and put all our stuff in this bag; then we had to go down this other hall and sit in this room with about six or seven other girls in there watching TV. They'd call us one by one and take us out.

"I got in the room. There was a little table, a little bed thing…those things with the stirrups. Those scare me. I'd never been to a gynecologist but I kind of knew what to expect.

"Two men and a lady were there. I don't know what they were all for. I didn't care. I just wanted to get it over with. She told me to get up on the table, and I did. She gave me a shot, and in about a minute, I was out...The next thing I know, somebody was telling me to wake up."

Against her medical advice to rest, Kathy went to a party that night where Tom would be performing. She was too late; he had already left. She did see him again, but says they never talked about the abortion. In the end, her fear of losing him came true. He left, according to Kathy, not because of the abortion, but because he had found another girlfriend.

Judge Nice continues to feel he made the proper judgment in Kathy's case. Asked in an interview four months later how he determined that Kathy was not mature, he told *Ms.*, "I based it on her looks...just something that comes across when you talk to her...her credibility." Nice has stated publicly, as reported in the local press, that "I don't think anybody's for abortion. But in proper cases it should be considered." Those cases include rape, incest, and "other situations," which he did not specify.

Nice also told *Ms.* that he did not try to appoint Wendy Crew to represent the fetus in this case. However, he said he strongly believes the fetus should have an attorney. "After all, the fetus has a part in it...whether the fetus is going to exist or not. And, as it is now, you have no one to represent anybody but the mother and say that she should have an abortion." He said that in minors' consent cases he would consider not only what is in the minor's best interest, but what is in the fetus' best interest as well. Asked if it would be hard to approve an abortion under these conditions, he replied, "Might be."

The difficulty Kathy faced in getting her abortion approved is somewhat unique. In the other states with parental consent laws, most teenagers are granted abortions after their judicial hearings. In Massachusetts, for example, 99 percent of petitions are approved. According to Janet Benshoof, director of the American Civil Liberties Union's Reproductive Freedom Project, it takes exceptional maturity for a teenager to endure the legal process, so the minors who go before a judge always fill the criterion that demands they be mature enough to consent to their abortion. "Secondly," she continues, "if someone wants an abortion, how can it *not* be in their best interest to have one?"

Many of the judges who grant the minors' abortions agree. "I believe the hearings don't have any value at all," Massachusetts Superior Court Judge Joseph Mitchell told *Ms.* "The laws make it as difficult as possible for these young ladies to have abortions." His evaluation of the hearings is shared by the six state court judges who heard at least 90 percent of the minors' abortion petitions in Minnesota, and who testified at the 1986 trial challenging the constitutionality of Minnesota's law.

Judge Gerald Martin told the court he did not "perceive any useful public purpose to what I am doing in these cases."

Parental consent (requiring written permission) and notification (requiring clinics to give advance notice to one or both parents) law are currently enforceable in 10 states, (see list at end of this chapter), although the degree to which each state complies with the laws varies. In Massachusetts, about 5,000 teenage girls have gone to the Superior Adult Court since 1981 to get permission to abort, appearing before the same judges who hear cases of fraud, blackmail, armed robbery, felony assault, rape, and murder.

Parental consent and notification laws have been on the books in 24 other states, but either they are inoperable because they fail to meet current judicial standards, or suits brought by groups such as the ACLU or Planned Parenthood have prevented them from being enforced. Before 1986, when its law was struck down, Minnesota had the second largest record of experience—approximately 3,500 girls went through its courts over the course of five years.

In all states, whether the law is parental consent or notification, the statutes have been developed and pushed through the legislatures by anti-choice groups. "They all emanate from model anti-abortion statutes," like those prepared several times a year by Americans United for Life Legal Defense Fund, said Janet Benshoof. Americans United for Life provides, along with its model statutes, line-by-line recommendations on how to write a bill that will withstand legal assault.

Kay James, Director of Public Affairs for the National Right to Life Committee, says that the passage of the parental consent and notification laws is among her organization's priorities. The laws are necessary, she told *Ms.,* because "I think when a child has to make a decision about abortion, it should be made within the context of the family, with those who have their best interests at heart, who cared for them from birth." To her, the law protects the children, "as they're making those decisions," and protects the "rights of parents to be involved in that decision making process." She believes the law forces children to deal with the consequences of their sexual activity. "When you're that age, you really need to be encouraged to deal with things that come up in your life. That's facing responsibility for your actions." If the laws decrease the number of abortions performed each year, she is pleased with that result: "I don't see that as the main purpose, but it would not disappoint me in the least."

Parental consent and notification laws, and the challenges to them, have forced the courts to make decisions about the right of a minor to an abortion. "*Roe v. Wade* held that abortion was a constitutional right, but left open the question of teenagers," said Dara Klassel, senior staff attorney for the Planned Parenthood Federation. In 1976 the Supreme

Court finally made a statement on minors' abortions. In *Planned Parenthood of Central Missouri v. Danforth,* the Court held that the state could not grant parents an "absolute veto" over a minor's abortion decision. But it was a Massachusetts case, *Bellotti v. Baird,* decided by the Supreme Court in 1979, which set forth the major guidelines concerning parental involvement. The Massachusetts law, originally enacted in 1974, required all minors to ask for their parents' consent. Only if the parent refused could the teenager go to court to get permission for an abortion. But the Supreme Court ultimately ruled that minors could go to court or through an administrative procedure *without first telling their parents.* This has come to be known as the judicial bypass.

While anti-choice groups continue to support consent and notification laws, they are not happy about the right of judicial bypass. Assemblyman Greg Beers, for example, the main sponsor of Alabama's law, states, "There is no question in my mind that a right to privacy of a minor girl does not supersede the right to knowledge of the parents."

The consent and notification laws often contradict other state laws about minors' rights. For instance, they often exist side by side in many states with laws authorizing minors to approve their own medical care. According to a 1986 ACLU booklet on parental notice laws, 40 states allow minors to consent to diagnosis and treatment of venereal disease; 27 states allow them to consent to prenatal care, including Caesarean section surgery; and nine states have developed "mature minor" laws allowing children under 18 to consent to all forms of medical treatment. The state of Alabama has all of these statutes.

Nevertheless, several statewide polls, commissioned by pro-choice groups and conducted by independent pollsters, have documented strong support for parental involvement laws. In Alabama, a University of Alabama survey found that 82.4 percent of those polled in 1986 favored the laws. Frequently both pro- and anti-choice advocates are for parental involvement, often sharing similar concerns. A 1987 study based in New England showed that among the major reasons voters across a broad political spectrum favored the laws were a belief that parents should be involved in the medical treatment of their children, a desire to increase parent-child communication about sex, and a desire to maximize the role of the family in the teenager's life.

Several parents *Ms.* interviewed in Alabama echoed the fear that their children might receive medical treatment without their knowledge. "Abortion is a surgical procedure and anything can happen," said Karen Snelling of Birmingham, who favors the law and is anti-choice. She is the mother of a 17-year-old girl. "If a parent is not aware her daughter has had the procedure and she starts hemorrhaging, the parents are going to be unable to help. It's just too serious a situation for a parent not to be involved."

Other parents believe the law will strengthen family ties at a time when "loose" social mores undermine the parents' influence on their children's lives. "It helps because it forces kids to turn back to their families," said the mother of a 15-year-old girl. "Peer pressure is really strong. It's easier for kids to turn to their friends." Still others want the system that holds them accountable for their children to be consistent. Said Marilyn Swaans, a Los Angeles mother of two teenagers, who describes herself as pro-choice: "I want something that will protect me as a parent. We get called and have to go to school because our children are failing gym, but we don't have to know that our daughters are pregnant and going to have an abortion?"

Swaans also feels that some parents who have been unable to impress upon their teenagers the seriousness with which they believe sex and abortion should be treated, hope that the law can do so for them: "Living in California, there is so much free sex, free drugs, so much money. Everything is a free ride with no prices to pay and no questions to answer." She thinks that maybe the court appearance could impress upon the girl—"unfortunately only the girl, the boy should have the responsibility, too"—the gravity of the situation.

A national survey conducted by the Alan Guttmacher Institute in 1980 showed that over half of the minors who had abortions at clinics had already told at least one parent about the pregnancy and planned abortion; the younger the teen, the more likely she was to have told a parent. The question is, can a law encourage the remaining young girls to tell their parents they're pregnant if they don't want to? According to Martha Kurz, manager of counseling programs at the Planned Parenthood Clinic of Greater Boston, "There are parents out there who would refuse to talk to the kids, kick them out of the house, hit them, do any number of unfortunate things." Letty Cottin Pogrebin, a child-care expert and editor-at-large at *Ms.*, agrees. "You can't legislate parent-child intimacy. Any child who is pregnant and doesn't go to her parents is saying, 'I'm afraid that my parents won't help me solve this.' In rare cases she's saying, 'My father or another relative may be the cause of this.'"

Although there are no national statistics to indicate how many, some portion of the young women who refuse to tell their parents they are pregnant are incest victims. Massachusetts Superior Court Judge Mitchell, who has heard some 500 teen abortion cases in the past three years, told *Ms.*: "We see incest…You ask who their boyfriend is, and they say, 'my father…my uncle.'" Experts like David Liederman, executive director of the Child Welfare League of America, say that often members of an incest victim's family deny the abuse and offer no help. The parental involvement laws put such girls in "a terrible position," said Liederman. "That's when kids get desperate and may try to abort themselves."

Ironically, the laws actually increase the health risks for many young women. The delays caused by the legal procedures increase the chances that an abortion will be performed later in the pregnancy when the procedure is more dangerous. In Minnesota, after the notification law was passed, the percentage of minors who had second trimester abortions increased by 26.5 percent. Because some minors travel out of state to get abortions in order to circumvent their own state's laws, the chances of receiving adequate follow-up care are reduced. A study in Massachusetts has estimated that 90 to 95 percent of pregnant minors each month go to nearby states like New York, Connecticut, or New Hampshire to have abortions, representing one in every three minor abortion patients in the state. And the girls who end up having babies because they put off talking to their parents or going to court are unlikely to get early prenatal care, placing the health of their babies—who are already more likely to be premature, to be of low birth weight, and to die in infancy—at even greater risk. These health consequences have led major professional associations such as the National Academy of Sciences, the American College of Obstetricians and Gynecologists, the American Academy of Pediatrics, and the American Psychological Association to oppose these laws.

At the bottom of all this, of course, is sex, and a society whose attitudes toward sex are hopelessly contradictory. In spite of the fact that the United States leads all industrialized nations in teenage pregnancy rates, only 15 percent of our schools offer timely and comprehensive sex education, and studies show that parent-child communication about sex is limited. A 1985 nationwide Louis Harris poll commissioned by the Planned Parenthood Federation showed that 67 percent of the parents polled had never discussed birth control with their children, and a follow-up survey the next year showed that 31 percent of 16- and 17-year-olds had never talked to their parents about sex.

The solution to the real problem is clear to experts like Nicki Nichols Gamble, executive director of the Planned Parenthood League of Massachusetts. "If you as a parent want to play a supportive role in your children's lives, you need to convey from a very early age that you want to help them, even when you and they may disagree…You need to talk to them about sexuality. You need to talk to them about contraception. You need to talk to them about the fact that contraception doesn't always work."

Kathy could never talk about sex with her mother or any other adult in her family. "My grandparents were real, real old-fashioned, and that's the way Mother was brought up," she said. Her mother married when she was 19, and had Kathy a year later. "She thought getting married so young was a big mistake, so I know if I got pregnant, she'd think that was a worse mistake, and she'd probably think an abortion was the worst mistake of all."

Kathy's abortion was the first medical treatment she had ever received without her mother's involvement. "All through the whole thing, I was wishing I could tell my mother," Kathy said. "Just to have her there with me would have made me feel better, or just knowing that I could tell her." Kathy still hasn't told her mother about the abortion and doubts that she ever will.

Although the abortion was very upsetting for her, Kathy believed neither adoption—"my stepfather would have surely found out"—nor keeping the child was a reasonable alternative for her. "I was seventeen years old. My job doesn't pay that much. We're kind of poor anyway with just us. With someone else, it would have been awful." As for birth control, "The way I did it, there was a time of the month you could get pregnant, and I'd just go around it. But my period got off and I didn't keep up with it." She never called it the rhythm method. She doesn't believe in using condoms, because they break, and is on the Pill now.

Kathy went for her medical follow-up visit to Summit six weeks after the abortion. The clinic offers post-abortion counseling, but few patients take advantage of this service and Kathy is no exception. Perhaps because she has not had the opportunity to speak to a counselor, Kathy is tormented with doubts about the abortion months later. "Every time I see something, like if I see something on TV about abortion...if I see a real tiny baby somewhere, I'll think, what did I do? Sometimes I wish I hadn't done it. I don't exactly like the idea of having an abortion. People think you killed a kid, you killed a life. I know I didn't. I didn't!" By now Kathy is crying. Tears fall, but she does not make a sound.

Kathy quickly recovers, however, as she has, it seems, so much of her life. What about the future? Marriage? Children? She smiles and says, "One, maybe one. And I want to be very in control of my life. I want to have a nice job, a husband, and a decent cash flow to support the kid and a place to live." She smiles again. "I've been thinking about becoming a lawyer."

Notes

1. This article originally appeared in *Ms.*, April 1988. Reprinted by permission, © *1988, Ms. Magazine.*

2. Some of the details of Kathy's life have been changed to protect her anonymity.

A State-by-State Guide to Parental Consent and Notification Laws for Minors' Abortions[1]

A total of 34 states have passed statutes at some time regulating the access that teenage girls—those under the age of 18—have to abortion. The statutes require that a minor who wants an abortion have the consent of one or both parents, agree to have the abortion provider notify one or both parents, or obtain the permission of a judge.

The laws on the books are categorized below as enforceable; enjoined by court order and therefore not operating, at least temporarily; or inactive—that is, not operating and considered to be unconstitutional on their face by Supreme Court standards.

Parental Consent Laws (21)

Enforceable (7)
- Alabama
- India
- Louisiana
- Massachusetts
- Missouri
- North Dakota
- Rhode Island

Enjoined by Court Order (7)
- Arizona
- Arkansas
- California
- Florida
- Kentucky
- Mississippi
- Pennsylvia

Inactive and Unconstitutional (7)
- Alaska
- Colorado
- Delaware
- New Mexico
- South Carolina
- South Dakota
- Washington

Parental Notification Laws (13)

Enforceable (3)
- Maryland
- Utah
- West Virginia

Enjoined by Court Order (8)
- Georgia
- Illinois
- Maine
- Minnesota
- Nebraska
- Nevada
- Ohio
- Tennessee

Inactive and Unconstitutional (2)
- Idaho
- Montana

SOURCE: Information provided by the National Abortion Rights Action League and the Reproductive Freedom Project of the American Civil Liberties Union.

Teen Pregnancy and Abortion in the United States

One out of every 10 women aged 15-19 becomes pregnant each year—about 414,000 young women.

40% of all girls in the U.S. will become pregnant at least once in their teens.

11.5% of all abortions in the U.S. are performed on women under the age of 18 —about 182,000 women each year.

85% of the 1.1 milllion teenage pregnancies each year are unintended; 50% of sexually active young women always use contraceptives. Of these, only one in two relies on the most effective methods. The most common reasons for not using contraceptives are believing that risk of pregnancy is small and failing to anticipate intercourse.

32 states currently have parental involvement laws on the books.

Pregnant teenagers have higher rates of maternal mortality, toxemia, and anemia. They also have more complications at birth. Infants born to teenagers have a higher rate of infant mortality, are more likely to be premature, and have higher rates of birth injury, low birthweight, and neurological problems.

SOURCES: "Parental Consent and Notification Laws," NOW Legal Defense and Education Fund, 1989; *Reproductive Rights Update,* 6/27/90, ACLU Reproductive Freedom Project; information from Alan Guttmacher Institute as quoted in the *New York Times,* 6/27/90.

Reproductive Issues Are Essential Survival Issues for the Asian-American Communities

Connie S. Chan

When the Asian-American communities in the United States list their priorities for political action and organizing, several issues concerning basic survival are usually included: access to bilingual education, housing, health care, and child care, among others. Yet the essential survival issue of access to reproductive counseling, education, and abortions is frequently missing from the agenda of Asian-American community organizations. Why is the reproductive issue perceived as unimportant to the Asian-American communities? I think there are several reasons—ignorance, classism, sexism, and language barriers. Of course, these issues are inter-related, and I'll try to make the connections between them.

First, let me state that I am not an "expert" on the topic of reproductive issues in the Asian-American communities, but I do have first-hand experiences which have given me some insight into the problems. Several years ago, I was a staff psychologist at a local community health center serving the greater Boston Asian population. Most of our patients were recent immigrants from China, Vietnam, Cambodia, Laos, and Hong Kong. Almost all of these new immigrants understood little or no English. With few resources (financial or otherwise), many newcomers struggled to make sense of life in the United States and to survive in whatever fashion they could.

At the health center, the staff tried to help by providing information and advocacy in getting through our confusing system. I thought we did a pretty good job until I found out that neither our health education department nor our ob-gyn department provided *any* counseling or information about birth control or abortion services. The medical department had interpreted our federal funding regulations as prohibiting not only the performance of abortions on-site, but also the dissemination of information which might lead to, or help patients to obtain, an abortion.

Needless to say, as a feminist and as an activist, I was horrified. When I found out that pregnant women who inquired about abortions were given only a name of a white, English-speaking ob-gyn doctor and sent out alone, it seemed a morally and ethically neglectful practice. One of the nurse-midwives agreed with me and suggested that I could serve as an interpreter/advocate for pregnant women who needed to have abortions, or at least wanted to discuss the option with the English-speaking ob-gyn doctor. The only catch was that I would have to do it on my own time, I could not claim any affiliation with the health center, and I could not suggest follow-up care at the health center.

Not fully knowing the nature of what I was volunteering for, I agreed to interpret and advocate for Cantonese-speaking pregnant women at their appointments with the obstetrician. It turned out that over the course of three years I interpreted during at least a hundred abortions for Asian immigrant women who spoke no English. After the first few abortions, the obstetrician realized how essential it was to have an interpreter present, and began to require that all non-English-speaking women have an interpreter during the abortion procedure.

As a middle-class, educated, bilingual Asian-American woman, I was aware of the importance of having the choice to have an abortion, and the necessity of fighting for the right to choose for myself. I had been unaware of how the right to have an abortion is also a right to survival in this country if you are a poor, uneducated, non-English-speaking immigrant.

The women I interpreted for were, for the most part, not young. Nor were they single. They ranged in age from 25 to 45, with a majority in their late twenties and early thirties. Almost all were married and had two or more children. Some had as many as five or six children. They needed to have abortions because they had been unlucky enough to have gotten pregnant after arriving in this country. Their families were barely surviving on the low wages that many new immigrant workers earned as restaurant workers, garment factory workers, or domestic help. Almost all of the women worked full-time: the ones who had young children left them with older, retired family members or did piece-work at home; those with older children worked in the factories or hotels. Without fail, each woman would tell me that she needed to have an abortion because her family could not afford another mouth to feed, that the family could not afford to lose her salary contribution, not even for a few months, to care for an infant. In some ways, one could not even say that these women were choosing to have abortions. The choice had already been made for them, and it was a choice of basic survival.

Kai Ling was one of the women for whom I interpreted. A 35-year-old mother of four children, ages 2 to 7, she and her husband emigrated to the United States from Vietnam. They had no choice in their emigration; they were refugees whose village had been destroyed and felt fortunate to escape with their lives and all four of their children. Life in the United States was difficult, but they were scraping by, living with another family in a small apartment where their entire family slept in one room. Their hope was that their children would receive an education and "make it" in American society; they lived with the deferred dream for the next generation.

When Kai Ling found out that she was pregnant, she felt desperate. Because she and her husband love children and live for their children, they wanted desperately to keep this child, this one who would be born in America and be an American citizen from birth. Yet they sadly realized that they could not afford another child, they could not survive on just one salary, they could not feed another one. Their commitment was to the children they already had, and to keeping their family together.

When I accompanied Kai Ling to her abortion, she was saddened but resigned to what she had to do. The $300 that she brought to the clinic represented almost a month of wages for her; she had borrowed the money from family and friends. She would pay it back, she said, by working weekends for the next ten weeks. Her major regret was that she would not be able to buy any new clothes for her children this year because of this unexpected expense.

Kai Ling spoke very little English. She did not understand why she had to go to a white American doctor for her abortion instead of receiving services from her Asian doctor at the health center. She had no real understanding of reproductive rights issues, of *Roe v. Wade*, or of why there were demonstrators waving pictures of fetuses and yelling at her as we entered the clinic. Mercifully, she did not understand the questions they shouted at her in English, and she did not ask me what they had said, remarking only that the protestors seemed very angry at someone. She felt sure, I think, that they were not angry at her. She had done nothing to provoke anyone's anger. She was merely trying to survive in this country under this country's rules.

It is a crime and an injustice that Kai Ling could not receive counseling in her language and services from her doctors at the Asian neighborhood health center. It is a crime that she had to borrow $300 to pay for her own abortion, that her Medicaid benefits did not pay for it. It is a grave injustice that she had to have me, a stranger, interpreting for her during her abortion because her own doctor could not perform the procedure at her clinic. It was not a matter of choice for her to abort her pregnancy, but a matter of basic survival.

Kai Ling speaks no English. Kai Ling will probably never attend a march or a rally for choice. She will not sign any petitions. She might not even vote. But it is for her and the countless thousands of immigrant women like her that we need to continue to struggle for reproductive rights. Within the Asian-American communities, the immigrant women who are most affected by the lack of access to abortions have the least power. They do not speak English; they do not demand equal access to health care; their needs are easily overlooked.

Thus, it is up to those of us who are bilingual, who can speak English, and who can speak to these issues, to do so. We need to insure that the issue of reproductive rights is an essential item on the Asian-American political agenda. It is not a women's issue; it is a community issue.

We must speak for the Kai Lings, for their children, for their right to survive as a family. We must, as activists, make the connections between the issues of oppression based upon gender, race, national origin, sexual orientation, class, or language. We can and must lead the Asian-American communities to recognize the importance of the essential issue of reproductive rights for the survival of these communities.

Pro-Choice Activism
Springs From Many Sources

Ann Baker

Operation Rescue, which is more accurately called Operation Bully, was launched in 1987 at the annual Pro-Life Action Network conference by Joe Scheidler (author of *Closed: 99 Ways to Stop Abortion*) and Randall Terry of Project Life in Binghamton, New York. To date, clinics in 173 cities in 44 states, two Canadian provinces, and the District of Columbia have experienced this anti-abortion scourge.

Prior to this, anti-abortion militants had attacked clinics sporadically as a form of "guerrilla warfare," conducting sit-ins at which they were quickly removed by local police. A devoted and tightly knit core of about 100 had been built by Scheidler. At any given time a couple of dozen could be called upon to travel to a designated city and conduct a sit-in. By 1986 they had decided to call these actions "rescues."

The 80% Majority Campaign started collecting arrest lists in August 1985 when 62 anti-abortionists blocked the entrance to Reproductive Health Services (the Missouri abortion clinic in the *Webster* case). It was apparent from the lists that a significant number of those arrested had travelled to St. Louis to participate in the blockade. It is now clear that many are repeat arrests. Of 32,000 arrests in 1988-9, about 12,000 people were arrested only once, and 5,750 people account for the remaining 20,000 arrests. This data accords with the experience of pro-choice activists who observe that the same people are repeatedly involved in blockades.

Before Operation Bully, the direct action strategy had failed to expand the ranks of the anti-abortion movement, and they were losing ground in the press. Initially the media had shown an interest in Scheidler's proclaimed "Year of Pain and Fear," in which he threatened abortion providers with ongoing harassment. "Operation Rescue" was devised to re-energize the anti-abortion crusade by drawing press coverage, both to well-staged clinic blockades with hundreds of people waiting to be arrested, and to the courts.

Additionally, Operation Bully also assumed that it could make an impact in the 1988 presidential elections. As Randall Terry wrote in the first flyer for Operation Rescue, "Picture if you will, a wave of righteous uprising spreading across America. A movement so large, so encompassing, that politicians have to decide between jailing thousands and thousands of good, decent people, or making child killing illegal again!"

Operation Bully has consistently tried to portray itself as the contemporary civil rights movement. Their original flyer observed, "One of the greatest things that could ever happen in the cause of the children would be for hundreds and hundreds of decent citizens to be in jail together for a day or two, for trying to rescue children from death. In the civil rights movement, the sight of hundreds and hundreds of blacks jailed together for peaceful protest against the injustice of segregation helped win the sympathy of the nation to their cause."

At the same time that Operation Bully seeks to identify with the civil rights movement, it demonstrates how distant it really is from that heritage. The big differences are obvious: blocking access to abortion clinics is not much different from blocking access to schools, voting booths, and public accommodations.

But there are more subtle differences. Local leaders of Operation Bully emphasize that they are "ordinary people," "clean cut," "middle-class Americans." They are really saying to the public that they are the all-American good guys, not the scruffy people who fought for social change in the 1960s, and especially not poor, Southern blacks. "Acceptable" protest by middle-class Americans is sanctioned only for a reactionary agenda.

From its inception, Operation Bully was a prescription for anti-abortion violence. For them, non-violence is nothing more than a tactical decision of the militant leaders rather than a basic philosophical approach to making social change. Consequently, it was only a matter of time until discipline broke down among their ranks and hostility was directed at women or anyone who did not cooperate with their goals, such as judges, law enforcement personnel, and the media.

Starting with their week of actions in Los Angeles in March 1989, violence has escalated in direct proportion to the failure of the militants to achieve their public relations aims. Those who have attempted to block clinics have resorted to breaking doors, turning over dumpsters, and invading waiting rooms. The tactic of clinic invasion is used when they do not have enough people to block entrances for hours at a time. During these invasions they use Kryptonite locks to secure themselves to clinic furniture and prevent police from removing them quickly.

Another tactic when they do not have enough people to keep the clinic closed for hours is to crawl under one of their vehicles and chain themselves to it. Failing that, they crawl under police buses or throw themselves in front of patients' cars.

Verbal assaults have become more intense. At many blockades women and older men actually block the clinic, while the younger men roam about harassing the escorts and police officers. Since the leadership talks repeatedly about the coming civil war over abortion in America, it isn't any wonder that violence has become a characteristic of their activities.

What the entire anti-abortion crusade doesn't understand is that the civil rights movement made changes not just because of their tactics but because of their vision of a just society and the moral imperative to struggle to bring it about. They summoned the conscience of most Americans to live up to great human ideals. The intolerance and self-righteousness of the anti-abortion crusade cannot elicit that kind of response.

Operation Bully has been an incredible catalyst for galvanizing pro-choice activists. Many providers who have lived through blockades were already targets of anti-abortion harassment. But in other communities where Operation Bully has hit clinics, providers had never had any trouble with the anti-abortion movement and the attacks came as a rude awakening. Staff had to be trained and new protocols developed to assist patients on the day of a blockade. The delivery of a medical service had become politicized.

This unprecedented direct attack on access to abortion has spawned pro-choice coalitions all over the country made up of providers and activists. The massive pro-choice turnout of 600,000 in Washington, D.C. for the March for Women's Equality and Women's Lives on April 9, 1989, was made possible not just by the threat of the pending *Webster* decision, but because the pro-choice sleeping giant had been aroused by Operation Bully and was then fueled by *Webster*. It has become clear to the political establishment that it can no longer count on a quiescent pro-choice majority to passively sanction anti-abortion votes.

National and statewide pro-choice organizations have been swamped with calls since *Webster*. Tens of thousands of people who took the right to reproductive choice for granted now want to get involved with the defense of this right at all levels. Candidate support is an area where the impact has been felt almost immediately.

Perhaps the most commonly heard admission of these new activists is that they had never before actively identified pro-choice candidates and voted for them. They had not made support for choice a condition for giving their support to a candidate. As a result, for the past

16 years, politicians in most state legislatures have responded to the highly active anti-abortion movement by voting against abortion in whatever legislative package was offered to them. Although they knew the majority of their constituents were pro-choice, they also believed correctly that few of them would actively support a candidate solely based on his/her position on abortion.

This has changed. Newly activated pro-choice supporters and pro-choice organizations have pledged to make abortion an issue in every election and to make their support for candidates hinge on the candidate's position on choice. In elections since the *Webster* decision, the pro-choice electorate has sent an unmistakable message to politicians all over the country, from a special election in California to gubernatorial elections in Virginia and New Jersey. Using a voter identification project developed by the Westchester Coalition for Legal Abortion, one which has been employed there successfully since 1984, the pro-choice community intends to identify voters who will cross party lines to vote for pro-choice candidates. Anti-abortion incumbents will be defeated.

The newly re-activated pro-choice movement is visible in all political arenas, electoral and grassroots. All over the country, groups are organizing rallies and continuing clinic defense and patient escort activities. The movement is able to undertake projects and programs it had only dreamed of a short while ago. Elected officials, the media, and popular opinion are all responding to these organizing efforts.

Despite the shift, the "war" continues at the clinics, though in a scaled-down mode. Public opinion is very much opposed to the actions of Operation Bully. What has not happened is a changed climate at the clinics for the patients and the staffs. We need a popular voice saying to opponents of abortion that it is unacceptable to generate media coverage by harassing the women who need abortions and the women who provide those services. We need to generate more support for abortion providers so that they can create a better climate for the provision of abortion services. In particular, since the opposition to abortion originates in some churches, other churches in the community should find ways to discourage people from participating in Operation Bully. As a movement, we are faced with a remarkable opportunity. We have the chance to complete a process begun in the 1960s when our country was coming to the conclusion that it did not make any sense to perpetuate illegal abortion. For 20 years and more, the general public has understood that the government was not qualified to intrude in private reproductive decisions. These conclusions are reflected in the polls, which have clearly demonstrated strong majority support for legal abortion.

In 1973, *Roe v. Wade* was a response to what had become an obvious fact—illegal abortion was no longer acceptable in this country. However, during the decade of debate and discussion that had preceded the Court's decision, it had been the feminists who had urged the availability of abortion for all women, allowing every woman the right to make that decision for herself. The legal and medical communities were promoting reform of abortion laws, but they did not go so far as to suggest that the right to choose abortion should be a right for every woman.

Although *Roe* was a great victory for the feminist vision, the victory was obtained before it was a widely accepted point of view that abortion should be a generally available right. The Court ruling cut short the national discussion, and allowed for the strident opposition, representing a minority viewpoint, to take center stage. With the resurgence of the pro-choice movement, we now have the opportunity to resume the discussion and finally obtain widespread agreement for reproductive choice. The next Court decision that acknowledges this right will not sound like a brief for physicians. It will make clear and unequivocal statements about personal liberty and non-intrusive government.

By advancing legislation that will lead ultimately to a constitutional amendment to protect abortion rights, we have the opportunity to protect future generations from an intrusive government and a well-financed crusade against reproductive rights. What comes of this opportunity is entirely up to the character of our activism.

Whenever coalitions have been made up of the mainstream pro-choice organizations—not necessarily feminist—and groups with a more radical approach—also not usually feminist—there has been tension which has sometimes undermined the ability of these coalitions to respond effectively to Operation Bully, and to the legislative initiatives of abortion opponents. We should draw lessons from the places where differing theories about the goals and tactics of clinic defense have been transcended by the need to work together.

This is crucial at a time when the split in anti-abortion ranks has been magnified by continued clinic blockades, officially opposed by some powerful anti-abortion groups like The National Right to Life Committee. We need to project a feminist vision of all women free to plan their lives and grow with a sense of self-worth. Ultimately that is the issue. The struggle for reproductive rights is an intrinsic aspect of freedom and dignity for women. When there is competition among pro-choice organizations and lack of respect for each other's efforts, we fail to live up to our own vision. I urge us to come together at this time. The stakes are enormous.

Civil Rights and Reproductive Rights

The adoption of the tactic of civil disobedience is their right, but the appropriation of the moral imperative of the civil rights movement is all wrong. The civil rights struggle sought to extend constitutional rights to all Americans and have those rights enforced. Today's anti-abortionists, quite to the contrary, are attempting, in the Operation Rescue protests, to deny American women their constitutional right to freedom of choice. They want the constitution rewritten...

—from a Press Conference, January 1989.
Participants included 14 veterans of the civil rights movement: Julian Bond; Dorothy Cotton,* Southern Christian Leadership Conference; Connie Curry,* Student Non-Violent Coordinating Committee (SNCC); James Farmer,* Congress on Racial Equality; Dorothy Height, National Council of Negro Women; Jesse Jackson; John Jacob, Urban League; Mary King,* SNCC; Joyce Lander,* SNCC; Joseph Rauh, civil rights lawyer and activist; William Taylor,* U.S. Commission on Civil Rights; Roger Wilkins; Andrew Young; Dorothy Zellner,* SNCC.
(Reprinted from *The Campaign Report*, 2/6/89.)

Choice is the essence of freedom. It's what we African-Americans have struggled for all these years....This freedom—to choose and to excerise our choices—is what we've fought and died for...Somebody said that we were less than human and not fit for freedom. Somebody said that we were like children and could not be trusted to think for ourselves....

Now once again somebody is trying to say that we can't handle the freedom of choice. Only this time they're saying African-American women can't think for themselves and, therefore, can't be allowed to make serious decisions....There have always been those who have stood in the way of our excercising our rights, who tried to restrict our choices. There probably always will be. But we who have been oppressed should not be swayed in our opposition to tyranny, of any kind, especially attempts to take away our reproductive freedom...

—from "We Remember:
African-American Women Are for Reproductive Freedom,"
Byllye Avery; Rev. Willie Barrow, Operation PUSH; Donna Brazile, Housing Now; Shirley Chisholm, National Political Congress of Black Women; Rep. Cardiss Collins; Romona Edelin, National Urban Coalition; Jacqui Gates, National Association of Negro Business and Professional Womens Clubs; Marcia Ann Gillespie, Ms. Magazine; Jewel Jackson McCabe, National Coalition of 100 Black Women; Julianne Malveaux, San Franscsico Black Leadership Forum; Eleanor Holmes Norton, Georgetown University Law School; C. Delores Tucker, DNC Black Caucus; Patricia Tyson, Religious Coalition For Abortion Rights; Maxine Waters, Black Women's Forum; Faye Wattleton, Planned Parenthood.

Organizational affiliations listed for identification purposes only.
* Indicates former affiliation.

Operation Oppress You:
Women's Rights Under Siege[1]

Dázon Dixon

When the sister called, I had to instruct her how to get to the clinic and to wait for someone in a bright-colored staff T-shirt to escort her to the clinic. She was worried about confronting the TV cameras and the newest members of one of the oldest hate groups in our country—"Operation Rescue." She had every right to be worried. The truth of the matter, though, is that getting into the clinic is not a serious concern; most clinics are prepared for intervention by the so-called "pro-lifers" and the news media. The real worry is that these people could conceivably succeed in this violent effort to deny women legal and safe access to abortion as a choice.

Since the beginning of the Democratic National Convention in July, 1988, Atlanta has been "under siege" by fundamentalist Christian soldiers in a war against women—a war against a constitutionally guaranteed right to life and freedom of choice. Five abortion clinics have been picketed, barricaded, and invaded almost daily. Atlanta, as the "Home of the Civil Rights Movement," is the choice location of this protest. "Operation Rescue," dominated by middle- and upper-middle-class Euro-American men and women, actually identifies its cause for the fetus with the struggle of African-Americans in this country. The idea is as absurd as it sounds.

The sister called back and said she wasn't coming if I was not there to meet her. On the way across the street we were met with graphic pictures of mutilated infants, professed to be fetuses, and a hateful mob of Bible-quoting fanatics. The client I was protecting seemed to handle the pleas to "save her baby from these murderers" very well—she realized that these people just didn't understand her or care about her. But when a young-looking, blonde and blue-eyed man screamed charges at her that the Rev. Martin Luther King, Jr. would "turn over in his grave for what *she* was doing" and that she was contributing to the genocide of African-Americans, she broke. She stopped, stared him in his eyes with tears in hers, then quietly and coolly said, "You're a white boy, and you don't give a damn thing about me, who I am or what I do. And you know even less about Martin Luther King or being Black. What you have to say to me means nothin', not a damn thing." He was silenced and she walked on.

What I witnessed that morning was a quiet politicization of a woman who had to defend her own morals and choices because of her color and her sex. This really is nothing new, just a new tactic. For 15 years, anti-abortion forces have waged senseless and insensitive attacks on women and women's clinics. Where they have failed to change the minds of the pro-choice majority, both in Congress and in the courts, they have taken their fight to the streets and news media. What they do not realize in their effort to reverse *Roe v. Wade* is that, legal or not, women will continue having abortions. Whether someone agrees or disagrees with the morality of the choice is insignificant. What is significant is the fact that, as long as abortion is legal, it is a safe option. We cannot return to the days when well-to-do women had safe abortions and poor women had to risk their lives and dignity with back-alley abortionists.

Anti-abortion sentiment is precisely that: a sentiment. As the civil rights and other movements have proved, individuals have the right to their own beliefs, including the right to voice those beliefs. Using those rights, however, to prevent a woman from exercising her own guaranteed protections is an abuse of our democratic process. It is also an abuse particular to white supremacy. It should not be a surprise to us that the same people protesting against women's rights usually are protesting against civil rights, gay and lesbian rights, and rights of the poor and homeless. We can identify the enemy because it is, almost always, one and the same.

A few days after this incident, I received a letter from the sister. In her letter, she thanked the health center for being there for her, and she thanked me. She was glad she confronted the man who had insulted her. The last point she made was that, of all her experiences of oppression, this was the worst. It took an act of injustice based on both the color and shape of her skin that called her to respond. The insanity and hate she saw in that man's eyes prompted her to tell him just what she thought—that until he experienced being Black and female, her experience was as foreign to him as his was to her. Their worlds were too different to compare. She thought he had definitely overstepped his personal boundaries simply to see how far he could stretch into hers. She did not identify with his cause of giving more importance to the fetus than the woman, and she wished they would all stay home and control their own lives.

Notes

1. Reprinted with permission from "Common Ground—Different Planes," The Women of Color Partnership Program Newsletter, December 1988.

Every Sperm is Sacred[1]

Cynthia Peters

Parodying the self-righteous, hymn-singing Operation Rescue demonstrators that gathered outside a Boston abortion clinic, pro-choice activists offered the following version of their own tribute to the sanctity of human life, singing: "Every sperm is sacred; every sperm is great. If you waste them, God gets quite irate."

The misogynist plea that anti-abortion activists direct at women to protect and value the life of the unborn over their own is thus turned back on this group of mostly middle- to upper-class white men who have taken it upon themselves to come out on this cold Saturday morning to rescue unborn babies. "What happened to all the potential life you wasted last time you jerked off?" one of the women yelled from the crowd. For those of us boiling with anger and frustration at the incredible assault on women's autonomy that constitutes the "rescuers'" mission, this moment of embarrassment and utter mortification for all those on the other side of the police barricades was more than satisfying. We were on the offensive now. The "rescuers" seemed to be momentarily stunned by the explicit language and by the very idea that attention should be focused on so private a matter (and to them, so abhorrent) as masturbation. This unplanned and very brief guerrilla strategy had worked in an important way. Some had slowed their picketing, others stood with jaws hanging slightly ajar. Their very own and very precious idea—the sanctity of potential life—had been stretched to absurdity. Meanwhile, attention had been focused on male participation in the creation of life. Parody offers a mirror, bringing into sharp focus what is most ridiculous. What a startling reflection it must have been for them.

Atlanta

My sister Marcia works at an abortion clinic in Atlanta, Georgia, a focal point of Operation Rescue. Ever since the summer of 1988, when this group of right-wing Christians decided to take advantage of the influx of national media to Atlanta during the Democratic National

Convention, there has been a persistent showing of anti-abortionists at her clinic. The violence, hatred, fear, and misogyny this "operation" has thrust into her life have taken their toll. As a clinic worker, she must cope daily with the throngs of people who collect outside her workplace and consider her a baby killer. She must deal somehow with the heightened level of guilt and anxiety experienced by her clients—heightened because whatever social, cultural, and political messages these women may have picked up in their lifetimes which implicitly preach their lesser worth are now being given powerful voice just outside the door. Hence, the mother bringing in her 16-year-old daughter to get an abortion feels sufficient safety and legitimacy to say, in front of her daughter, "I just want you to know that I'm only here to support my daughter. Otherwise I'd be out there with them."

Taking circuitous routes home from work may make it difficult for the anti-abortionists to discover my sister's address and plague her with hate mail or worse. Attempting to politicize her work as an abortion provider may ease her sense of isolation and helplessness. She tells me she is currently ending her explanation of the procedure to each group of clients with the proviso, "I have just described to you a legal abortion. The Supreme Court will soon be reviewing a case that could make this scenario illegal. Here is a petition we are circulating in support of a woman's right to choose. Please sign it and get involved in this struggle in whatever way you can." But the profound weariness and frustration brought about by being so categorically on the defensive are what have moved her to search for ways to turn the whole thing on its head, to respond militantly and creatively to the madness waiting for her at work every day.

So rather than lashing out at the "rescuers" who are up in her face reciting verses from the Bible as she makes her way from the parking lot to the front door of the clinic, she simply looks at them directly and, with all the self-assurance in the world, stuns them into silence with a list of words like "penis, masturbation, intercourse, ejaculation..." "It's a miracle," she says, "how quickly a path opens up before me." On other days, when perhaps she's feeling less verbal, she goes in and out of the clinic with an unwrapped and unrolled condom pinned to her blouse. "If they're going to invade my life with their moral indignation and self-righteousness, I'm going to come back at them with my own reality."

She believes in affirming sexuality; she supports contraception and safer sex; she honors women's privacy and their public right to choose. And she's willing to flaunt it.

Ithaca

A gay activist, Mickey J. Wheatley (a.k.a. Maybelline Gurleen), on his way into Ithaca, New York, with his lover for a gathering of radical faeries, noticed a small anti-abortion demonstration happening outside a Planned Parenthood clinic. They pulled their car up to the curb opposite the demonstrators and began to boo the 10 or so men, women, and children carrying placards asking for an "end to the second holocaust." For the radical faeries, who are part of a loosely defined anarchist movement concerned with pagan spirituality and reclaiming their connection to the earth and the "feminine," their oppositional response seemed little more than a yelling match, leaving them feeling ineffective while boosting the morale and self-righteousness of the anti-abortionists. But they regrouped, keeping in mind the advice of their peers that a faerie action is not taken in opposition to something but rather "comes from askance." As Wheatley wrote in the *Gay Community News* letters column,

> We walked past the group, ignoring them, and took up residence against a tree about ten feet from the end of the picket line and began necking. Their resolve began to quickly melt. Within two minutes, a young mother took her two children out of the picket line and hurriedly ushered them away from the scene lest our evil influence corrupt them. Then a woman removed herself from the other members and stood between us and the others, using her placard to try and shield the picketers from the view of our amorous display. We moved to just the other side of the placard and intensified our efforts. The woman quickly skulked back to the safety of her heterodyne peers.

Wheatley and his lover were empowered (and much more effective) when they shifted the focus onto themselves and their sexuality, rather than sitting in the car trying to yell louder than the others. They stepped outside the narrow framework of being for or against abortion and, instead, restructured the moment so that they were at the center of it. Thus, they were able to gain the upper hand, put the demonstrators on the defensive, and dissolve their morale. Someone from the clinic rushed out and thanked them on behalf of the staff inside.

Not A Damn Thing

Two 16-year-old Black women were being harassed by the anti-abortionist who comes regularly to the clinic, looking official and full of authority in her nurse's outfit, complete with a stethoscope around her neck. Her strategy is to scare each client away from the clinic by inundating them with lies about the side-effects of abortion. On this particular day, she followed the two 16-year-olds into a nearby Burger

King, confusing them by exercising her supposed authority in such an unlikely place, and embarrassing them deeply with her public harassment regarding their choice to end their pregnancies. Scared and distraught, the two girls managed to get back to the clinic, where they were told that the "nurse's" harassment was inexcusable and illegal and they had a right to file a complaint with the police. They did so, amazed and newly empowered to find that they were not the guilty parties in this case, as the nurse would have them believe.

In Charlotte, North Carolina, workers at the Carolina Women's Clinic have come up with creative disguises to get women in and out of the facility anonymously. At the Commonwealth Women's Clinic in Virginia, pro-choice activists have solicited donors to pledge a certain amount per arrest of an Operation Rescue demonstrator. Outside the clinic, a large sign shows the amount raised for the cause of reproductive freedom every time someone from the other side gets arrested. The "Pledge-A-Picket" fund is being used to pay for poor women's abortions. In New York City, pro-choice activists infiltrated Operation Rescue in order to find out which hotels they would be staying at and where their prayer meetings would be held. Thus, activists have been able to take the offensive, changing the site of the protest from the clinic to the prayer hall, and forcing the "rescuers" onto the defensive.

In a similar move in Seattle, Washington, local reproductive rights activists chained shut the exit of a church parking lot where anti-abortionists had gathered to register to participate in a clinic shutdown. After Operation Rescue managed to unhinge the locked gate, the pro-choice activists sat down in the driveway, further delaying Operation Rescue's attempt to shut down the clinic. According to Vivien Sharples, reporting for *Gay Community News,* spokespeople from the group made it clear that "their intention was not to impinge on the anti-abortionists' right to demonstrate, but to prevent them from limiting women's rights."

Long-time activists for reproductive freedom say that responding to Operation Rescue is the most defensive our movement has ever been. This is especially true in the realm of public debate, where the central question is still considered to be whether or not a fetus is human, leaving out entirely the question of the *woman's* humanity and protection and honor for her conscious choices regarding her reproductive ability, her sexuality, etc.

Despite the current defensive posture of the reproductive rights movement, there are individuals and groups who have discovered ways of responding militantly and creatively to the anti-choice Right. I have tried to tell some of their stories here. As we continue to rally in response to recent attacks on abortion rights, we should pay attention to those who have found ways to take the offensive; they have a great deal to teach us about asserting our humanity as we work to defend our already-won rights. Nor can we afford to lose sight of what we are defending. Everyone's heard a story of an illegal abortion. Here is the one playing over and over in my head as I write this article.

It was the mid-1950s. My friend was young, poor, and recently married to a man who was just beginning a long and difficult battle with cancer. She was also pregnant. Her illegal abortion left her with such a severe infection that she was rushed to the hospital, where she hung on the edge of death for days. As it turned out, she had to fight off much more than a lethal infection. Police came into her room and endlessly harassed her for the name of the abortionist. She refused to give it to them. They threatened her with arrest and warned her she would have to stand trial when (and if) she was able.

Meanwhile, doctors gave her the news that she would never be able to have children. The bungled abortion had caused too much damage.

Within months, however, she was pregnant again. Although her circumstances still made motherhood the last thing on her agenda, she would not risk another abortion and the possibility of never being able to have a baby.

By the time her trial date rolled around, her pregnancy was showing. The prosecuting attorney dropped the charges, believing that her impending motherhood would garner too much sympathy from the jury.

What we are *defending,* and demanding, is a woman's right to end her pregnancy if she so desires. In the instance described above, this right would have allowed this woman to choose a safe abortion; it would have saved her from near death, the injustice of police harassment, the potential loss of her capacity to have children, and the sexist irony of having her second pregnancy provide her delivery from prosecution and imprisonment more effectively than her own voice or argument. These are immense gains. Quantitatively, they have saved women's lives. Qualitatively, they have given us more control over what happens to our bodies, freeing many of us to make choices about sex, childbearing, and careers that were not available to an earlier generation. Defending these gains is of critical importance. We cannot go back to the days when women risked their lives to end unwanted pregnancies, or, indeed, pregnancies that were wanted but were financially or otherwise impossible to carry out.

I know a woman who takes a metal coat hanger with her practically everywhere she goes. It serves as a graphic and terrifying reminder of what lies in store for those who cannot afford a safe abortion. But we are fighting for much much more than the right to medical practice beyond the coat hanger. Even a legal abortion would not have offered the woman whose story I just told everything she would have needed to make the necessary choices in her life. Access to abortion would not have freed her to pursue the career of her choice because, being poor, this was not open to her anyway. Nor would a legal abortion have made it possible for her to raise children later on under reasonable conditions. As much as she wanted children, contending with the health care system's treatment of her progressively ill husband, racism, and the daily struggles of the poor in Washington, D.C. would have made (and, for many, have made) raising a family an incredibly difficult burden—something that is done against all odds, rather than as a socially supported choice. Indeed, pushing even further, having abortion be a legal option would not necessarily have changed the mindset of a public that thinks what is transpiring inside a woman's body is of more importance than her subjectivity.

Legal abortion does not stop sterilization abuse; it does not affirm the reproductive freedom of gays and lesbians; it alleviates the middle-class woman's fear of unwanted pregnancies, but it does not address the fears of those who cannot afford abortions; it brings a degree of sexual liberation to the heterosexual practicing vaginal intercourse, but does nothing to acknowledge or affirm other forms of sexual expression; it does not give us day care, a lower infant mortality rate, safer contraception, men who take responsibility for parenting, or a legal system that is not convinced it has the right to legislate what happens inside a woman's body.

We will do what is necessary to defend our clinics. But we must bring with us more than coat hangers as the symbol of what we are fighting *against*. We must bring with us all the symbols of what we are fighting *for*. Whether it's an unrolled condom pinned to your blouse; open expressions of homosexual desire; a powerful race and/or class identity; a consciousness that does not turn misogyny inward, but makes guilt-free, life-affirming choices—we must bring symbols of *our* world and the world we hope to create to the struggle for reproductive freedom.

Are these responses a little shrill, vaguely offensive, invasive of others who are exercising their right to make their values known? When you think shrill, think of the police harassing my friend in her hospital bed as she fought for her life. When you think offensive, think of the white man invoking the name of a civil rights leader against a Black woman attempting to claim some bodily autonomy.[2] When you think invasive, think of the sheer audacity of those who wish to control whether or how we become mothers.

Women and men must take the offensive now: to begin to shape the debate and go public with the things we care about. To respond everywhere and always, to those who would remove this most basic right, that we are not simply about scrambling to preserve the narrowly-defined right to abort a fetus. Rather, we are about affirming our sexualities, and the autonomy of our bodies, and our right to have children (if we want them), and to have them in a society that offers decent health and day care. We are about changing forever the mentality that says someone can dictate what happens inside a woman's body—whether forced pregnancy or forced sterilization. We are about removing, once and for all, the conditions that make it possible for this country to have one of the highest infant mortality rates among industrialized nations, and for over one-third of our urban children to be living in poverty. We are about *constructing* a world that reflects our needs and desires, in all their multitude.

Notes

1. This article originally appeared in *Zeta Magazine,* April 1989. Reprinted by permission.

2. See Dázon Dixon's article (page 185). This is in reference to her story which was previously quoted in this article.

Clinic Violence and
Harassment of Abortion Providers

- In 1985, 47% of abortion providers were harassed. The most common types of harassment were: bomb threats; blocking entrances to prevent patients and staff from entering or leaving; mass scheduling of no-show appointments; invasion of facilities; property destruction; assault of staff and patients; jamming phone lines; death threats; tracing patients' license plate numbers; picketing the homes of staff members.

- 80% of all abortion providers have been picketed.

- Between 1977 and 1988, there were 42 reported arson attacks on abortion providers, 37 attempted bombings and arson attacks, 216 bomb threats, 65 death threats, 2 kidnappings, 20 burglaries, 162 incidents of hate mail, and 220 incidents of vandalism. The violence has increased since 1983.

- Targeted clinics experience higher security and legal costs and more lost leases and staff members. They have had their insurance cancelled, faced new license requirements, and had difficulty obtaining hospital back-up support.

SOURCE: *Facts on Reproductive Rights: A Resource Manual,* NOW Legal Defense and Education Fund, Fact Sheet #11, 1989; "Violence and Harassment at Clinics Providing Abortions," Planned Parenthood League of Massachusetts.

RU-486

Judy Norsigian

RU-486 (mifepristone), a steroid drug which effectively terminates pregnancies within the first nine weeks of gestation, generated substantial controversy and media attention during the late 1980s. Given its potential to make abortion easier and more accessible, the anti-abortion movement opposed efforts to distribute it in France and to develop it in the United States. Pro-choice groups in the United States view RU-486 as a means for expanding options for abortion, as well as a potential obstacle to classic anti-abortion tactics. It will be much harder to harass all the physicians and clinics that might offer RU-486 than to harass the relatively few clinics now providing abortions.

Petitions to bring RU-486 to the United States are being circulated by a number of pro-choice organizations.

As a long-time activist in the women's health and self-help movement, I am intensely interested in RU-486. Initially many feminists were skeptical of the claims being made about RU-486. Even now, some women of color organizations are far from convinced that RU-486 represents a significant benefit to them, in part because the clinical trials to date have involved primarily white women. In addition, there is mistrust of a system that has so often been abusive and insensitive to the needs and concerns of women of color.

We need therefore to understand the primary mode of action, available data on safety and efficacy, the initial response of women using the drug in France (the only country making it available as of January 1990), its potential to alter women's experiences with abortion in the United States as well as in developing countries, the impact of conflict between two drug companies with major research involvement in this field, and other issues raised by this new method of fertility control.

How does RU-486 work?

By blocking the normal action of progesterone in the uterus, RU-486 can prevent implantation of a fertilized egg or bring on menses even if implantation has already taken place. This "anti-progesterone" is most effective when used within seven weeks of the last menstrual period and when accompanied 48 hours after ingestion by a dose of prostaglandin (either suppository or injection). Approximately 96 percent of women who receive both drugs during this early stage of pregnancy have a complete abortion within one day of receiving the prostaglandin.

Because a pregnancy is not "medically" established until after a fertilized egg has implanted, RU-486 is not necessarily acting as an abortifacient in the technical sense. Even after fertilization and after implantation (which can take several days), several steps are required for proper development of the embryo. To recognize the continuum of the reproductive process (and most likely to reduce the likelihood of anti-abortion opposition), French researcher Etienne-Emile Baulieu, the primary developer of RU-486, coined the term "contragestive" (a contraction of "contra-gestation") to describe this drug. He views the term "abortion pill" as negative and guilt-inducing, as well as not totally accurate. Whether use of the term "contragestion" will serve to clarify this drug's mode of action or simply confuse non-professionals remains to be seen. It certainly won't alter the degree of opposition from anti-choice individuals and groups.

Is RU-486 safe and effective?

RU-486 has been tested in over a dozen countries, mostly on a small scale. In France, however, over 30,000 women have used the drug as of late 1989. (Currently, about one-third of all abortions in France are done using RU-486.) So far, RU-486 appears relatively safe in the short term. There are negative effects such as cramps (sometimes severe), dizziness, diarrhea, and nausea. About one woman in 1,000 will experience bleeding sufficient to require a transfusion. Ongoing follow-up of women using this drug is essential to determine long-term effects, if any. However, the fact that RU-486 has a short half-life (about 30 hours) and does not remain in the body as do other hormones augurs well and may limit harmful effects.

RU-486 in combination with a prostaglandin is successful 96 percent of the time when used within seven weeks of the last menstrual period. When it fails, a suction abortion or D&C will be required. If a pregnancy should continue after administration of RU-486, the effect on the growing fetus is unknown. It is reasonable to expect that RU-486, as a steroid, might cause birth defects, so women should be aware of this. There are, however, three known cases where a woman took RU-486, did not subsequently take the prostaglandin, and went on to have a baby that appeared normal in all respects.

RU-486 can be used alone, with lower success rates, as has been demonstrated in studies in Los Angeles and elsewhere.

What has been the experience of French women to date?

Several women's health activists, including representatives of the Feminist Women's Health Centers in Los Angeles and the Routh St. Clinic in Dallas, Texas, visited France in the spring of 1989. Their report indicates a most favorable response to this early abortifacient. When women compare RU-486 to a surgical abortion, they overwhelmingly prefer the former. However, it is important to note that first trimester abortions in France (and in most of Europe) are performed under general anesthesia. The experience of surgical abortion is understandably a more stressful physical event than it has to be under such circumstances.

A woman's attitude toward surgery and her assessment of the skills of the abortion provider will influence her decision regarding what type of abortion to choose. A medical abortion using RU-486 may be far more attractive than a surgical one if a woman is particularly concerned about uterine perforation or about the risk of infection. On the other hand, as long as RU-486 abortions remain a two-step procedure (currently, one has to return to the clinic or doctor two days after receiving RU-486 to obtain the prostaglandin), some women will choose surgical abortion in order to save time, or to avoid extra hours off from work, or simply to get the experience over with as quickly as possible. In the United States, where general anesthesia is rarely used for first trimester abortions, the preference for RU-486 over surgical abortion may not be the same as in France.

How might RU-486 affect women's lives in the United States and in developing countries?

Because RU-486 can be administered in a doctor's office as well as in a clinic setting, women will more easily be able to avoid the anti-abortion picketers and harassment so common at many abortion clinics in the United States. It is likely that many physicians and other practitioners not involved with the provision of surgical abortions will offer RU-486, once it is available in the U.S.

For women who are aware of their unwanted pregnancies in the earliest stages and who would want to end their pregnancies as soon as possible, RU-486 offers advantages. Also, some women who suspect they are pregnant but would rather not know for sure will want access to RU-486 without having to obtain a positive pregnancy test. Although this drug is unlikely to be made available in the near future to anyone without a confirmed pregnancy, it is possible that this option will develop over time.

Women who have little awareness of their unwanted pregnancies until after eight or nine weeks will not be able to use an early abortifacient such as RU-486. Possibly, greater media attention to this method will educate more women about the early signs of pregnancy and thus expand the number of women who would be able to choose a very early means of having an abortion.

Some feminists have been concerned that RU-486 would privatize the abortion experience and further isolate women from one another. They pictured a woman going in and out of a doctor's office or clinic to take RU-486, returning two days later for the prostaglandin, and then going home to have a very early miscarriage, possibly alone and without support. In fact, because most French women have developed strong contractions quite soon after receiving the prostaglandin, they are choosing to remain in the clinics, in the company of other women, and to wait for the miscarriage to take place there. In a few instances, women wanted to stay overnight rather than go home. While this avoids isolation and also ensures medical back-up should something go wrong, it also means that RU-486 will, like surgical abortion, be controlled by the medical establishment, with all the attendant problems. It also means that harassment by anti-abortionists can continue.

Women in developing countries have expressed great interest in RU-486, especially in settings where abortion is illegal and maternal mortality rates due to illegal abortion are high. On the one hand, they are concerned about the long-term effects of RU-486, the possible short-term problems that might appear with poor and malnourished women (something the French studies cannot address), and the unsafe situation for the one in 1,000 women who will bleed seriously but not have access to transfusions. On the other hand, they acknowledge the current dangers of common practices, such as inserting unsterile objects and caustic solutions into the uterus. In hospitals, as well, infection may pose a serious problem. Even without proper medical backup, some women argue, use of RU-486 would provide a safer overall situation, since the risk of infection would be greatly reduced by avoiding use of instruments in the uterus. Others have suggested that clandestine use of RU-486 would be easier than the clandestine provision of surgical/suction abortion by trained providers (lay or professional). What this shows us is the importance of looking at drugs like RU-486 in different contexts and being sensitive to the ways in which poverty, geography, etc. will shape the effects on women's health. It should also emphasize for us the importance of continuing to advocate for expanded health services for women and children in developing countries. RU-486 is not a substitute for adequate reproductive health services, including surgical abortion.

What are current prospects for marketing RU-486 outside of France?

Unusual circumstances surrounded the initial marketing of RU-486 in France and most likely have influenced the cautious approach of Roussel-Uclaf, the company which developed and now markets this drug in France. After the French government approved the drug in September 1988, Roussel responded to pressure from anti-choice groups and withdrew RU-486 from the French market in late October 1988. Immediately, about 2,000 of the 9,500 physicians attending the World Congress of Gynecology and Obstetrics in Rio de Janeiro signed a protest petition, complaining to both Roussel and the international media.

More importantly, just two days after the drug's withdrawal from the market, the French Health Minister ordered Roussel to resume marketing or risk transfer of the patent for RU-486 to another company. (Since the French government had over one-third interest in the company, it had the power to take such action.) This order was well-received by the company, since it took the moral burden for marketing RU-486 off Roussel. Many observers wonder to this day if the whole incident was not carefully planned and enacted by the French Health Ministry and Roussel, though both parties deny this to be true.

Hoechst, a large German pharmaceutical manufacturer and the parent company of Roussel, has also been pressed by anti-abortion/anti-choice groups. Its chief executive officer has met with the head of the National Right to Life Committee in the United States and is reported to share anti-choice views with groups like the National Right to Life Committee. The extent to which Hoechst has influenced corporate decision making at Roussel is not totally clear. However, most stockholders are probably more concerned with the great profit potential of RU-486 (a likely billion-dollar market in the United States alone) than with the "moral" issues as defined by anti-choice organizations. Many with financial interest in the companies also believe that RU-486 offers a substantial contribution to the health and well-being of women.

In late 1989, Roussel and the French government agreed upon a price of 250 francs for each dose of RU-486 paid for by the government. As the drug is distributed by more conventional means (along with other drugs), rather than in the highly controlled fashion that characterized its initial use, the potential for a black market increases. In January 1990, Roussel announced plans to market RU-486 in Britain, Scandinavia, and the Netherlands, possibly by spring. Several U.S.-based companies have also approached Roussel about the U.S. market, so it may not be long before it appears here, too. Given the high quality and extensive nature of the French clinical data, it is likely that the FDA review process will go fairly smoothly. The Chinese government also has approved RU-486 (it did so just before France gave its approval) but currently does not have the means to mass produce the drug (or a similar one). In January 1990, Roussel announced its intention to help China and India build plants that would manufacture RU-486.

What about a "combined" pill?

A "combined" approach is, in fact, possible. A woman could take RU-486 plus a prostaglandin in a delayed release form, and thus avoid an extra trip to her clinic or practitioner's office. (In a developing country this extra trip could involve substantial travel.) Both Roussel-Uclaf, the French manufacturer of RU-486, and Schering, the German pharmaceutical company which has the patent on the idea of a combination of an anti-progesterone with a prostaglandin, have decided to suspend further research on abortifacients for the time being. Thus, women will be waiting a long time for improvements over the current drugs.

Some women's groups have suggested a letter-writing campaign to both Roussel-Uclaf and Schering to urge cooperation on this matter. Others are calling for feminists to consider forming a company for research, development, and distribution.

Other issues for consideration

It is crucial that rigorous post-marketing surveillance of RU-486 be conducted to determine long-term effects, if any, as soon as possible. Clinical trials involving women of different racial, cultural and socio-economic backgrounds are also essential to demonstrate safety and efficacy for women of different backgrounds and in different conditions. For example, would malnutrition play an unforeseen role in outcomes with RU-486?

Should RU-486 become more widely available, suction and surgical abortion services must still be preserved for women who need or want them, especially in instances where a later abortion is required. Unfortunately, if current abortion clinics face substantial competition from other providers who choose to offer RU-486, it is possible that some of these clinics (including women-controlled health centers) will be forced to go out of business, thus limiting access to suction/surgical abortions. This possibility may make a strong case for limiting distribution of RU-486 to abortion providers, if they are present in a community.

RU-486 also has potential as an occasional menses inducer, to be taken several days before a woman's period is due. It could not be used regularly, however, because of its tendency to disrupt the menstrual cycle, making it difficult to know when the next menstrual period would be due. Similar drugs may offer more promise as a once-a-month menses inducer and need to be researched further. Such an approach to fertility control does not require a positive pregnancy test and could be used by women who suspect they might be pregnant but would rather not delay action, seek testing, etc. Many women are advocating further research into this potential use of RU-486.

Conclusion

As an early abortifacient with a good safety and effectiveness record to date, RU-486 offers a substantially new approach to fertility control that will attract many women with unwanted pregnancies. Feminists, those in the medical and public health fields, consumer groups, and others will have to work hard to preserve a political climate that will speed up its entry into the United States. Once here, we must conduct rigorous post-marketing surveillance to determine its long-term safety, especially for groups of women with particular medical conditions. And, as with other forms of abortion, we must also fight to make RU-486 safe, legal, and accessible to all women.

Fighting Back to Save Women's Lives[1]

Brenda Joyner

Recall how you felt the day that the U.S. Supreme Court handed down the *Webster* decision. Women were saying things like, "There will be no going back. We are not going to allow Supreme Court Justices or legislators to make fundamental decisions about our reproductive lives…We are going to do whatever is necessary to help women get safe abortions…We are not going to sit back and let them play games with women's lives."

I read and understood *Webster* to have devastating and frightening implications for women. For me and other abortion rights proponents, the question was, "What do we do to save women's lives?"—which we translated into a question about how to impact the political process to prevent *Webster* from happening in our state.

After *Webster*, Bob Martinez, the governor of Florida, called a special session of the legislature, which he hoped would pass severe restrictions on abortion rights of the sort that the Supreme Court had legitimized in the *Webster* decision. Despite the fact that the word was out that not much would happen in the session, we had no choice but to take his call as a direct threat. The special session was not THE PROBLEM. After *Webster*, it was more like adding insult to injury.

It was clear that we had to respond to the governor's challenge, but it was also clear that we shouldn't focus on the legislators. They had indicated in advance where they stood. Responding to the political mobilization at all levels, from the grassroots to within mainstream political parties themselves, legislators were not prepared to pass restrictive legislation in a state where the pro-choice majority was so strong and organized. Mainstream women's groups organized statewide memberships to write letters and otherwise lobby legislators. We made contact with the legislative Black Caucus and, once assured of their 100 percent pro-choice support, focused our attention elsewhere.

The Tallahassee Feminist Women's Health Center had helped build a grassroots coalition of progressive groups who have worked together for several years on a variety of issues. This coalition came together again after *Webster* to engage in the kind of political activity the mainstream was not prepared to tackle. We saw a role for everybody; ours was to keep the issue visible in creative ways, refusing to allow anti-abortion propagandists to set the terms and conditions of public debate. Our activities included: a recall campaign calling for the governor's resignation after he announced the special session; a Capitol Re-decoration Project, in which pro-choice graffiti was stencil painted in strategic places; and a Coat Hangers Project, which involved sending the governor hundreds of coat hangers with messages attached in brown bags. Although these activities were very well received by the public and the media, mainstream pro-choice groups tried to distance themselves, especially from the Capitol Re-decoration action. They seemed to be trying to marginalize us and to insulate themselves from our more radical stance and tactics.

We saw our activities as another way of saying to the legislature, "We will not allow you to do this to women." We saw the need to speak out and say that we will do whatever is necessary to help women get safe abortions. We are not going to sit back and let them play games with women's lives. So we participated in every aspect of the organizing around the special session. We helped mobilize people to demonstrate at it. We were prepared on July 3 and called a press conference putting forth our position as a coalition. We appeared on television and at community forums. We had daily pickets at both the Capitol and the governor's mansion. We performed street theatre at the Capitol. All of our efforts were directed toward education and politicization—helping people to understand what was at stake, and broadening their understanding of the meaning of *Webster*.

The threat was not new. Florida has a long history of efforts by the anti-abortion movement to pass restrictive legislation against state Medicaid funding and the abortion rights of minors, and an ongoing saga of clinic restrictions. We also have a long history of violence and harassment directed at clinics—bombings, arson, picketing. And we have been flooded with anti-abortion propaganda. Some of us have participated in many years of consistent struggle against these efforts. We have tried to keep the abortion issue visible in ways that help women. It was only because of *Webster* that the massive mobilization took place. Many who had been silent began to speak out.

As a result, the governor's effort to restrict abortion was unsuccessful. He was soundly defeated in the special session. This was even more significant because he had been so insistent on calling the session even when urged to call it off, even when Florida court rulings made it clear that judges in Florida would not look as favorably on restrictive legislation as the Supreme Court had done in *Webster.* In spite of statewide polls indicating that 85 percent of Floridians favored existing laws and opposed further restrictions, the governor persisted, and we defeated him. Coming on the heels of *Webster,* the whole country was watching. The media touted this as a significant victory for the pro-choice movement.

I see it more as a standoff than a victory. We won because we did not lose, but no gains in rights were made. In these times, however, this was a victory, the result of the confluence of many social, political, and historical factors.

Our ability to organize successfully after *Webster* was based on the foundation we had built over the years. TURF—Tallahasseans United for Reproductive Freedom—was a grassroots, people-based coalition. Groups involved included Students Organized for Reproductive Freedom, the North Florida Rainbow Coalition, Veterans for Peace, the Women's Center, the Black Student Union, the Center for Participant Education (these three from Florida State University), progressive faculty and attorneys, and other like-minded individuals. The coalition had been together for a long time. We had worked together on the first statewide abortion rights conference; on clinic defense; against apartheid, racism at home, U.S. militarism, and violence against women; and for the election of the Reverend Jesse Jackson. After *Webster* we were able to reach more people, and our task changed because of the urgency of the matter.

Role of the Tallahassee Feminist Women's Health Center

The Tallahassee Feminist Women's Health Center played a significant role in pulling this coalition together. Our political history put us in a position to be effective. Even our location is politically significant: we are in a low-income Black community in the center of the city, four blocks from the governor's mansion and a few blocks from the university. We are a non-profit women's health clinic. The Center was founded in 1974 by a group of feminist self-helpers who were part of the Federation of Feminist Health Centers (directed by Carol Downer, considered to be the mother of feminist self-help). These Centers promoted a certain view of women's health which emphasized women's power and knowledge and community control of health care. Many of the other self-help clinics have closed in recent years, primarily because of the political climate. The Tallahassee Center remains and continues to be committed to the original goals. We are trying to keep the embers burning.

I have been at the Health Center for 10 years. I've got it under my skin. This organization has transformed my life and my understanding of what is going on in the world for women. The central questions really are: who is going to control women's bodies?; who is going to control women's lives? Our work is guided by the belief that women must be in control. This is what we are fighting for—a feminist politics and philosophy that are not like the mainstream image. It is a feminism which realizes that the issues of reproductive control are broader than just the fight for gender equality. It is a feminism which understands the world simultaneously from race and class as well as gender perspectives. In line with this, the Center has adopted a policy which mandates us to have proportional, multinational representation at both the board and staff levels. We have tried to represent the diversity of our clientele. We do not have a top-down structure dominated by white middle-class women and men. The medical professionals we work with are employed by us.

Our own understanding of feminism and reproductive choice has been expanded through our work. We started a prenatal clinic because of a real need in the community. Very few doctors will see pregnant women who are on Medicaid. Even the doctors working with the Health Department have a documented history of not wanting to serve poor women. They went on strike because they wanted to be paid at a higher rate than Medicaid was reimbursing them. Their attitude was one of contempt for poor people. If they were forced to deal with poor women, they wanted to extract a price.

The Health Center fought to change that situation. There are now adequate programs to meet the prenatal health care needs of poor women in Tallahassee, although the outreach is still inadequate. We have tried to be a voice in the community to say that poor women have a right to have healthy children, and we have tried to advocate for the services that make this happen.

The Feminist Women's Health Center has had a fight back posture for as long as it has existed. We have had to. When it first opened, two local doctors tried to run the Center out of town because it was committed to self-help and because it provided abortions for $150 when the going rate at that time was close to $1,000. The Center sued the doctors under the Sherman federal anti-trust laws, and after a five-year legal battle, we won a precedent-setting victory. The case went to the United States Supreme Court; we won. Before it was over, the Florida Medical Association and the American Medical Association had joined the doctors, while the American Public Health Association and the Southern Poverty Law Center had joined the Health Center. These were real "heavyweights" going at each other. This victory required a large expenditure of resources. It politicized us and our community. We even had to sue our own lawyers, who tried to make off with the damages money!

We won against them too. Through all of this—a number of political, legal, and social issues were put before the community with the Health Center in the thick of it.

We have consistently been involved in abortion politics. We are picketed by anti-abortionists every single Saturday, and we always hold counter-demonstrations. We would never just let them have their way. There is an analogy here to the K.K.K. If the Klan announces a cross burning at your house, you don't just allow them to come and do as they please. You stand your ground because they are threatening you and your family. This is how we think of the anti-abortion attacks on the Health Center.

Standing our ground has sometimes involved us in arrests. In fact, a significant turning point occurred one Saturday in July 1982 when the anti-abortionists engaged in a planned attack on the clinic. On that day we didn't expect what we got. The streets were blocked off. I had been a political activist for some time but had not been prepared for the possibility of serious violence. But we stood our ground, and despite the fact that we did no violence, but had violence done to us—despite the fact that we broke no laws—we were still the ones arrested, not the anti-abortionists. Three of our co-directors went to jail, a true rainbow of women. There was police brutality directed at us and conspiracy between the police and the anti-abortion demonstrators. Not only were we witnesses to this, but our children were as well. We had never been afraid to bring the children; we had never before been concerned for their safety.

We were able to use this experience as an opportunity to educate the public about the ties between the police and the anti-abortion movement. It turned out that the assistant chief of police and the state attorney were on the board of the Christian Action Council, the anti-abortion group attacking the clinic. These public officials had allowed their official titles to be used on anti-abortion literature and provided the anti-abortion group with a meeting place at the police station. We encouraged the community to protest this, which it did. The media was of course quite interested. This exposure proved to be quite a source of embarrassment for both public officials.

We see activism on the abortion issue as part of our work. Serving women in the clinic, we just cannot allow them to be subjected to terrorism, picketing, and harassment. Women going to a clinic should have some protection and should not be forced to face alone picket lines and aggressive demonstrators. Providing that protection is our role.

If there is anything that I have learned throughout all of this, it is the need to maintain a fight back position in the face of the opposition. Otherwise we will fail. If the pro-choice movement had fought back sooner, we wouldn't be where we are now. We have just come out of two terms of Reagan's anti-abortion politics. For many years the anti-abortion movement has been allowed to do incredible damage to women by restricting access to abortion and by influencing public opinion with well-financed propaganda campaigns. This went on much too long virtually unchecked by the women's movement. Many organizations which project themselves as protecting women's rights were afraid to touch the abortion issue. NOW, for example, feared that abortion would hurt their ERA campaign, until they finally saw that masses of people were very strongly pro-choice. Then, and only then, did NOW decide to do something active on the issue of abortion.

Had we seen this kind of public outcry and mobilization of resources to oppose the Hyde Amendment in 1976 that we have seen against *Webster*, perhaps there would not have been a *Webster*. Why wasn't that support there when the Hyde Amendment eliminated the right of women on Medicaid to obtain an abortion? Because of racism and elitism in the women's movement. Because Hyde knocked on the doors of poor women and *Webster* knocks at the doors of white, middle-class women. Because of a narrowness and self-centeredness among many white, middle-class feminists who seem to mobilize only when their own self-interest is directly threatened.

I do not think that the situation is very different now. I do not see the pro-choice movement looking out for the interests of the majority of American women—working and poor women. Individuals and organizations who had been silent now want to be publicly associated with the pro-choice position. It is almost as if one gains political prestige in this way. This is not real concern for the lives of poor women. Instead I see it as opportunistic. A real threat to the lives of poor women is being used to build the political careers of those who have not taken stands in the past. These mainstream groups have attempted to manipulate our TURF coalition and have claimed credit for all pro-choice organizing that is and ever has been. This kind of posture widens the gap between the mainstream, white organizations and those of us who are long-time grassroots organizers. We see them as trying to marginalize us and insulate themselves from our more radical stances and tactics.

Racism also continues to be a factor. The leadership of most mainstream organizations remains mostly white, at both the local and national levels. Women of color cannot participate in any group that is not actively fighting racism. And the racism, classism, and elitism that I see within our movement must be opposed. I have identified as a feminist for over 20 years but not as the kind of feminist being promoted by mainstream organizations. I am committed to fighting for a more broad-based feminism and movement. The women's movement must begin to deal seriously with racism. If not, there will continue to be many movements which lack the ability to work together and therefore lack the power that would come with that unity.

At the Health Center, we see ourselves as serving the needs of *all* women. Each of us gives a piece of our lives every day to women of all races and classes through our work. And this is how it should be. The Health Center is a model of the way the world can work.

In the reproductive rights battle we are fighting to make abortion safe and accessible for all women. We concur with the Federation of Feminist Women's Health Centers' position. There will be "No Going Back." Of necessity, women will learn and practice self-help techniques, including menstrual extraction. Women must demand and produce aggressive and well-funded research on the safety and efficacy of RU-486 and herbal abortifacients. If abortion is made illegal, we will be creative about making it accessible. We will re-think and do what is in the best interests of women. We have been and will continue to try to be where we are needed, to raise the hard questions, and to be a voice for all women's lives.

Notes

1. This article is based on a telephone interview with Brenda Joyner, a co-director of the Tallahassee Feminist Women's Health Center in Florida. She and the clinic participated in the successful effort to defeat state anti-abortion initiatives proposed by the governor of Florida.

The Female War Saga

Sharon Cox

III.

I used to laugh when I saw the mostly male
groups lying their bodies down outside of
abortion clinics
how funny I thought no longer to hear them say
"Get rid of 'it' " and " 'it's' not mine"
Now they are calling "us" murderers and claim
to be protecting the unborn—men with a holy
mission? I think not
I can almost hear them saying
"So you want choice
the back alleys are still there"

IV.

Message from the front
Wish you were here today, but we
the rank and file want you to know
we are holding-on

The voices of propaganda suggest that our liberation
is almost a reality and the movement is dead
the treaty ready for signing
but these mere words are not enough
to drown out the sounds of the war drums
we the rank and file hold-on
Open doors for some, small token gifts of Phds
CEOs Mds and law degrees are recognized for the
trojan horses they are and are not enough to make
us blink or deflect our aim
we the rank and file hold-on

Threats of re-instituting slavery through the womb,
back alley abortions, surrogacy and supposed

ticking of biological clocks are not enough to
break the will of those who have been bloodied
in the trenches
we the rank and file hold-on

Homelessness, welfare hotels, loss of custody in
the courts and the forced use of underground
networks to protect the young, not even economic
sanctions are enough to make us capitalists
we the rank and file hold-on

Though beaten, raped, and murdered in our homes,
freeway killers, Green River murders all acts
of terrorism designed to make us bolt are not
enough to make us desert our post on the front-lines
Yes we the rank and file are holding-on.

EXPANDING THE AGENDA: BUILDING AN INCLUSIVE MOVEMENT

Survival, Empowerment, and Activism

Roxanna Pastor

I gave this speech a few days before the April 1989 March for Women's Equality and Women's Lives in Washington, D.C. At the time I was director of a high school-based day care center for the children of teenage parents, and I continued to be an activist in the Latino community. Speaking from these experiences, I hoped to convey the limitations of any "exclusive" movement and ideas about how we can build an effective coalition. The main principle is the need to expand our definition of what is "politically correct" so we can live our daily lives in a way that facilitates change in all areas.

I am going to talk about the people who are not going to the March and why. I am a Latina activist. I live in Boston and have been in this country for the last 10 years working with women and children. What I want to talk about is empowerment and about taking risks and about the things we need to understand so that all of those people who are not going to this March could come in the future. People who live in third world countries, people who live in poor neighborhoods in this country have so many daily struggles. Staying alive is a struggle. Having food on the table is a struggle. Being able to understand the teacher at school is a struggle. Understanding the transportation system is a struggle.

I want to talk about why we need to dispel myths and why we need to take risks and put down stereotypes. The only way that all of us can work together is if we not only respect differences, but value them. I go a step further. I am not asking you to respect me, to tolerate me; I am asking you to value me. If we cannot value differences, then we cannot understand other people's struggles. If we have stereotypic ideas about being politically correct and about people, then we cannot join forces. The reality is that we don't win struggles on an individual basis, and the reality is that many of the women who are being affected by decisions like those on abortion are not getting involved in some of these movements. We need to find out why. It is not o.k. to say they just don't come, they have to work three jobs, historically they are against abortion, or that the church has a big influence in the Hispanic community. These are superficial reasons.

I want to tell you about some of the people that I work with to give you an understanding of how the issues that affect them are their primary issues, for valid reasons. In order for them to join your struggle, you have to join their struggle. This does not mean that you have to be an activist on every issue in this world—nobody can do that. It means that you have to understand these connections and make changes in your own life and in the way you conduct yourself on a daily basis.

One of the people that I want to talk about is a teenage mother who is originally from the Dominican Republic. She has a one-year-old child. She had the child not because she did not know about birth control, not because she decided to have that child, but because there were many circumstances in her life that made that choice an alternative. She was 17, failing in school because, when she first came from the Dominican Republic, they put her into a classroom where children spoke only English and the teacher spoke only English. They did this because she needed to learn English in order to make it in the United States. She never really learned how to read, but they passed her along anyway because there are people who are more concerned about statistics than about education. Chyrell was failing school because she could not read, and Chyrell didn't feel very good about herself because she wasn't blonde and because she wasn't pretty and she wasn't thin.

But there was something that would make her feel good about herself. There was something that would give her status in her community. And that was being a mother. The day that Chyrell gave birth everybody on her block congratulated her and told her how beautiful her baby was.

Is Chyrell going to the March? No, Chyrell is not going to the March. Does Chyrell care about the March? No, Chyrell doesn't care about the March. If we were to think about what would help Chyrell make a conscious choice about her reproductive rights, we would need to look to a school system that is a failure. Her issue, or the issue that most affects her, is a lousy school system. My role in working with her is not to tell her about Washington but to try to do something about the school system.

I want to tell you about one other person; her name is Maria. She is 23 years old and has two children under the age of two. She is somebody I worked with a number of years ago. She is from Puerto Rico. One of the things that I do is work with the movement against U.S. intervention in Central America and the Caribbean. Very often, when I am with activists, they ask me, so where are the Latinos? Where are the

Black people? How come you guys don't get involved? Every time they ask me that question, I tell them about Maria.

Maria lived in Roxbury with her family. Over a number of years they acquired a house, which then burned down. When their house burned, some of the family moved back to Puerto Rico and others stayed in Boston, not by choice but because they could not all afford to go back to Puerto Rico. Maria was one of the people who stayed in Boston. She ended up in an apartment that she could barely afford. It didn't have any heat, and the oldest of her two daughters happened to have special needs. She was concerned about the fact that the right side of the body of her two-year-old didn't work very well. So I came to her home and found her in this apartment that by any legal standard should be condemned. To her, however, it was a wonderful home. She did not want to be on the street. The next day Maria called me saying she was sorry to be calling and that I must think she was an opportunist. She went on, "I don't really know you but my two kids have fevers of 104. I don't have enough money for a cab, so I have to take a bus but I can't carry the two kids. Can you come help?" I went with her and spent the next six hours in a clinic waiting for the doctor to see her. Then the doctor couldn't communicate with her, and when they finally gave her a prescription and we went to get it filled, the pharmacist screamed at her because she had Medicaid and not cash. We finally got back to her home. A month later, Maria was out on the street because the landlord needed to give the apartment to his son.

Do you think Maria cares about the militarization of Puerto Rico? No, she is not part of the anti-intervention movement. Maria eventually went to live in a shelter where people shut the lights off at 9:00; it doesn't matter if you are not sleepy. She lived in a shelter where she had to go out every day to look for an apartment, even if it was snowing or raining, and she had to be out with her two kids. Maria eventually found an apartment in Lynn, a small impoverished town close to Boston but far enough away so that she left all of her support system behind. It meant that her kid lost special needs services and that she lost her friends. She was alone in this community, but she had an apartment. For Maria, if I had to think of the issue that I worked with her on, it was housing. I babysat her kids in my office while she went from one apartment building to another. I talked to her about what to say and what not to say in an interview. We went and put her name on every mailing list that you could imagine. Maria needed to do that; she couldn't talk about abortion. She needed to talk about housing. She needed to worry about how to get her kids off the street.

What I am saying is that these are real issues that are affecting real people who are not against your issues. In order for all of us to work together we need to make those our issues. This doesn't mean going to every march. It does mean the way you live your life every day, how you speak out, when you speak out. When we think of politics as a spectrum where different people do different things depending on their needs and where they, their community, and their culture are at, then the circle is much larger. There are many expressions of politics, and until we value all of them, we will not create a whole movement.

We need to redefine our concepts and value our differences. I am proud to be different. I don't want to be the same. I don't work actively every day to get rid of my accent, and I want people to value me for who I am, as I value people for who they are. Until we all do this, many people will not be joining our struggle.

I want to end by giving you an example of something that is currently going on in Central America and affects my life very deeply. Five Central American Presidents got together and said what they wanted to do in their region. One of the things they said was they wanted to get rid of the *contras*—the mercenary army that was created by the U.S. government to attack the Sandinista government of Nicaragua. The Bush administration had its own plan; it was going to preserve the mercenary army until the United States thought it was time to get rid of it.

This is exactly the same line of thinking as saying to a woman, you do not have a right to decide when you can have an abortion. The government is saying to people, you are not capable of making your own decision. The government of the United States is saying to five Central American countries, you tried really hard to come up with a democratic plan but it doesn't work. The U.S. government will tell you what works.

We need to make these links and create a space where we can all take risks, so that it is safe to work in coalitions, so that we do feel that we are working together rather than using one another. We need to make links so that we can create a country, and a world at large, that allow all of us to be participants and to feel that we have something to contribute. We need to make links so that we are not tokens but real participants in the struggle together. The issues are always there; the struggles are always there. Today your issue may be on the front line, tomorrow mine.

La Mujer Puertorriqueña, Su Cuerpo, y Su Lucha por la Vida: Experiences with Empowerment in Hartford, Connecticut

Cándida Flores, Lani Davison, Enid Mercedes Rey, Migdalia Rivera, and María Serrano

The story of empowerment of Puertorriqueñas is the story of struggle. This is a social, political, economic, and historical struggle—carried out both individually and collectively.[1] For Puerto Rican women, especially those living in the barrios of the United States, it is waged on many different terrains: from the inner self to the family, from the home to the workplace, from the welfare office to the emergency room, from the courtroom to the streets. The history of Puerto Rican women is colored by struggle. But the first and most important site of Puertorriqueña struggle is the female body. The body represents the unique and culturally revered capacity to procreate, symbolizes the taboo realm of sexuality, and carries with it the honor or shame of the family. The body is at once a valued (often exploited) instrument for social survival and an object for enforcing social control. The Puerto Rican woman cannot begin down the road to empowerment until she has confronted the many ways her body has been used, the purposes it has served, and in whose interests it has toiled.

Feminists have made this same argument about empowerment strategies for Euro-American women.[2] However, its expression in the struggle of Puerto Rican women provides it with a unique coloring. Sexuality, reproduction, motherhood, and family need to be redefined in light of the experiences of colonization, inter-lingualism, and the development of capitalism in Puerto Rico.[3]

Amigas Latinas en Acción (A.L.A.S.), a Latina feminist collective in Boston (one of us—Rivera—was a member), was among the first to develop a perspective about Latina women and their bodies. Other groups have followed suit, including the new National Latina Health Organization, Comisión Feminíl Mexicana National, Comité de Mujeres Puertorriqueñas Miriam Lopez Perez, Mujeres Unidas, the "Centro de Educación del Embarazo" project of the Massachusetts Department of Public Health, and M.A.N.W.A. (Mexican American National Women's Association). The authors of this paper have been involved in a project called Mujeres en Acción Pro Salud Reproductiva: Northeast Project on Latina Women and Reproductive Health, based at the Hispanic Health Council in Hartford, Connecticut.

Mujeres en Acción Pro Salud Reproductiva

The Mujeres en Acción Pro Salud Reproductiva Project ultimately aims to empower Latina women, especially Puerto Rican women, who comprise the largest Latina population in the Northeast. It does so using a multi-stranded approach that includes: a) collecting primary data on reproductive illness and using these data to advocate for policy and program change in the interests of Puertorriqueñas; b) designing and testing a culture/gender-appropriate educational support model for Latina leadership and confidence-building (one which could be replicated elsewhere); c) developing and distributing bilingual, bicultural educational materials sensitive to Puerto Rican women's informational needs about reproductive health and sexuality.

The first component, the Mujeres en Acción Research Project, entailed interviews with 40 Puerto Rican women aged 20-45[4] and a 225-household random survey of women in the same age group living in the highest density Latino neighborhoods of Hartford.[5] We wanted to engage poor and working Puerto Rican women in a dialogue about reproductive health experiences, gender relations, the use/misuse of the female body, personal and cultural identity, and social conditions. Our interviews were designed to examine the relationship between reproductive illness and women's wider social experience.

We found that such dialogue enabled women to think about and discuss matters that might be difficult to speak about in other contexts, thereby helping them to gain perspective upon their past and present experiences. This is a critical first step in enabling the women to construct a new, self-affirming identity. Through this process, women developed a new understanding of how socialization plays an important role in shaping gender relations. The women discussed the humiliation of not being able to fulfill the role obligation of "bueno proveedores" (good providers) and how it contributed to their compañeros' anger and physical aggression.[6] Puerto Rican men and women have undergone tremendous suffering as a consequence of the political-economic transformation of the island over time. This message was not difficult to transmit to the women, who were all too familiar with the suffering of their people—men and women alike.

Our individual discussions with the women lasted several days. Many mentioned that they had "never before spoken about these things" and that they "felt isolated and afraid." Since speaking, they said, they feel better about themselves and about how they have acted in their lives. They all had feelings of release and wanted to help other women talk too.[7] This information helped to shape the format and content of the support group leadership development model which was the second component of the project.

"Cosas de Mujeres" or "Issues Affecting Women" is a bilingual, bicultural support group for poor and working Puerto Rican women with limited formal education. The group is designed to enhance personal self-confidence, leadership skills, and self-esteem as well as to encourage the development of socio-political awareness of what has been called "the Puerto Rican experience."[8] The group is guided by the premise that empowerment for poor Puertorriqueñas begins with a heightened understanding of and greater sense of power over their own bodies, especially in matters related to reproduction and sexuality.

The program provides participants with information about risks to their general well-being, as well as to their reproductive health. Raising women's awareness about these risks is a vital aspect of the project, since in large part, the feelings of powerlessness, depression, and anger held by many of them stem from the fact that they have been misinformed about their bodies.[9]

"Cosas de Mujeres" runs in 10-week cycles, and has 12-15 women in each group. Each group selects the topics it wishes to cover for a particular cycle, and a series of bilingual outside speakers, films, videos, diagrams, and other educational materials are featured. Topics covered include: Puerto Rican history and cultural pride, the role and status of women in Puerto Rican society, domestic and other forms of violence, physical/sexual/emotional abuse, types of love and feelings for others, changes in the female body, reproductive technologies, medical experimentation, sexually transmitted diseases including AIDS, menopause, and differences between the male and female body.

At the center of the group are two bilingual, bicultural facilitators, familiar with the life issues of Puertorriqueñas in Hartford's barrio, and trained in sexuality, counseling, psychology, history, and support-building.

In "Cosas," there is a strong emphasis on generating educational outreach materials on various topics selected by the group, which is the last of the three components of the overall Mujeres en Acción Pro Salud Reproductiva Project. In contrast to the majority of resources that exist for Latina women about reproduction, these materials are bilingual and bicultural and focus on women's symptoms rather than on medically defined conditions. They use familiar words, traditional idioms, and cultural symbols and include graphics that clearly illustrate the problems described. Many materials developed in the project avoid the traditional handout or pamphlet format in an effort to make them more appropriate to the cultural and social background of poor and working Puertorriqueñas. For instance, the most recent "Cosas" group designed and made their own poster and T-shirts. With the words "Cosas de Mujeres" painted down the side in brightly colored lettering, the T-shirts and posters celebrate Puertorriqueñas as "luchadoras y valientes" (fighters and courageous survivors) who will continue to fight, struggle, and survive no matter what. Ultimately, the strength of all the materials stems from the input and feedback of the group participants as well as the project staff who work with these and other Puerto Rican women every day. The production of these materials in and of itself has been an empowering process for the women, since these materials will be sold as a means of generating income for the group so that it can become self-sustaining at the end of project funding.

Origin of Mujeres en Acción Pro Salud Reproductiva

The Mujeres en Acción Pro Salud Reproductiva Project is the product of a long history of work conducted by the Hispanic Health Council on Puerto Rican Women and Reproduction. This work began in 1979, when a health needs assessment conducted by the Council found that over 50 percent of Puerto Rican women from a random sample of 153 households in Hartford had been sterilized, revealing one of the highest sterilization rates in the world.[10] Council staff subsequently conducted in-depth inteviews with a sub-sample to find out why women had undergone la operación (sterilization) and under what circumstances. Four reasons were identified: medical (46 percent), the desire not to have more children due to housing/economic difficulties (42 percent), family-related issues (7 percent), and doctor's decision (5 percent). Medical reasons included past history of birth-control problems, pregnancy-related problems, numerous Caesarean births, other reproductive problems, and chronic problems like asthma which became worse during pregnancy. Family issues included women's concern about the poor health of their children, and a feeling that partners were not "living up to their standards." Doctor's decision meant women were sterilized at the recommendation of a physician for some medical problem.

One of the most blatant examples of women's vulnerability was the fact that many women (some as young as 22 years of age) were using la operación as a birth control method because they understood it to be reversible, that their tubes "could be untied" just as easily as they "had been tied." Also, the study found that it was first suggested to many women that they should have la operación just after they had gone through the agony of a long, hard delivery. Others were not able to understand what was being explained, the consequences of the procedure, or potential alternatives. One woman reported that she was sterilized and told about it by her doctor two days later.

Until the ongoing Mujeres en Acción Pro Salud Reproductiva Project, the Council was not able to obtain support to look further into the kinds of health problems that lead Puerto Rican women to be sterilized, nor how women were coping with these medical problems. The Council did, however, publicize its findings, and was able to bring about a policy change at the main hospital in Hartford used by Puerto Ricans. The new policy mandates that doctors not discuss sterilization with women within the month prior to or following delivery. Also, several local health care facilities were successfully influenced to hire more bilingual staff who could carefully explain birth control alternatives at out-patient ob-gyn clinics.

Not long after the end of the initial study, the Council received support from the U.S. Department of Health and Human Services for a major national demonstration project called the Comadrona Program. This project was designed to train and organize lay women into groups for information sharing and social support in order to reduce pregnancy risks. The project also offered translation and assistance for pregnant women having problems with the health care system. Other projects subsequently developed by the Council that focused on reproduction include: a) Project APOYO, designed to support Latina mothers whose infants were hospitalized in neonatal intensive care; b) Clinica Atabex, a permanent reproductive health clinic offering free medical services, reproductive health education, pregnancy testing, birth control, and counseling to Latinas; and c) the Infant Mortality Review Project, a community-centered study of infant deaths in Hartford examining not only biological, but also behavioral, institutional, and social correlates of neonatal mortality.

However, the most important influence on the Mujeres en Acción Pro Salud Reproductiva Project was a women's self-help support group for single mothers run for a full year in 1984 on a voluntary basis by two staff members of the Hispanic Health Council (Flores and Serrano). Known as "Mujeres en Acción," this group met weekly and helped women confront and successfully cope with personal experiences of domestic violence, family conflict, poor self-image, stress, adjustment to the United States, unemployment, and racism. The group functioned as a means by which women could meet new friends, get out of their homes, give and receive support, raise their self-esteem, and obtain information about their new environment, including available community resources and services. "We wanted them to see that there were alternatives to staying isolated in their homes." In the words of Mariá Serrano, one of the founders, "We wanted to raise their self-awareness so that their sense of self-worth and self-esteem would improve."

Additionally, "Una Carta a la Mujer" (A Letter To Women) was developed by the facilitators and printed in Spanish language newspapers and flyers for distribution to the community. Written in clear, popular Spanish, the letter urged women who felt "confused, depressed, and isolated" to "come and join the group." Free child care and transportation were provided to all participants. For Thanksgiving, turkeys were given to all participants, and for Christmas, gifts were purchased for each of their children. This approach, expressed by the cultural concept of *personalismo,* was essential to the success of the project. Such concern indicated to participants that the facilitators cared about them as people and functioned to create enduring bonds while enhancing group solidarity. Although most of the participants have since moved to other cities including back to Puerto Rico (reflecting the high rate of geographic mobility in the Puerto Rican population), a few remain. Facilitators continue to maintain contact with these women and their families, and are planning a reunion for them and for the current participants of "Cosas de Mujeres."

The founders of "Mujeres en Acción" were single parents with children. Both had undergone many of the same personal struggles experienced by program participants. The shared experience of facilitators and participants was central to the success of the group. The women came to feel comfortable talking about painful and embarrassing experiences, learned from one another, and drew strength from the knowledge that they were not alone. Seeing that other women, women whom they had come to admire and respect, had gone through similar experiences helped them to overcome the guilt and sense of shame they had endured. In the process, the women began to redefine themselves and their place in the world.

Women in consciousness-raising groups were not simply giving voice to already formulated women's perspectives; they were creatively constructing them. In telling stories about their experiences, they were giving them meanings other than those granted by patriarchy, which sees women only as seductresses or wives, as good or bad mothers.

Many women in the group began to demonstrate their new strength by saying they wanted to "take better care of themselves" and to "be concerned" about how they presented themselves to others. By the end of the year, some had decided to go back for a G.E.D. (the equivalent of a high school diploma); others taught themselves or learned English through ESL programs. Some women left abusive family situations, and others became economically and emotionally independent.

Development of "Cosas de Mujeres" Support Group Model

"Cosas de Mujeres" utilized many of the same strategies as "Mujeres en Acción" in recruiting women and involving them in the difficult process of unraveling their social conditioning as women and reweaving the strands into a new, healthy image of Puerto Rican femaleness. At the outset, what differed for "Cosas de Mujeres" was that it centered on sexuality and the body as the first step in empowering women to articulate their unique identities and to reclaim their rights as Puerto Rican women.

A.L.A.S. had utilized this approach through their *encuentros* in Boston, as had several other feminist Latina groups overseas (Taller Salud, Cidhal). Other groups, such as Mujeres Unidas and the Comité de Mujeres Puertorriqueñas Miriam Lopez Perez, also in the Boston area, had centered on domestic violence as a catalyst in changing women's views of themselves through a focus on the body. In Hartford, there were few comparable efforts, although there were two groups—a support group based at the Sexual Assault Crisis Center for Latina survivors of abuse and a therapeutic support group for Latinas being run by one of the "Cosas" facilitators at the Hartford Community Mental Health Center—that had some parallel objectives. There was also the work of one of the authors (Rivera) in individual and group therapy at Hartford High School, but with adolescents rather than adults.

"Cosas" had to deal with the fact that emigration has had negative effects on the psychological and physical health of Latinas. Coupled with forced economic exodus from the island were the pressures and strains of acculturation and the deterioration of supportive interpersonal networks. It was therefore not surprising that among Puerto Rican women there was a high incidence of depression, somatization, *nervios* (nerves), anxiety, feelings of powerlessness, fear of losing control, inadequacy, negative self-appraisal, frustration, and anger.

It was clear that in order for Puerto Rican women to change their lives, they had to confront and struggle against two forms of colonialism and oppression—the socio-political systems imposed on Puerto Rico first by Spain and later by the United States. They also had to fight the religious and cultural values stemming from and perpetuated by these systems. Puerto Rican women have been socialized to subservience through the education system as well as through their role and status as women of color in the United States. They have been taught to believe that they are inept, incapable, and unworthy of aspiring to positions of societal power. Confronted with double standards and conflicting messages about personal and cultural identity as well as acceptable norms of behavior, Puerto Rican women harbor strong feelings of self-criticism and self-blame for the negative experiences they endure. Despite this bleak reality, however, Puertorriqueñas have not surrendered, nor have they been passive receptors in the process.

With all of this in mind, we developed a set of topics and distributed them during the first session, along with a personal questionnaire about their social and demographic situation and background. It was explained from the beginning that, while the group could continue to meet at the Hispanic Health Council, formal facilitation by the organizers would last only for 10 weeks. During the first cycle, the most commonly requested themes were: a woman's body and its functions, changes in a woman's body, health and sexuality, STDs, AIDS, the history of Puerto Rican women, violence against women, and cultural and socio-political sensitivity-building.

For each session the facilitators created a message, or slogan, capturing the essence of what they wanted the women to think about and to serve as a symbolic support for helping them change their views of themselves and their bodies. Slogans included: "Mujeres Puertorriqueñas: Luchadoras y Valientes" ("Puerto Rican Women: The Brave and Struggling Survivors"); "Recordemos la Dignidad de Ser Mujer" ("Let Us Always Remember the Dignity of Being Female"); "La persona oprimida tiende a tener un cuadro distorcionado de su situación en el mundo en el que vive" ("A person who is oppressed will have a distorted view of her situation in the world in which she lives"); "Tengo derecho a conocer mi cuerpo" ("I have the right to know my body"); "No hay peor lucha que la que no se pelea" ("There is no worse cause than the one you don't fight for"); and "Altas tasas de depresión de la mujer estan relacionadas con que está siendo violentada y ultrajada por la sociedad" ("High rates of depression among women are directly related to the fact that they are being abused and violated by society").

The facilitators would state the slogan at the beginning of each session and integrate it into the discussion throughout the evening. At the end of the session the facilitators would encourage the women to call out the slogan together with them and, finally, encourage them to call it out in loud voices. This exercise was done to reaffirm what had been discussed during the session, but, more importantly, to instill a sense of unity within the group.

"Cosas de Mujeres" also entailed the women's participation in wider social actions, as well as activities they had planned and organized. For instance, the women chose to be part of the "March for the Decolonization of Puerto Rico," held in New York on August 12, 1989. None of the women had ever taken part in a demonstration before. They designed and painted a large banner with a message of support for the referendum of self-determination with "Cosas de Mujeres" across the bottom. They also wore the T-shirts they had made. As a contingent, they received much attention from the press and other organizations. This event was an opportunity for the women to try out and put into practice the information they had been learning, and it also symbolized their consolidation as a group. The march boosted the entire group's self-esteem and confidence and was another significant marker along the road to empowerment.

We are currently facilitating the transition of the first group of "Cosas de Mujeres" participants into other self-affirming activities before doing outreach for the next cycle of "Cosas." This has been the most difficult aspect of the project since many of the women wanted to continue with the group. As one woman commented at the end of the "Cosas" graduation ceremony, "You'll never get rid of me. You cannot close the door on me. I will do anything I can to keep on...You see, we are luchadoras y valientes."

Facilitators placed a strong emphasis on the need to prevent dependency; they encouraged the women to find ways to support one another and utilize what they had learned throughout the summer to confront issues on their own in their personal lives. There is also a commitment on the part of facilitators to ensure that the women were "not left hanging," and that they became involved in other community activities as well as leaders in their own right. Still, carrying through the follow-up work is a difficult task since many of the women are in a general state of crisis. As one of us recently commented to a local newspaper reporter wondering why Latinas aren't more involved in the abortion issue: "Puerto Rican women live in crisis. They have to react to so many outside pressures—housing problems, feeding their children, dealing with transportation issues, helping a family member out of jail. You name it, they're dealing with it. They're concentrating on everyday survival. That's what their lives are about. Their own bodies are the last item on their list of priorities, yet their bodies are the first to be abused."

In spite of these difficulties, several members have committed themselves to continuing in the group, in addition to joining new efforts. Almost all of the women have taken part in "Communidad y Responsibilidad," a new AIDS prevention education project at the Hispanic Health Council that trains lay women in AIDS risks and prevention strategies, and offers paid support to them in the organization of home-based *charlas* (educational house meetings of family and neighbors). Others have joined a Puerto Rican feminist collective in a local cultural center called Centro Juan Antonio de Corretjer. Known as "Cimarronas" ("Maroons," in commemoration of female slaves who rebelled against the Spaniards), the collective is engaged in dialogue about the role of women in Puerto Rican history and culture.

Women in "Cosas de Mujeres" felt that the group had played an important part in facilitating their personal growth, and enabling them to have a broader understanding of who they are as women and as Puerto Ricans. It also helped women learn about their bodies in ways that had not been possible before. Finally, "Cosas" helped the women feel they had the right to question their own and others' actions as these related to the body/self, and to be able to analyze such actions in a different ideological framework.

Our experience with both the "Mujeres en Acción Research Project" and "Cosas de Mujeres" demonstrates that there are very real steps which can be taken to empower Puerto Rican women. Doing so involves altering existing relations of power in the home, in the community, and in society. The collective voices of silenced people from all corners of the earth must join in the struggle for social transformation.

Acknowledgements

The authors would like to extend their appreciation and recognition to María Victoria Cruz, Noemí Valentín, and M. Idalí Torres for their many hours of work on the "Cosas de Mujeres" support group effort. Without their help, the project could never have been what it has now become. We also wish to extend our deepest gratitude to Merrill Singer, Ph.D., Director of Research at the Hispanic Health Council, for his excellent comments, suggestions, and editorial contributions to this paper. In addition, we are extremely grateful to the funders and funding staff who supported this project: June Zeitlin at the Ford Foundation, Sashi Hohri and Susan Dickler at the Ms. Foundation, Joellen Lambiotte and Carolyn Sauvage-Mar at Joint Foundation Support, June Makela at the Funding Exchange, and Martha Newman at the Fisher Foundation and Wenner-Gren Foundation for anthropological research. Finally, we thank all of the courageous Puerto Rican women with whom we talked, laughed, and cried over the course of this project, and whose inspiration has become a lesson for us all.

Notes

1. Zavala-Martinez, Iris, 1986, "En La Lucha: Economic and Socioemotional Struggles of Puerto Rican Women in the United States." In: *For Crying Out Loud: Women and Poverty in the United States*. New York: Pilgrim Press, pp. 111-124.

2. Boston Women's Health Book Collective, *The New Our Bodies, Our Selves*. New York: Simon and Schuster, 1984, Preface; Rusek, S.B., *The Women's Health Movement*, New York: Praeger, 1978.

3. A.L.A.S., nd, unpublished manuscript on Latinas and sexuality, Somerville, MA; Rivera, Migdalia, "Sexuality of Latinas: Theoretical Formulations and Therapeutic Implications." Department of Education, University of Massachusetts. Unpub-

lished manuscript; Espin, Olivia M., 1986, "Cultural and Historical Influences on Sexuality in Hispanic/Latin Women: Implications for Psychotherapy." In: *All American Women: Lines That Divide, Ties That Bind.* "Edited by J.B. Cole. New York: Free Press. pp. 272-284; Soto, Elaine and Philip Shaver, 1982, "Sex-Role Traditionalism, Assertiveness, and Symptoms of Puerto Rican Women Living in the United States." *Hispanic Journal of Behavioral Sciences,* Vol. 4, No. 1:1-19.

4. Davison, Lani, 1989, "Gender and Reproduction Among Puerto Rican Women in Hartford, Connecticut." Paper presented at the Annual Meetings of the American Anthropological Association, Washington, D.C., November 18, 1989; Davison, Lani, Cándida Flores, Migdalia Rivera, M. Idalí Torres, and Zaida Castillo, 1989, "Gender, Life Experience, and Reproductive Illness Among Puerto Rican Women in Hartford, Connecticut." Paper presented at "Primer Congreso Puertorriqueño Mujer y Salud," San Juan, Puerto Rico, November 9-10, 1989.

5. Davison, Lani, "Los Cosas Que Las Mujeres No Hablan: Life Adversity and the Social Construction of Reproductive Illness in a Puerto Rican Community," Ph.D. Dissertation, Dept. of Anthropology, University of Connectcut (in progress).

6. Victor De La Cancela, "Labor Pains: Puerto Rican Males in Transition," *Centro de Estudios Puertorriqueños,* #2 (1988), pp. 40-55.

7. Davison, Lani, 1989, *op. cit.;* Davison, Flores, et al. 1989, *op. cit.*

8. Centro de Estudios Puertorriqueños, 1979, "Labor Migration Under Capitalism. The Puerto Rican Experience." New York: Monthly Review Press.

9. Espin, Olivia M., 1986, *op. cit.;* Zavala-Martinez, Iris, 1988, "En la Lucha: The Economic and Socioemotional Struggles of Puerto Rican Women." In: The *Psychopathology of Everyday: Racism and Sexism.* New York: Harrington Park, pp. 3-25; Comas-Diaz, Lillian, 1982, "Mental Health Needs of Puerto Rican Women in the United States." In: *Work, Family and Health. Latina Women in Transition,* Monograph No. 7, Hispanic Research Center, Fordham University, pp. 1-10; Amaro, Hortensia, 1988, "Considerations for Prevention of HIV Infection Among Hispanic Women," *Psychology of Women Quarterly* 12:429-443.

10. Gonzalez, María, L. Victoria Barrera, Peter Guarnaccia, and Stephen L. Schensul, 1982, " 'La Operación': An Analysis of Sterilization in a Puerto Rican Community of Connecticut." In: *Work, Family and Health: Latina Women in Transition,* Monograph No. 7, Hispanic Research Center, Fordham University, pp. 47-62.

Shared Dreams:
A Left Perspective on Disability Rights and Reproductive Rights[1]

Adrienne Asch and Michelle Fine

Women have the right to abortion for any reason they deem appropriate. Newborns with disabilities have the right to medical treatment whether or not their parent(s) wishes them to be treated. Both rights are unequivocal, consistent, and currently protected by statute. Both sets of rights are, however, under severe attack—the former from the Right and the latter from the Left. And together they have been juxtaposed as a contradiction. We argue here that both sets of rights are essential to preserve and are compatible from a leftist, feminist perspective. In fact, this compatibility forces us to struggle with the reality that in both cases—women's right to abortion and disabled infants' right to treatment—the institutions and services that translate these rights into realities are currently denied appropriate levels of financial and social support, often rendering these rights hollow and irrelevant for those who most need them.

The rights of women to abortion and of newborns with disabilities to medical treatment are, in fact, separate rights that have been linked by the Right in an anti-feminist and allegedly "pro-family" position, and by the Left out of ignorance of the meaning and politics of disability. In this chapter, we review some of the recent controversies over disability rights as they relate to women's right to abortion, amniocentesis, and more generally a Left politic. To make our argument, we cover three topics: (1) the bias against people with disabilities inherent in most of the reasons offered for non-treatment of infants with disabilities; (2) the bias against women and a woman's right to control her own body inherent in the arguments against amniocentesis and abortion of fetuses with disabilities; and (3) the continuing problematic distinction between a fetus residing in the body of a woman and a newborn infant, as it relates to the question: whose body is it anyway? Because the only voices from the Left—including feminist organizations—that have spoken for the rights of ' disabled newborns to treatment have been those publicly identified with the disability rights movement, we turn first to the issues of infants with disabilities. Unfortunately, these voices have been relatively ignored thus far and must be given serious weight in this debate.

Rights of Newborns

In our earlier writing on this subject, we challenged the prevailing assumption in the reproductive rights movement that any woman *would* have an abortion if she were diagnosed as carrying a fetus with a disability.[2] We urged the reproductive rights movement and other feminists not to presume nor prescribe any reason (for example "the tragedy of the 'defective fetus'") for an abortion. Just as we would not advocate the "tragedy of the female fetus" as a legitimate reason for an abortion—many of us abhor the use of abortion for sex selection—activists can not continue to exploit the disabled fetus as the good or compelling reason to keep abortion safe, legal, and funded. Abortion must be safe, legal, and funded on the basis of women's rights alone—not to rid our society of some of its "defective" members.

Recently the controversy has emerged in all its complexity: Baby Jane Doe, an infant born on Long Island with a series of disabling conditions including spina bifida and microcephaly, was denied an operation by her physician and parents acting jointly. Earlier, a Bloomington, Indiana, boy (also called Baby Doe) was born with a diagnosis of Down syndrome and an esophagus unattached to his stomach. Routinely an infant's open esophagus is corrected by surgery, but Baby Doe's parents decided against surgery based on the diagnosis of his mental retardation. Despite some dozen offers of couples to adopt him, Baby Doe died of starvation at six days old. Even more recently and less well known, an infant boy was born in Illinois with a heart problem, and a "hand like a claw." His father, a well-known veterinarian, was handed the baby in the delivery room. On seeing the child he threw it to the floor, killing him. The community has rallied around this man, claiming that everyone has a psychological threshold beyond which he or she is not responsible. For him, it was the presumed tragedy of having a disabled child.

The reasons used to justify denial of medical treatment to these infants have been the reasons given by people who believe that living with a disability is either not worth living, too costly to the family, or too costly to the rest of non-disabled society. But no one ever questions the use of costly treatments to ameliorate or cure all sorts of neonatal medical problems if those procedures result in a perfect, "normal" child. The question arises only when no amount of medical treatment will relieve all of an infant's medical or mental problems, and that infant will remain a person with some level of disability throughout its life. At that point, leftists and feminists have, for the most part, joined in the arguments that such treatment wastes limited societal resources, harms non-disabled parents and siblings, harms society, and does not benefit the child. All these arguments arise from confusing what is inherent in disability with the problems imposed on disabled people by a discriminating society—one without national health insurance or adequate financial and social supports for persons with disabilities, one which prizes profit over human needs and persists in discriminating at the level of medical treatment, education, employment, and housing.

Unacknowledged by those who would deny treatment is this discrimination against people with disabilities. Such prejudice is found throughout the population and thus it is no surprise, although it is dismaying to see people who decry discrimination on the basis of race, ethnicity, gender, sexual orientation, or social class urging that public policy embody their fear, terror, revulsion, and ignorance of disability and people with disabilities. Millions of citizens with biological limitations would assert that their main obstacles to fulfilling lives stem not from these limitations but from a society that stresses mental and physical perfection and rugged individualism, that often rejects, isolates, and segregates them, assuming that disabled people are unpleasant, unhappy, helpless, hopeless, and burdensome.

Such stereotypes lead inevitably to the first of three major arguments given for non-treatment: that the child's quality of life will be intolerable. We ask: intolerable to whom? How do we know? And, if that child's quality of life is less than someone else's, how much do we as a society contribute to its impoverishment by denying needed health care, education, independent living, rehabilitation, and social supports to ensure a better life? We do not know what the lives of any children will be like when they are born. People who decide that Down syndrome or spina bifida automatically renders children or adults "vegetables" or "better off dead" simply know nothing about the lives of such people today—much less what those lives could be in a more inclusive, person-oriented society.

Persons with Down syndrome or spina bifida represent a broad range of potential. Many lead intellectually, economically, socially, and sexually fulfilling lives. Others don't. We don't know how they would live in a society that did not systematically deprive children of opportunity if they do not meet norms of appearance, intelligence, and autonomy. Some parents who gave their children with Down syndrome cosmetic surgery have found that their children's social and intellectual skills improved once they no longer carried the stigma of "Mongoloid" appearance. We cannot separate the essence of disability from the social construction of disability, and we must continue to struggle to ensure a life free of the kinds of oppressions we have described so that disability can refer to the physical or mental limitation alone.

The second major argument against treatment is that even if the child could have a "meaningful" life, its presence would unduly burden or deprive non-disabled family members. Some feminists have argued that deinstitutionalizing disabled people and saving disabled newborns constitute yet another means by the Right to keep women in their homes, bearing the "double burden" of the pathetic disabled child. Women, it is argued, are oppressed by deinstitutionalization and medical treatment to ensure life for infants with disabilities, and siblings will resent the attention and emotional and financial resources given to the disabled child.

This argument is based on the assumption that disabled children contribute nothing to family life, which even in today's society can be denied by thousands of parents and siblings who attest to the pleasures as well as the problems of living with disabled people. Moreover, it blames the disabled child and suggests eliminating that child, rather than blaming society for causing problems of inadequate resources for all. In the United States it is often quite expensive to care for a child with a disability, but sometimes it is not. When it is, we must struggle politically for well-funded medical, social, and caretaking public programs. We can neither locate the problem inside the child with the disability nor the solution with the individual mother of that child. In Sweden, national health care and a full range of social services enable parents of disabled children to easily partake in infant stimulation programs, integrated day care and schools, respite care, and a host of other services that contribute to their lives and their children's lives. Adult relationships do not flounder; siblings without disabilities are not neglected. A supportive context diminishes the alleged negative impact—which we contend is massively overestimated—of having a child with a disability. We would also argue, however, that a parent unable or unwilling today to care for a child with a disability be offered the option of placing the child up for adoption or in foster care temporarily, and we would agitate for adoption agencies to recruit actively and to aggressively support adults interested in adopting or providing foster care for a child with a disability.

We come to the last argument against treating newborns with disabilities: society's resources are limited already and should thus not be spent on people who cannot measure up to the standards of what we think people should be. Obviously, this argument rests on our first point—the assumption that disabled people cannot have a valuable existence. It also assumes that society's resources are limited rather than misallocated. We know that under current political arrangements, military spending grossly overshadows spending for social programs. Saying that we should not treat disabled children because resources are scarce, existing services inadequate, and futures uncertain is like saying that poor people and Black people should not have children because society is hostile to poverty and deeply racist. No progressive would accept that. Nor should it be accepted where children with disabilities are concerned. We should all fight to transform social arrangements and allocation of resources so that needs are better met for all of us.

Progressives should fight not against deinstitutionalizing disabled people, as some have, and not against treatment for Baby Janes, as many have, but for community based residential centers, independent living policies, educational and employment opportunities, and the civil rights of all disabled children and adults. All the arguments against treatment rest on the assumption that disabled people are less than human. It is this assumption that should be questioned, not the rights of these children and adults to the societal goods to which the non-disabled members of the community are entitled.

We believe that all children with disabilities deserve treatment regardless of parental wishes. How then can we support a woman's unquestioned right to an abortion if that abortion may stem from learning that the fetus being carried has a disability? We do so because we believe that abortion of a fetus and killing an infant are fundamentally different acts.

Women's Right to Abortion

Women have won the right to abortion as a part of the right to control their bodies. As a society, we have decided that women are not simply vessels to reproduce the species. While a fetus resides within her, a woman must retain the right to decide what happens to her body and her life. Otherwise we ask that women bear not just unwanted children, but also the unnecessary physical and psychic burdens of sexual acts, burdens that men do not share. Since we have decided that each heterosexual act need not be linked in mind or fact to reproduction, we must permit women to decide what becomes of their bodies and lives during a pregnancy.

When a woman decides that she wants to abort, rather than carry to term a fetus with Down syndrome, she makes a statement about how she thinks such a child would affect her life and what she wants from rearing a child. Every woman has the right to make this decision in whatever way she needs, but the more information she has, the better her decision can be. Genetic counselors, physicians, and all others involved with assisting women during amniocentesis should gain and provide far more and very different information about life with disabilities than is customarily available. Given proper information about how disabled children and adults live, many women might not choose to abort. And many will still choose to abort. While a fetus resides within her, a woman has the right to decide about her body and her life and to terminate a pregnancy for this or any other reason.

May we argue that a woman has a right to abort a fetus diagnosed with Down syndrome but also that an infant with Down syndrome has a right to treatment despite her or his parents' desires? Yes, we can and do. We must recognize the crucial "line" separating the fetus—residing in the body of her mother—and the infant, viable outside the womb. The fetus depends on the mother for sustenance and nourishment. We argue that the "line" of birth makes an enormous difference. Once that living being survives outside the mother, that mother cannot eliminate it because it does not meet her physical and mental specifications. As a society, our Constitution accepts personhood as starting at birth. We cannot simply decide that "defective" persons are not really persons and not entitled to all the care and protection we grant other citizens.

The existing laws against murder, the recently passed child abuse amendments of 1984, as well as the provisions of Section 504 of the Rehabilitation Act, prohibit institutions and parents from withholding treatment to persons merely because those persons have disabilities.[3] If parents and doctors would use the disability of a newborn as a reason to withhold treatment and nourishment, and if such treatment and nourishment would permit life for that infant—not a dying infant but an infant with a disability—the social collective as a whole and not the individual parent(s) bears the responsibility for that infant's protection. Parents do not have unlimited rights over their children. Children are not their property. Just as state and federal laws now protect children from parental abuse and just as courts have intervened to insist upon medical care and education for minors when their parents oppose these for religious reasons, the federal government can appropriately intervene to protect newborns from being killed because their parents and doctors find them inconvenient, distasteful, and/or burdensome.

Some will say that the government should not intervene in this private family matter—contending that parents are suffering a tragedy, that they are already going through a terrible time, and that they should be left alone. Socialist-feminists have learned to be wary of such privacy-of-the-family arguments, aware that the family as we've known it has long been abusive to women and children. Grief-stricken, shocked, and anxious parents who may seek to end the lives of their "imperfect" infants should be counseled, educated, and told that the child will receive treatment whether or not the parent(s) agrees. We should work toward a policy in which the government picks up the medical expenses associated with such treatment; where parents are given extensive information about what it means to have a disability, have access to disability rights organizations and parents' groups, and are assured of informed consent in which they are informed that should they wish they can put their infant up for adoption or foster care.

Parents may be removed *if they so desire* from responsibility, at which point the state acts to protect infants. If non-treatment is contemplated when treatment would benefit the child, it should be rendered nonetheless. If state intervention is necessary to ensure treatment, then we should opt for state intervention. We already opt for state intervention in all manner of other situations where one person's or group's rights are infringed upon by another. Denial of treatment means denial of life, the most basic right of all.

This argument for treatment of newborns is not the same as that of the Reagan administration or the Right to Life movement. Unlike these supporters of the disabled—who care about them only when they are in the intensive care nursery and who slash budgets for needed educational programs for them and try to deny them civil rights to education, housing, and employment once out of the nursery—we believe that the government has major responsibility for assisting disabled children and their families throughout life. Not only does the government have the obligation to absorb the medical and social service expenses that children with disabilities entail, it has the obligation to provide parents with extensive information about life with a disability. In addition, the government must assist parents in finding alternative homes for children if parents do not feel prepared to raise them.

Information about disabilities must include materials developed by parents of similarly disabled children and advocacy groups of disabled adults. It cannot merely consist of medical, diagnostic, or prognostic information without including facts about the social meaning of disability and the ways people manage in today's world. Disabled adults are among the most important advocates for disabled children, and they must participate in any decisions about the lives and policies affecting the lives of these children.

Like feminism, the disability rights movement entails a commitment to self-determination and a shared sense of community, recognizing that the one is meaningless without the other. Thus, as disabled adults increasingly advocate for the rights of children with disabilities, they seek to ally with feminists and others on the Left to grapple with remaining questions. In short, they seek to put forward a shared dream of a just and inclusive society.

When disability rights groups and the American Academy of Pediatrics put forward a statement on the rights of newborns to treatment in November 1983, no known progressive or feminist groups signed the document. We urge that all of us on the Left rethink positions taken out of deep-seated terror and repugnance at disability and out of almost equally deep-seated—but in this case knee-jerk—opposition to the Right's attack on women and the pro-choice movement. We have conceded the issue of disability to the Right. We can and must commit ourselves to the lives of newborns with disabilities while protecting our hard-won gains as women.

New political contradictions will emerge in this struggle: for example, how to mobilize against physicians and medical researchers who systematically prolong the lives of dying infants in order to afford expensive equipment, research laboratories, and sophisticated technology at the expense of the pain and finances of the parent(s) involved; how to deal with late abortions, viable disabled infants who survive abortion procedures or could be kept alive with new technological interventions; or how to deal with infant disabilities that may arise because a woman refused some form of medical intervention during delivery (for example, a woman recently refused a Caesarean section recommended because of an active vaginal herpes sore, producing a now blind infant). Such questions cannot halt us but must be incorporated into our political struggles as contradictions always have been.[4] Indeed if we can create a society that supports the newborn with a disability, perhaps the most defenseless of all citizens, we can create a society humane enough and just enough for us all.

Notes

1. This article appeared originally in *Radical America* 18(4):51-58 (1984). Reprinted by permission.

2. Michelle Fine and Adrienne Asch, *Reproductive Rights Newsletter,* November 1982.

3. In *Bowen v. American Hospital Association* et al., 106 S.Ct. 2101 (1986), the U.S. Supreme Court ruled that Section 504 of the Rehabilitation Act did not apply to instances in which parents and physicians agreed on the particular course of medical treatment or non-treatment. The Court reasoned that because Section 504 applied to the conduct of institutions, the statute did not cover situations in which hospitals acceded to parental wishes. The Court indicated, however, that if a hospital regularly brings proceedings when parents refuse "medically necessary" treatment, but fails to do so in the case of a severely disabled child, such inaction by that hospital would appear to constitute illegal discrimination.

4. For a detailed feminist discussion of emerging issues in reproductive technology, see S. Cohen and N. Taub, *Reproductive Laws for the 1990s* (Clifton, N.J.: Humana Press, 1988). See, in particular, A. Asch, "Reproductive Technologies and Disability," for a full-scale treatment of how these emerging issues affect the disabled population.

The Abortion/Baby Doe Controversy: A Disability Perspective[1]

Marian Blackwell-Stratten, Mary Lou Breslin, Arlene Byrnne Mayerson, Susan Bailey

Just as the mothers of disabled children have a different perspective when considering parenting issues, so too do disabled women have a different perspective when examining abortion rights and the Baby Doe controversy. The disabled woman is concerned not only with abortion rights but also with the right to be free from involuntary sterilization. Further, the Baby Doe controversy involves the disabled woman both as a parent or potential parent and as a disability rights advocate.

The disabled woman's concern with the right to be free from involuntary sterilization stems from an important difference in the social roles of disabled and non-disabled women. In the past, feminists have struggled with being cast only in the limited role of mothers. As a U.S. Supreme Court case justifying the enactment of protective work legislation for women stated, "And as healthy mothers are essential to vigorous offspring, the physical well being of women becomes an object of public interest and care in order to preserve the strength and vigor of the race."[2]

The perception that women are weaker than men and are to be seen primarily as mothers has sometimes resulted in protective legislation. Disabled women, however, have never been considered fit as mothers. One psychologist comments, "Historically, child custody suits almost always have ended with custody being awarded to the non-disabled parent, regardless of whether affection or socio-economic advantages could have been offered by the disabled parent."[3] The presumed inferiority of the disabled person has been translated frequently into social policy that condones the involuntary sterilization of mentally retarded boys and girls. In 1930, for example, 28 states had sterilization statutes on the books.[4] In light of this history, it is imperative that reproductive rights activists advocate social policy that insures all women the right to decide whether or not to have a child.

The second issue, the Baby Doe controversy, is a hotly contested debate involving the right of a parent to withhold life-sustaining medical treatment from a severely disabled infant. In "Baby Doe" situations, the infant is born with a severe disability and needs medical attention to survive. If given, the medical treatment will prolong the life of the child, but it will not lessen the child's disability. An example is that of an infant with Down syndrome. She or he has a permanent mental impairment that may range from mild to severe. Let us say that shortly after birth the infant develops a blood infection and needs medical treatment to save its life. But the treatment, which may be very expensive, will not lessen the infant's mental impairment. These parents decide they would rather withhold treatment, thus pitting their right to privacy in making decisions regarding the welfare of their child against the right of the disabled child to live. Part of the parents' rationale for withholding medical treatment relies on the telethon "disability as tragedy" theory. That theory holds that a disabled infant imposes such an emotional and financial burden on the family that the state has no right to prohibit the parents from relieving themselves of the burden. Viewed from the parents' perspective, the argument appears compelling. Take away the blinders imposed by the "disability as tragedy" theory, however, and the Baby Doe issue becomes a clear-cut case of civil rights. Viewed from a civil rights perspective, a disabled infant should not receive a different standard of medical care solely because of her or his disability. If a non-disabled infant developed a blood infection, there would be no question of a right to life-sustaining medical treatment.

In a recent case involving the validity of regulations prohibiting discriminatory treatment of disabled newborns, two public-interest law firms representing disability rights and women's rights[5] filed a joint friend-of-the-court brief. They argued that the civil rights protections that apply to disabled adults should also apply to disabled infants, noting that the outdated stereotypes once used to exclude women and minorities from medical care (society's perception that women and minorities are "subhuman," "sick," or "inferior") are now used to limit a disabled infant's right to medical care.[6]

The cooperation between the women's movement and the disability rights movement in the Baby Doe controversy illustrates how effectively coalition work can function when viewed in the context of civil rights.

Notes

1. This article is excerpted from "Smashing Icons: Disabled Women and the Disability and Women's Movements" by Marian Blackwell-Stratten, Mary Lou Breslin, Arlene Byrnne Mayerson, and Susan Bailey; in *Women With Disabilities: Essays in Psychology, Culture, and Politics,* edited by Michelle Fine and Adrienne Asch, Temple University Press, 1988. Reprinted by permission.

2. *Muller v. Oregon,* 208 U.S. 412 (1908).

3. Vash, C., 1981. *The Psychology of Disability.* New York: Springer.

4. Burgdorf, R. and M. Burgdorf, 1977. "The Wicked Witch Is Almost Dead: Buck v. Bell," *Temple Law Quarterly,* 50:995.

5. The Disability Rights, Education and Defense Fund and the Women's Defense Fund.

6. *Brief of Amici Curie for Petitioners, Margaret M. Heckler v. American Hospitals Association,* no. 84-1529 (2. Cir. 1985) Cert. Granted.

Women's Reproductive Rights in the Age of AIDS: New Threats to Informed Choice[1]

Hortensia Amaro

My personal passage in the last three years through the sickness and death of my closest sibling, my brother Armando, brought AIDS "home" at a very intimate level. My research in the last six years on drug use among adolescent girls and women in the inner city, and more recently my research on prevention of HIV infection among Black and Latina women, has also brought me in painful touch with the devastating effects of this epidemic on individual women, their families, and communities. These experiences in my personal and work life have included a profound sense of frustration with the inadequacies of policy, research, and services directed at the prevention of the spread of HIV infection and with the inadequacy of the services available for those most directly affected, especially the women most at risk for HIV infection.

The AIDS epidemic has had a severe impact on women's reproductive choices and poses new threats to reproductive rights. There are specific policy issues which affect women's reproductive services and choices, and which are unique to the over 100,000 women estimated to be infected with HIV (according to the *Public Health Service, 1988*) and the approximately 4,000 women currently diagnosed and living with AIDS in the United States.

As the most disenfranchised of all groups affected by HIV infection and AIDS, women have also been among the most ignored groups in this epidemic. But the effect of this epidemic on women is potentially very broad. HIV infection and AIDS are new and fertile soil for encroaching on the reproductive rights of women in general. The curtailment of the rights of women has been facilitated by the public's fear of AIDS, by the stigma associated with this illness, and by the fact that AIDS is increasingly a public health problem that affects women who are disen-

Women and AIDS

100,000 women are infected with HIV; 11.4 million women are in the highest risk categories.

Women with AIDS are primarily Black (52%) and Latina (20%), the majority (76%) between the ages of 13 and 39.

In New York City, AIDS is the leading cause of death for women aged 25-34.

AIDS among women is growing, as reflected in yearly incidence rates of diagnosed AIDS cases: 1981, women were 3%; 1985, 6.6%; 1988, 10.3%; 1989, 11.1%. In certain states the rates are much higher. In New Jersey, Connecticut, Puerto Rico, New York, 12-20%.

Infected needles and paraphernalia used in shooting intravenously-injected drugs are the primary route of transmission for women—52% of women with AIDS are infected this way; 61% are infected through heterosexual contact with an infected partner.[2]

franchised, based not only on their gender but also on their social class, ethnicity, and addiction.

The response to AIDS as a public health problem in this country has been thwarted by a climate of societal, political, and judicial conservatism and a period of economic crisis, budget cutbacks, and reduction of social programs. This social and political context has framed our national response—or lack of response—not only to the AIDS epidemic overall but also to the specific concerns of women in this epidemic.

Women with AIDS and at risk for HIV infection are distinctly different in key demographic, social, economic, and health characteristics from most men diagnosed with AIDS.[3]

The AIDS epidemic among women is one which affects primarily poor and minority women whose lives are affected by their own addiction or their partners' addiction. This picture contrasts directly with the profile of the majority of men diagnosed with AIDS, among whom the primary route of transmission is sexual contact with another man (81 percent), and who are white (60 percent) and older (67 percent are 13 to 39 years of age). Since most of the women diagnosed with AIDS are poor and have limited access to health care and economic and social resources, the services which they need and the policy issues which have emerged in relation to their illness are unique and need to be considered in research, policy, and program development.

Framework of Current Response to HIV Infection and AIDS Among Women

One distinct way in which women differ from men is their ability to bear children. This simple and important fact has in large part been the lens through which public health issues of women and AIDS have been focused. Women are discussed in scientific or policy questions related to AIDS, as "vessels of infection" and "vectors of perinatal transmission."[4] As a result, much of the attention to issues of women and AIDS has been limited to the role of sex workers in the spread of HIV, to the infection of children during pregnancy, and to pediatric AIDS. While there are many more women than children infected, a disproportionate amount of scientific literature and attention to policy issues is focused on pediatric AIDS in comparison to the problems women face as infected persons.

This perspective fits well into a historical context that has defined women through their reproductive capacity. We can see this in public health and in medicine where women's health is almost exclusively seen as "maternal and child health," that is, those aspects of health related to reproduction, childbearing, and childrearing. In fact, "maternal and child health" refers more to maternal behavior which may adversely impact neonatal growth, infant development, or child health than to the mother's (woman's) health. It is valid and quite important to address health issues related to maternity, and it is also true that in many circumstances the health and well-being of children are closely linked to the health and well-being of mothers. However, women's health is not encompassed solely by this very limited definition of "maternal" health. The consequence of this myopic vision of women is that many women's health issues are never addressed, and women's experiences related to health and health care are rendered invisible.

This way of viewing women is simply a logical extension of how women's health has been (or not been) interpreted in medicine and public health. It is an example of institutional sexism, which, I would argue, is the first factor that has framed this country's response to the prevention of HIV infection and treatment of AIDS in women.

In addition, there are several other factors which play a major role in framing research, policy, and prevention related to women. The second key factor is institutional racism. The fact that the majority of women who have been diagnosed with AIDS and who are infected with HIV are Black and Latina is not insignificant. This society's devaluation and oppression of people of color are central to how issues of AIDS and HIV infection among women are being framed.

A third factor is socio-economic class. While poor women are most affected by AIDS and HIV infection, as with most other problems affecting the poor, they have little say in the priority given to the problems which so brutally shape and, in this case, end their lives.

Finally, societal values and norms which place drug addiction within the realm of morality rather than within the realm of illness have also contributed to the societal response. Entry into drug treatment is jeopardized by multiple obstacles. This is especially the case for women with children or women who are pregnant. There are only a handful of programs nationally that accept pregnant women or can accommodate child care for inpatient treatment. Models for the treatment of drug addiction, especially among women, have received insufficient funding and research attention.[5]

The impact of these factors and biases can be clearly observed in the policies and practices which affect the reproductive choices of women infected with HIV. Attorney Katherine Franke, from the AIDS Discrimination Unit of New York City's Human Rights Commission, notes that the epidemic of stigma surrounding AIDS has unleashed a new wave in the manifestation of racist, classist, sexist, homophobic, and xenophobic notions of morality. These notions of moral superiority have manifested themselves in policy, research, and clinical practices in the treatment of pregnant women at risk and of women who are infected with HIV. These moralistic norms and their applications to AIDS are particularly important not only because they directly infringe on the service needs of women who are infected, but also because they embody a new approach to the limitation of women's reproductive choice.

"Routine Testing" as an Example

One of the most controversial topics in the AIDS epidemic has been the issue of HIV antibody testing. A variety of policies for mandatory testing which affect women are in effect: people requesting a marriage license, people entering the military, people in correctional systems, prostitutes, etc. However, the single policy which will affect the largest group of women at risk is routine counseling and testing of pregnant women and women seeking family planning services (which is called for by the Public Health Service Guidelines).

According to the Public Health Service, the rationale for these guidelines is that "identifying pregnant women with HIV infection as early in pregnancy as possible is important for ensuring appropriate medical care for these women; for planning medical care for their infants; and for providing counseling on family planning, future pregnancies, and the risk of sexual transmission of HIV to others."[6]

There is no question that women have the right to be informed about HIV transmission and the HIV antibody test. There is also no doubt that many women who would benefit from this information do not currently receive it. Knowing whether a woman has been exposed to the AIDS virus can be critical in assisting the health care provider to better plan the prenatal and postpartum care for both the woman and her infant. Yet serious potential dangers also accompany the implementation of "routine counseling and testing" programs. This "routine" approach to testing encourages confidential rather than anonymous testing for the HIV antibody. This means that a woman's HIV antibody status will most likely be part of her medical record, and this information will be available to the many health and social service staff who have access to such records. This practice places the woman at risk for inappropriate disclosures of this information and potentially for discrimination based on knowledge of her antibody status. With anonymous testing, on the other hand, test results are provided only to the individual being tested, and it is then up to the individual's discretion whether to share this information with health care providers and others.

The full extent of the potential misuses of results from confidential testing among high risk women is yet to be seen. However, considering the recent court cases in which women have been charged and sentenced for child abuse and neglect resulting from their use of illicit substances during pregnancy and the enactment of laws in several states and pending bills in 14 other states criminalizing willful transmission of HIV,[7] it is not unforseeable that in the near future women infected with the HIV antibody who become pregnant could be charged by the state (on behalf of the fetus) with intentional homicide or child abuse.

While this may seem like a preposterous or unlikely possibility, we have already seen that concerns with the "rights of the fetus" have been successfully employed to place judicial restrictions on women's physical activities, including mandated Caesarean sections and other medical procedures.

To date, the women most likely to be subjected to court-ordered obstetrical interventions such as Caesarean sections, intrauterine transfusions, and hospital detentions have been women receiving care in teaching-hospital clinics or receiving public assistance, women who are Black or Latina, and women who are non-English speaking.

As medical knowledge progresses in the treatment of perinatal transmission of HIV infection and as treatments with drugs such as AZT become part of standard clinical practice, we are left to wonder whether women could be ordered by courts to submit to these during pregnancy. Many doctors already think that pregnant women who refuse medical advice and "endanger the life of the fetus" should be detained in hospitals or other facilities so as to ensure compliance. They would like to see the precedent set by the courts in cases requiring emergency Ceasarean sections for the sake of the fetus extended to other procedures that are potentially lifesaving for the fetus. In this context, the policy of "routine testing" of pregnant women, instituted in order to ensure that HIV infected women receive appropriate medical care, may eventually render women vulnerable to a judicial battle over what the state regards as the "rights of the fetus."

If women know or suspect that a positive HIV antibody test could be used against them (as in the loss of a job or in the loss of custody through a child abuse or neglect charge), women at most risk of HIV infection may choose not to seek prenatal care or family planning services. If the inappropriate use of HIV antibody tests serves to discourage women from seeking services, the resulting impact on women's health could be serious. Participation in prenatal care is already low in the United States, especially among poor and minority women.[8] For example, in Massachusetts, where there are fewer financial barriers to prenatal care than in other states, more than 40 percent of Black and Latina women receive inadequate prenatal care.[9] Women at most risk for HIV infection, those who use illicit drugs, are the most likely not to receive any prenatal care. At Boston City Hospital, 80 percent of women who delivered after having received no prenatal care were users of cocaine and IV drugs.[10] Testing policies and practices that do not protect women from discriminatory actions and legal liabilities will most likely further deter women at highest risk from seeking prenatal care. Current policies and laws that prohibit discrimination against those infected need to be extended to protect the specific circumstances of infected pregnant women.

Those recommending "routine counseling and testing" say that women will systematically receive counseling regarding testing, that prevention of HIV infection among those not yet infected can be facilitated through counseling before and after testing, and that counseling can result in risk reduction among those infected so as to reduce risk of infecting others.[11] However, due to constraints in staff time and clinic resources, there is a great risk that the "counseling" component of the "routine counseling and testing" program will be shortchanged. For most people, the decision to be tested is very difficult and stressful. It typically involves a series of conversations with a health care professional or counselor who should be well informed and trained in counseling. This person should also be able to devote time during several visits to answering client questions and concerns. Yet the majority of women at risk for HIV infection, who are poor, Black, or Hispanic, and live in the inner city, obtain their prenatal care either at community health clinics or at local public hospitals. Staffing and resources in these health care settings are almost always extremely constrained, and as such, the implementation of "routine counseling and testing" programs in prenatal care poses considerable problems. The wait to obtain a prenatal appointment can be several weeks or even months. Women with appointments wait hours to see a physician. It seems unrealistic to expect that under these circumstances the clinic staff will be able to dedicate the time necessary for adequate counseling.

The risk of testing without counseling is that women will be tested without genuine "informed consent." On the other hand, there may be women who would benefit from being tested who do not get tested because they receive insufficient information or inadequate counseling. In either case, the woman's right to make a decision is hampered or violated.

In order to ensure that women at risk of HIV infection are not denied the right to information or to make their own decision, implementation of "routine counseling and testing" programs needs to be carefully designed.

While counseling is currently reimbursable through Medicaid and alternative test sites, the amount allotted for this service does not allow for the time required to support an individual through a decision about testing or the adjustment to a positive result. More adequate reimbursement for risk reduction counseling, preferably through alternative test sites, is also needed.

There is also a critical need to develop education and counseling strategies that are effective in assisting women to reduce the risk of infection.

Right to Choose: A Double-Edged Sword

In post-test counseling, women who test seropositive are supposed to be provided with information about their "choices and alternatives" to continue or terminate the pregnancy. This includes a presentation of the facts about the probability of infection of the infant, the implications of that for the health, treatment, and care of the infant, and the possible medical effects of pregnancy on the progression of HIV infection and AIDS in the woman herself. The client's ability to care for herself and her child, as well as the sources of social and material support, also need to be explored and discussed.

In practice, post-test counseling often falls short of this ideal, sometimes failing to meet the mental health needs of clients undergoing a crisis and undermining a woman's right to exercise her choice to continue or to terminate her pregnancy. The obstacles for HIV positive women wishing to exercise their right to terminate the pregnancy are the most familiar. The passage of the Hyde Amendment in 1976 and the continued restrictions on the use of Medicaid funds for abortion place a very real obstacle in front of poor women who are infected and who wish to terminate their pregnancies. In addition, the recent decision by the Supreme Court in the *Webster* case makes it constitutional for states to prohibit abortions from being performed in public facilities and will add further barriers to access in some states.

Even when abortion is legally available and when there are no economic barriers to obtaining an abortion, HIV seropositive women face barriers to obtaining abortion services. An investigator from the AIDS Discrimination Division of the Law Enforcement Bureau of the New York City Commission on Human Rights made an appointment for an abortion, identifying herself as a potential client seeking an abortion. After the appointment was made, she disclosed that she had tested HIV antibody positive. Two-thirds of the providers (30 clinics and private doctors) would not keep the appointment for an abortion after a woman identified herself as being HIV positive. The rationale as well as the comments made by providers indicated not only a lack of knowledge about HIV infection but also deep-seated animosity and hostility toward women who are infected.[12] Thus, women who are HIV positive and who seek to terminate their pregnancies face not only possible legal and economic barriers but also discrimination by health care providers.

In addition to the barriers faced by women who want to terminate their pregnancies, the new hitch introduced by AIDS into reproductive rights issues is the potential coercion of HIV positive women into having abortions. While no federal agency has to date recommended directly that HIV positive pregnant women be encouraged to have abortions (which of course would reveal a suspicious philosophical contradiction to federal actions in the realm of abortion during the last decade), statements and recommendations from federal agencies have indirectly pointed in that direction. While federal funds have been severely restricted with respect to counseling women who are *not* HIV infected about "pregnancy options," this restriction has not yet been placed on federally-funded AIDS projects. In fact, among women at risk for HIV, it is not only acceptable but expected that health care providers will do "counseling on options" (i.e., abortion) to pregnancy.

Prenatal testing for HIV is viewed by many in the field as an important strategy for prevention of pediatric AIDS.[13] This policy assumes that the logical response to HIV infection during pregnancy is abortion. In some states, educational materials strongly advise that infected women should choose to abort. Policymakers and providers have assumed that testing women is an effective method for reducing perinatal transmission because they assumed that knowledge of HIV status would discourage women from becoming pregnant. This is not the case. A study in New York City showed that 24 percent of 70 seropositive women and 22 percent of 121 seronegative women became pregnant one or more times after knowing their antibody status. Simply testing women does not result in behavior change. Ongoing education and counseling must be provided in order to assist women in changing risky behaviors and in maintaining behavior change.

The psychological, cultural, and social factors that make pregnancy a rational alternative, even if a woman is HIV seropositive, need to be understood and addressed. For many HIV positive women, a 50-80 percent chance of having a child who is not infected may be the best odds she has ever had. In fact, knowing HIV test results is not a determining factor in women's decision to carry out or terminate a pregnancy.

An HIV positive woman who was a recovering IV drug user told me that her two-year-old son had been diagnosed with ARC and that she wanted to have this baby because it might not be infected. For her, this pregnancy provided hope. For many women infected with HIV or at risk of being infected, AIDS is number 10 on a list of immediate concerns which include addiction, abuse, violence, lack of housing and food, immediate health problems, threat or actual loss of custody of children, and many others.

Involuntary sterilization of infected women and involuntary HIV antibody testing are also proposals likely to receive support from some sectors. A moment of reflection on the history of population control among women in developing nations and forced sterilization among Black and Latina women in the United States should be sufficient to help us recognize that such coercive practices have been employed before and could be employed again among HIV infected women, especially because they are among the most disenfranchised and least capable of fighting back. Supporting these policy directives are attitudinal norms in sectors of our society: that "these women" are dispensable; that they are not fit to be mothers; that they have no right to get pregnant; and that, since they and their babies are going to die anyway, there is no point in their carrying on their pregnancies. These attitudes and judgments, when held by health care professionals who are supposed to be assisting women to make informed decisions regarding their pregnancies and health care, result in coercion (whether it is to terminate their pregnancy or to carry the pregnancy to term) and constitute a violation of a woman's right to make her own decisions in these matters.

AIDS prevention targeted to women at risk must not seek to isolate risk of infection from the social and economic context in which women live. Counseling has to incorporate these concerns and assist women in obtaining the services they need in order to first create sufficient stability in the life of the client that then enables the client to turn her attention to prevention of infection and transmission.

Notes

1. A longer version of this article was presented as an invited address to the Division of the Psychology of Women at the 97th Annual Convention of the American Psychological Association, New Orleans, Louisiana, August 1989.

2. Morgan,W.M. and Curran, J.W. (1986). "Acquired Immunodeficiency Syndrome: Current and Future Trends." *Public Health Reports,* 101, 459-464; Guinan, M.E. and Hardy, A. (1987). "Epidemiology of AIDS in Women in the United States." *Journal of the American Medical Association,* 257(15), 2039-2042.

3. Centers for Disease Control. *HIV/AIDS Surveillance* issued August 1989. U.S. Department of Health and Human Services.

4. Wofsy, C.B. (1987) "HIV Infection In Women." *Journal of the American Medical Association,* 257 (15), 2074-2076; Stephens, P.Clay (1988) "Women and AIDS in the U.S." *New England Journal on Public Policy,* 4 (1), 381-401.

5. Franke, K. M. (1989). *HIV-related Discrimination in Abortion Clinics in New York City.* A report by the AIDS Discrimination Division.

6. "Recommendations for assisting in the Prevention of Perinatal Transmission of human T-lymphotropic virus type III/lymphadenopathy-associated virus and Acquired Immunodeficiency Syndrome. *Morbidity and Mortality Weekly Report* (1985); Vol. 34(48), 721-732.

7. Franke, K.M., "Turning Issues Upside Down," in *AIDS: The Women,* Inez Rieder and Patricia Ruppelt, eds., Cleis Press, 1988, pp. 226-232.

8. Brown, S. S. (1989). "Drawing Women Into Prenatal Care." *Family Planning Perspectives,* 21(2), 73-80.

9. Massachusetts Department of Public Health, Vol. 1, 1989.

10. Keith, personal communication.

11. Centers for Disease Control, "Public Health Service Guidelines for counseling and antibody testing to prevent HIV infection and AIDS," in *New York State Journal of Medicine,* Feb. 1988, Vol. 82, No. 2, pp. 74-76; Minkoff, H.L. & Landesman, S. H. (1988). "The Case for Routinely Offering Prenatal Testing for HIV." *American Journal of Obstetrics and Gynecology,* 159(4), 793-796.

12. Franke (1989), *op. cit.*

13. Wofsy, C.B. (1987), *op. cit.*

Court-Ordered Caesareans: A Growing Concern for Indigent Women[1]

Janean Acevedo Daniels

Health consumers, medical professionals, scholars, and maternal and child health advocates watch with growing alarm as the national Caesarean section rate climbs steadily each year. In 1985, the figure hit 22.7 percent of all live births.[2] While the incidence of C-section is troublesome, this article addresses a related phenomenon that is less widespread but equally problematic: court-ordered Caesarean deliveries. Physicians and hospitals across the country are seeking court orders to perform C-sections that their patients have refused to undergo for a variety of reasons but that the clinicians believe are medically necessary to safeguard the health of the fetus and the mother. In most cases, courts are willing to follow doctors' recommendations and order the surgery, often despite vigorous opposition by the women against whom such orders are directed.

The increase in court-ordered C-sections has coincided with new medical technologies that allow specially-trained physicians to see the fetus, spot abnormalities, and at times correct them. A growing number of these physicians view the fetus as the "second patient" and may view a pregnant woman's refusal to agree to a Caesarean section as irrational.[3] At times, defensive medicine motivates court-ordered C-sections. Some physicians fear that parents will, in the end, sue if the surgery is not performed and the child is harmed. Thus, providers seek the protection of a court order to legitimize their ethical/legal concerns.

Although court orders mandating C-sections are few in number and generally go unnoticed, several cases have been reported in the last few years. Significantly, most cases involve defendants who are mostly low-income and minority women. Courts frequently appoint legal services attorneys to these cases on only a few hours' notice to represent clients in labor.

Because courts are forced to hand down such orders immediately, judges may not have sufficient time to consider the medical facts and legal principles involved. As a result, courts that override a competent woman's refusal to undergo major surgery by ordering C-sections often misinterpret the dictates of *Roe v. Wade* [4] and case law dealing with child neglect and rescue obligations. Furthermore, these court orders do not adequately address the widely recognized right to refuse medical treatment. Finally, court-ordered Caesareans interfere with the personal liberty and autonomy of the women involved in a manner that raises equal protection concerns.

Among the leading indications for Caesarean delivery are dystocia (which relates to problems of fetal position or size and is responsible for 31 percent of all Caesareans); repeat Caesareans (31 percent); breech presentation (12 percent); and fetal distress (5 percent). The indications contributing most heavily to the rise in the overall Caesarean rate are dystocia (contributing 30 percent to the rise), which has become known as a "catch-all" justification for C-sections, and repeat Caesareans (contributing 25-30 percent). Approximately 95 percent of all American women who previously delivered by Caesarean now undergo C-section in any subsequent pregnancy. [5]

In analyzing the socio-economic characteristics of women undergoing Caesareans, studies suggest that the C-section population is distinctly polarized: women who have the highest incidence of Caesarean sections are those with the least and most education, lowest and highest incomes, the youngest and oldest ages, most and fewest pregnancies, those who have public insurance only or who carry the most comprehensive private insurance, those who have had no prenatal care at all and those who have had the most extensive care, and women who use general municipal hospitals and exclusive private hospitals. [6] Expected infant birth weight and gestational age strongly affect who will undergo a Caesarean, with babies 2,500 grams or less and/or 36 weeks or less, and babies 4,500 grams or more and/or over 42 weeks being more likely to be born by Caesarean. The first figure is especially relevant for low-income women, who are likely to deliver premature, low birthweight infants. [7] For women receiving Medicaid, the Caesarean rate is slightly lower than for the general population. This may be attributable, however, to factors such as the younger age of Medicaid recipients giving birth. [8]

In contrast to the general distribution of C-sections overall, C-sections performed pursuant to court order are disproportionately directed toward low-income and minority women. A recent study published in *The New England Journal of Medicine* found that, among 21 requests by doctors and hospitals for court-ordered obstetrical intervention, orders were obtained in 86 percent of the cases. Eighty-one percent of the women involved were Black, Asian, or Hispanic, and 24 percent did not speak English as their primary language. All of the women involved were treated in a teaching hospital clinic or were receiving public assistance. Of the 15 orders sought for C-sections, all but one were granted, and minority women were again involved in greater numbers (47 percent were Black, 33 percent were African or Asian, and only 20 percent were white).[9]

Judicial reliance on child neglect statutes and the common law of rescue to justify compelled Caesareans appears misplaced. Legal scholars[10] and courts[11] have concluded that legislators did not intend for child neglect statutes to cover fetuses. Given the disparity between a parent's relationship to a child and a pregnant woman's relationship to a fetus, relying on child neglect law to justify a C-section may be "inappropriate and grossly oversimplified."[12] Equating a woman's refusal of a Caesarean to fetal neglect is improper, one author explains, because it focuses entirely upon the fetus and ignores the fact that a surgical intrusion upon the woman's body is also involved.[13]

This imagery brings to mind a troubling fact: with judicially compelled Caesareans, courts order a medical procedure, designed to aid another, that risks the health of the individual undergoing the treatment. Under common law, an individual is not ordinarily obligated to aid another who needs assistance unless the individual has a "special relationship" to the imperiled person, such as a parent to a child.[14] Whatever the relationship involved, however, the only rescues that may be legally imposed are those that can be performed without any danger to the rescuer. Yet by ordering Caesarean sections, which involve about four times the mortality rate of vaginal births,[15] courts are requiring women to undergo "risky rescues." Court-ordered Caesareans thus contravene the fundamental principles upon which rescue law is based, including freedom from physical invasion or involuntary physical activity and the right to refuse to subordinate one's preferences and needs to those of another. As one commentator observed, "If this freedom is important, it is as important for the pregnant woman as for anyone else."[16]

An individual's freedom from compelled surgery to aid another is buttressed by yet another legal principle: the right to refuse medical treatment. The right of competent persons to refuse treatment is supported by the common law right to bodily integrity and the constitutional right to privacy[17] and may be asserted even when refusal may result in death.[18]

Some courts, however, have overridden a competent adult's refusal of medical treatment. As one law review article explains, judicially compelled Caesareans ignore the mother's right to self-determination, intruding upon a woman's bodily integrity and violating "the fundamental moral principle that no one should invade or attack the body of another without consent—whether it is with a fist, a bullet, a drug, or a scalpel."[19]

Certainly, the fact that some fetuses may be harmed due to the woman's refusal is troublesome and may be morally unacceptable to those devoted to the protection of fetal life. It is important to recognize, however, that most pregnant woman who eschew Caesarean delivery truly believe, based on deeply held personal or religious convictions, that their decision is the best one for themselves and their babies. Exemplifying this point is the testimony of one judge who refused to order a C-section. The judge based her decision not only on the woman's fear for her health, but on the woman's belief in natural childbirth and her strong intuition that her delivery would turn out fine.[20]

Ordering women to undergo Caesareans also presents equal protection problems, since courts hesitate to impose bodily intrusions on citizens other than pregnant women. Furthermore, the only group of people that the courts can compel to undergo a Caesarean surgery are women. According to one scholar, "fetal rights laws," which allow infringement of a woman's constitutionally protected liberty and privacy interests in order to protect the fetus, "serve to disadvantage women as women by further stigmatizing and penalizing them on the basis of the very characteristics that historically have been used to perpetuate a system of sex inequality."[21]

Time Limitations

Beyond being obvious intrusions into the liberty and privacy interests of pregnant women, judicial proceedings mandating Caesarean delivery suffer from yet another shortcoming. Judges may not have time to consider sufficiently the numerous factors involved in such a decision. When a woman is in active labor and a court must render its opinion within hours, time constraints prevent a thorough examination of the facts and legal issues involved. Attorneys, especially those appointed at the last minute to represent the woman or the fetus, are often caught unprepared[22]; the woman herself will not be present; and the judge must necessarily make a rapid decision. The authors of the previously cited *New England Journal of Medicine* study believe that "the time required to weigh complex relative medical risks and benefits for both mother and fetus and then to balance these against the woman's rights is rarely, if ever, available."[23] In 88 percent of the cases in that survey, court orders were obtained in an hour or less, in some cases by phone.

Compounding the problem of the limited time available in compelled C-section proceedings is the judge's unfamiliarity with the procedure's risks. The judge is thus more likely to defer to the doctor's evaluation, which may or may not be based on current and correct medical data. Judges are usually unaware that C-sections have an average maternal mortality rate four times higher than that of vaginal births (41 deaths per 100,000 births for C-sections, as compared to 10 deaths per 100,000 vaginal births).[24] One study found a 27-fold increase in maternal mortality with Caesareans as compared to vaginal delivery, with one-third of those deaths occurring in cases of repeat C-sections.[25] Caesarean sections also involve five to seven times higher rates of maternal morbidity.[26] Although complications from Caesareans vary, the incidence of postpartum infection increases markedly among low-income women.[27]

The infant also faces greater risks from Caesarean delivery, including higher rates of medically-induced prematurity and respiratory distress.[28] This risk appears to be even higher for low-income and minority women's children, who are more likely to be born prematurely and/or with low birthweight. Data from New York City, for instance, show that for infants weighing less than 2,501 grams, Caesarean delivery presents a consistent neonatal mortality disadvantage as compared with vaginal births.

Medical Uncertainties

Contributing further to the uncertainty in determining the need for surgical delivery is electronic fetal monitoring (EPM), a procedure used increasingly in American obstetrical practice. Experts studying fetal monitoring have concluded that the dramatic rise in the C-section rate is closely related to the use of EPM, which may be responsible for as much as 50 percent of the increase in the Caesarean rate.[29] While 60 to 70 percent of labors in this country are monitored electronically, the machines often provide erroneous data. One comprehensive study of EPM found that the procedure can have a false positive rate (indicating fetal distress when none actually exists) of up to 80 percent.[30] Another investigation noted that doctors reading the same monitor strip disagreed in their decision to intervene surgically for distress in a significant number of cases.[31] Despite these variables, physicians may use EPM readings to bolster their assertions that women refusing Caesareans are endangering their fetuses and must therefore be ordered to undergo the procedure. Most likely, these doctors will succeed in convincing a sympathetic but often misguided judge to issue the order.

While the true impact of court-ordered Caesareans is not yet clear, the potential ramifications are startling. Many women who refuse surgical deliveries for personal or religious reasons may begin avoiding hospital deliveries or prenatal care altogether. In several cases, women who were targets of court-ordered surgery chose to forgo a hospital delivery and risk a home birth. The fact that low-income and minority women are more likely to be compelled by the courts to undergo surgical deliveries is especially troubling since a reluctance to seek prenatal care for fear of possible judicial action could have devastating effects on these women and their babies.

Furthermore, court-ordered Caesareans may be just the first step toward even greater medical and judicial intervention into the lives of pregnant women. Several fetal rights advocates suggest that, in addition to C-section, the law could require fetal surgery in utero, the institution-alization of mothers abusing drugs or alcohol, force-feeding of anorexic or neglectful mothers, compulsory hospital delivery instead of births attended by midwives or undertaken at home, and prenatal screening with a corresponding duty to abort defective fetuses.[32]

As these suggestions make clear, many doctors, lawyers, and judges do not appear to appreciate adequately the degree of intrusion involved in court-ordered obstetrical intervention. This may be due in part to the fact that the women involved have either acquiesced and submitted to surgery or have fled the court order. Perhaps only when reports begin to emerge of women in labor who continue to refuse surgery, requiring doctors to forcibly restrain and anesthetize them, will the true nature of compelled Caesareans become clear.

Notes

1. Reprinted from "Common Ground—Different Planes," The Women of Color Partnership Program Newsletter, December 1988, with permission from the National Health Law Program, which published the original, longer, version of this article in the February 1988 edition of the *National Clearinghouse Review*. For more information, contact Jane Perkins, National Health Law Program, 2639 S. La Ciega Blvd, Los Angeles, Ca. 90034.

2. *California Department of Health Services, Health Data and Statistics Branch, Data Summary, Report Register 87-02113* (Feb, 1987).

3. See Kolder, Gallagher, and Parsons, "Court Ordered Obstetrical Interventions," 316 *New England Journal of Medicine* 1192,1194 (May 7, 1987).

4. *Roe v, Wade*, 410 U.S. 113 (1973).

5. Telephone interview with Selma Taffel, National Center for Health Statistics (Aug. 11, 1987). According to Notzon, Placek and Taffel, "Comparisons of National Caesarean Section Rates," 316 *New England Journal of Medicine* 386 (1987), the U.S. rate of vaginal births after Caesarean (VBACs) (5 percent) is significantly lower than the rate in several European countries, such as Norway (43 percent VBACs), Bavaria (41 percent), and Scotland (39 percent).

6. Marieskand, "An Evaluation of Caesarean Section in the United States (1979)" (available from HHS, Washington, D.C.).

7. Rosenbaum, "The Prevention of Infant Mortality: The Unfulfilled Promise of Federal Health Programs for the Poor," 17 *Clearing House Review* 701, 703 (Nov. 1983).

8. National Institutes of Health, HHS, *Caesarean Childbirth: Report of a Consensus Development Conference* 130 (1981)(Publication No. 82-2067) [herinafter *Caesarean Childbirth*].

9. *Op. cit.*, Kolder, Gallagher, and Parsons.

10. *Ibid.*, See also Nelson, Buggy, and Weil, "Forced Medical Treatment of Pregnant Women: Compelling Each to Live as Seems Good to the Rest," 37 *Hastings Law Journal,* 703 (1986).

11. See e.g., *In re Steven S.,* 126 Cal. App. 3d 23,178 California Reporter 525 (1981); *In re Dittrick Infant,* 80 Mich. App. 219, 263 N.W.2d 37(1977); and *Jefferson,* 247 Ga. at 92 (Smith, J., concurring).

12. Rhoden, "The Judge in the Delivery Room: The Emergence of the Court-Ordered Caesareans," 74 *California Law Review* (1986), supra note 14, at 1960.

13. *Ibid.*, at 1968.

14. W. Keaton, D. Dobbs, R. Keaton, D. Owen, *Prosser and Keaton on the Law of Torts* 37577 (5th ed. 1984) [Herinafter *Prosser and Keaton on Torts*] 375-77.

15. *Caesarean Childbirth,* supra note 8, at 16.

17. *Superintendent of Belchertown State School v. Saikewicz,* 373 Mass. 728, 370 N.E. 2d 417 (1977) (incompetent patient's constitutional right of privacy may be asserted by guardian refusing lifesaving treatment for incompetent person); *In re Quinlan,* 70 N.J. 10, 355 A. 2d 647 (1976) (guardian may claim right of privacy on behalf of comatose patient to terminate life support).

18. *Saikewicz,* 38-73 Mass, at 739, 370 N.E.2d at 424.

19. *Op. cit.*, Nelson, Buggy, and Weil, supra note 15, at 719.

20. *Op. cit.*, Rhoden, supra note 14, at 1959.

21. Johnsen, "The Creation of Fetal Rights: Conflicts with Women's Constitutional Rights to Liberty, Privacy and Equal Protection," 95 *Yale Law Journal* 577, 620 (1986).

22. One attorney appointed to such a case described the chaos in the office as she sent a staff person to buy pantyhose for the unexpected court appearance, the attorney who specialized in tenant cases, began researching the case law on compelled medical procedures. Telephone interview with Gail Kleeman, Staff Attorney, Legal Services of Eastern Missouri, Inc. (July 20, 1987).

23. *Op. cit.*, Kolder, Gallagher, and Parsons, supra note 9 at 1195.

24. *Caesarean Childbirth,* supra note 8, at 255.

25. Evrad and Gold, "Caesarean Section and Maternal Mortality in Rhode Island: Incidence and Risk Factors," 19651975, 50 *Obstetrics and Gynecology* 594 (1977).

26. *Caesarean Childbirth,* supra note 8, at 260.

27. *Ibid.*, at 262.

28. Petitti, Olson, and Williams, "Caesarean Section in California—1960 Through 1975," 133 *American Journal of Obstetrics and Gynecology* 391 (1979).

29. Banta and Thacker, "Assessing the Costs and Benefits of Electronic Fetal Monitoring," 34 *Obstetrics and Gynecology Survey* 627, 631 (1979).

30. *Ibid.*, at 629.

31. Cohen, "Electronic Fetal Monitoring and Clinical Practice," 2 *Medical Decision Making* 79 (1982).

32. See e.g., Shaw, "Conditional Prospective Rights of the Fetus," 5 *Journal of Legal Medicine* 63 (1984); Robertson, "The Right to Procreate and In Utero Fetal Therapy," 3 *Journal of Legal Medicine* 333 (1982); and Myers, "Abuse and Neglect of the Unborn: Can the State Intervene?," 23 *Duquesne Law Review* 1 (1984).

Pregnancy and Drug Use: Incarceration Is Not the Answer[1]

Jacqueline Berrien

With popular attention focused upon the widespread use of crack cocaine and other illegal drugs, government officials at both the national and local levels have advanced myriad proposals to address the problem. Often addicted mothers are young and poor; they are victimized by the twin perils of poverty and racism. The specter of drug-addicted new-borns has caused a public outcry, which has led some lawmakers and law enforcement officials to take punitive measures against women on the basis of their conduct during pregnancy. One recent and disturbing trend among the plethora of government responses has been the effort to sanction, through criminal proceedings, the behavior of women during their pregnancies. These measures are a myopic response to an important public health issue. They frequently compromise or sacrifice important civil rights and liberties, as well as reproductive rights, while undermining the most promising solution to the problem—the provision of prenatal health care and, where medically appropriate, drug treatment tailored to the particular needs of pregnant and postpartum women.

A recent study conducted in 36 hospitals across the country revealed that approximately one in every 10 children born in the United States has been exposed to cocaine or another illegal drug. Doctor Wendy Chavkin, Rockefeller Fellow at the Columbia University School of Public Health, recently reported that the incidence of maternal substance abuse recorded in birth certificates, issued by the city, tripled between 1981 and 1987. Doctor Xylina Bean, Director of the High Risk Infant Follow-up Program at the Martin Luther King-Charles Drew Medical Center, in testimony presented to the California legislature during hearings on maternal substance abuse and fetal development, reported that in a three-year period in Los Angeles County, California, the number of fetal deaths associated with maternal ingestion of drugs rose from nine to 56.

Even though there are numerous indications that the problems of maternal drug use and drug-exposed infants are increasing, there is no parallel increase in the number of drug treatment facilities for pregnant women. A survey conducted under Dr. Chavkin's direction in New York City revealed that over half of the drug treatment facilities in the city refused to treat pregnant women under any circumstances. Dr. Chavkin also found that nearly 90 percent of the city's drug treatment programs refused to accept pregnant Medicaid recipients who were addicted to crack. The National Institute for Drug Abuse recognized over a decade ago that the inability to obtain child care prevents many women from participating in drug treatment programs. Nevertheless, Dr. Chavkin found that only two of 87 drug treatment programs in the city furnished child care for their patients who were parents.

While inner cities have clearly been affected by drug use among pregnant women, the problem is not confined there. Given the paucity of treatment facilities available to women in New York City, one can scarcely imagine the difficulty that a pregnant drug addict must face in obtaining treatment in more remote areas.

The problems of maternal drug use and drug-affected infants do not respect class. The proposed remedies for the problem, however, are far more race-, sex-, and class-conscious and, therefore, warrant careful scrutiny. Some lawmakers, prosecutors, and other public officials have proposed draconian "solutions" to this problem, opting to pursue sensational but shortsighted legislation and prosecutions, or undermining otherwise commendable programs with unnecessarily punitive measures. In every instance, the impact of such legislation will fall most harshly upon poor women and women of color, who are disproportionately dependent upon government-financed health care programs. In many instances, the programs for detection of maternal drug use are targeted primarily, if not exclusively, toward the conduct of these women.

For example, Senator Pete Wilson of California recently introduced legislation that would award grants to the states for the development and implementation of pilot projects for "outreach, education and treatment services concerning substance abuse to pregnant...[and/or] postpartum females and their infants."[2] While the Senator's proposal is laudable in providing funding for education and treatment programs for addicted women and their children, it is, regrettably, accompanied by punitive measures which would, if enforced, undermine the positive features of the proposal. For example, the bill provides that a state must "certif[y] that...it is a crime in such state to abuse a child, and that such abuse includes giving birth to an infant who is addicted or otherwise injured or impaired by the substance abuse of its mother during pregnancy."

Perhaps more alarming, in California, Florida, and Illinois, district attorneys have attempted to prosecute women who have given birth to infants testing positive for the presence of illegal substances. In each instance, the prosecutors attempted to apply existing laws concerning child abuse or drug trafficking in wholly unprecedented ways to criminalize the behavior of women during the pregnancies. In two of these cases, the women were frustrated in their efforts to locate drug treatment facilities that would accept them. Nevertheless, they were subjected to criminal prosecutions on account of their drug use during pregnancy. In another case, the woman was prosecuted on the basis of her alleged failure to furnish necessary care to her "pre-born" child. Her prosecution was triggered, at least partially, by a positive test for amphetamines in the urine of her newborn son. However, the prosecutor identified other behavior which he asserted contributed to the death of her infant, including her "refusal" to follow her physician's orders, which included advice to stay off her feet. There is no indication that the district attorney, in pursuing this novel theory of criminal liability, considered that the woman was a mother and primary caretaker of two small children. Nor did he appear to consider that the woman's poverty prevented her from paying for child care for the duration of her pregnancy. In short, the prosecution proceeded with the case even though this woman could only comply with the physician's recommendation to "stay off her feet" during her pregnancy if she was willing to abandon her care for her children.

While the behavior of pregnant women has, in some cases, led to criminal prosecution, there have been no prosecutorial efforts to arrest men for damage that secondhand cigarette smoke may cause to a fetus; men have not been required to avoid exposure to drugs or chemicals known to cause damage to the sperm; nor have the male partners of pregnant battered women been targeted by prosecutors for their infliction of injuries to the fetus in the course of physically abusing the women. *Ms.* magazine reports that a California district attorney prosecuted a woman, but not her male companion, despite the fact that one of the woman's allegedly harmful actions toward the fetus was to engage in sexual intercourse. Thus, the behavior of pregnant women is subjected to government scrutiny and punishment, but men are spared exposure to criminal sanctions for behavior which is equally or more harmful to the fetus.

Government programs for detecting drug exposure in infants are often objectionable, as well, because they target women who rely upon public health facilities. Lacking private health insurance and access to other funds, women of color are disproportionately dependent upon government-subsidized programs to address their health care needs. In a number of jurisdictions, women in government-subsidized facilities are routinely tested for drug use when women who can afford private health care are not tested under similar circumstances. Not only are the privacy rights of numerous women, the vast majority of whom are *not* drug users, violated by this system, but the system is also discriminatory, exposing poor women to testing and possible detection and prosecution while affluent women are not similarly affected.

Criminal investigations and prosecutions conducted under these circumstances also undermine a woman's relationship to her health care providers and destroy the confidentiality of this relationship. The law generally recognizes that it is important to facilitate honesty between physician and patient and that people must feel free to reveal all information necessary to ensure that their physicians can render appropriate and complete medical treatment. Certainly, if an individual fears that information rendered to a health care provider or facility could be revealed to law enforcement officials, the willingness to reveal potentially incriminating information will be greatly diminished. Predictably, in areas where women have faced criminal prosecutions on account of alleged drug use during pregnancy, health care providers and facilities have reported that some patients have lied to them; others simply refuse to obtain prenatal and other necessary health care.

There is no logical stopping point for efforts to police maternal behavior during pregnancy.[3] While the bulk of recent public attention has been focused upon illegal drug use by women during pregnancy, numerous other substances, including tobacco and alcohol, have also been demonstrated to have the potential to injure the fetus. A recent *New York Times* article discussed the prevalence of fetal alcohol syndrome among children born to Native American women and noted that a tribe "once locked up a pregnant woman who could not stop drinking."[4]

Despite the spread of punitive measures to address this issue, available evidence suggests that this is precisely the wrong approach. While considerable press attention has been devoted to the relationship between maternal drug use and newborn health, far less attention has been devoted to the more general and widespread problem of inadequate prenatal care. In an address to the American Civil Liberties Union's Biennial. Convention, Dr. Maxie Collier, Commissioner of Health of Baltimore, Maryland, observed that "urban settings bring unique problems that impact on the health of their citizens. Poverty is one of the single most important factors that influences health...problems of [racial] discrimination have gravely affected socio-economic status and health status, which are closely connected." Dr. Collier urged that the drug problem be viewed as a public health problem. Similarly, the maternal and infant addiction problem should not be viewed in isolation from its frequent accompaniments: economic deprivation and racial discrimination.

There is an undeniable nexus between race and infant mortality. The Children's Defense Fund (CDF) reported that in 1986, Black infants. were twice as likely as white infants to die before their first birthday, and, in some cities, nearly three times as many Black infants die in the first year of life. The lack of prenatal health care is by far the biggest threat to infant health. It is often exacerbated by poverty, youth, and/or lack of education of the mother. According to the CDF, "[t]he infants most likely to die tend to have been born prematurely, and to weigh less than normal babies; their mothers, often in their teens, tend to have had little or no prenatal care."

There are humane alternatives to the punitive measures appearing in response to the problem of prenatal drug use and fetal drug exposure. The late congressman Mickey Leland of Texas was a chief sponsor of legislation to extend Medicaid coverage to more poor women and infants; he recognized that this measure would help reduce the incidence of infant mortality. Senator Bill Bradley of New Jersey has sponsored the Healthy Birth Act of 1989, which would address many of the prenatal, neonatal, postpartum, and pediatric health care needs of poor people. Congress has also approved increased funding for the supplemental food program for women, infants, and children (WIC). People who are using drugs and the children born by these women must let elected officials know that they approve of humane, rather than punitive measures, and that they would also like to see additional funding directed toward drug treatment generally, and treatment for pregnant women particularly.

Prosecution and incarceration of women will not help anyone. Sensible, humane, and responsible public policy can.

Notes

1. This article originally appeared in "Common Ground—Different Planes," The Women of Color Partnership Program Newsletter, August 1989.

2. See Child Abuse During Pregnancy Prevention Act of 1989, S. 1444.

3. See McNulty, "Pregnancy Police: The Health Policy and Legal Implications of Punishing Pregnant Women for Harm to Their Fetuses," *NYU Review of Law and Social Change, XVI, 277 (1987-88)*.

4. Kolata, "A New Toll from Alcohol Abuse: The Indians' Next Generation," *New York Times,* July 19, 1989.

Punishing Women in the Name of Fetal Rights

- Florida: a 23-year-old woman was charged with child abuse for using cocaine during her pregnancy. There were traces of the drug in the baby's system at birth but no signs of addiction or withdrawal.

- Florida: a woman was arrested for child abuse for one-time cocaine use during pregnancy.

- Massachusetts: a 23-year-old woman was charged with distributing cocaine to a minor—her fetus.

- South Carolina: 18 women have been arrested and charged with either delivery of drugs to a minor or criminal neglect for allegedly using an illegal drug during their pregnancies. One woman spent several days in jail.

- Virginia: a guardian *ad litem* was appointed for the fetus of a pregnant woman in her first trimester of pregnancy in order that the woman be required to: "refrain from acts of commission or omission which tend to endanger the child's life, health or normal development"; specifically, to remain drug-free, keep all medical appointments, and follow through with recommended care instructions.

- Michigan: a young pregnant woman was charged with delivery of cocaine to a minor and second degree child abuse. She is subject to 24 years in prison.

- Washington, D.C.: a judge threatened to lock a woman up for the duration of her pregnancy because she was a cocaine user.

- Tennessee: a husband in the process of divorcing his pregnant wife got a restraining order to keep her from using alcohol or drugs. She is required to provide urine tests to a judge. Her husband has had his driver's license revoked for driving while intoxicated. He, however, is not under similar restrictions.

- Wyoming: a pregnant woman entered a hospital after being badly beaten by her husband. While waiting in the emergency room, she was arrested and jailed for endangering her fetus by drinking alcohol during her pregnancy.

- These cases are just a few examples of a growing trend which may increase significantly as a result of the *Webster* decision, which upheld language in a Missouri law stating that human life begins at conception. Some states will take this as a signal to "protect" fetuses from women.

SOURCE: ACLU Memorandum, from Kathyrn Kolbert, Lynn M. Paltrow, Ellen Goetz (Reproductive Freedom Project) and Kathy Moss (Women's Rights Project), 2/15/90, "Discriminatory Punishment of Pregnant Women" and ACLU Memorandum, "Case Update," 2/7/90 from Lynn Paltrow, Hilary Fox, and Ellen Goetz.

Gender Difference, Fetal Rights, and the Politics of Protectionism: Workplace Issues

Cynthia Daniels

In September 1989, the United States Court of Appeals for the Seventh Circuit upheld a "fetal protection policy" at the Johnson Controls Company in Milwaukee—a policy which excludes all fertile women from work producing automobile batteries, which the company argues poses an unacceptable "potential risk to an unborn child."[1] All women at Johnson Controls are now excluded from this work unless they can produce a doctor's note verifying that they are incapable of having children.

While no one knows how many jobs are now closed to women on the grounds of risk to fetal health, one federal estimate has put the number at 100,000. At least 20 million people nationwide work at jobs involving reproductive hazards.[2] Fears of liability suits have led some employers to screen for pregnancy when hiring women, to require women workers to report their reproductive status or use of contraception to their bosses, or to undergo regular pregnancy tests at work. With 1.5 million women giving birth every year, the potential impact of reproductive hazard policies in the workplace is extremely significant.

The presence of reproductive hazards raises serious policy questions. Is it possible to recognize biological gender difference in the workplace without reinforcing gender inequality? To what extent must the workplace change to accommodate women's ability to bear children? Most pregnant women are deeply concerned about workplace exposures and their lack of protection. Chemical exposures (such as benzene and methylene chloride) can cause infertility, miscarriage, genetic damage, or birth defects. Exposures to radiation (for health care and production workers) can also damage reproductive health. And recent studies of computer workers suggest that women who work more than 20 hours per week on word processors may have an increased risk of miscarriage.

Women are often torn between their fears of birth defects or miscarriage and the economic need to work. In many cases, pregnant women have to fight to get out of hazardous jobs—to be transferred to safer positions during their pregnancies. Fetal protectionism can provide some measure of security to pregnant women faced with immediate threats to their health. At the same time, however, we must ask: what is the political meaning of policies which focus almost exclusively on risks to the fetus and pregnant women, even where risks to male reproductive health are known? Within a "pro-life" era, where control over women's reproductive health is often a question for public debate, and where the answer to risk may be the exclusion of women from the workplace, these issues are of critical importance.

Health, Equity, and Gender Discrimination

Exclusionary policies or "fetal protection policies" have typically taken three forms. First, companies such as American Cyanamid have required women to prove their sterility before employing them in certain areas of work. In 1978, women working in their plant in Willow Island, West Virginia, were notified that they would have to prove that they were sterile in order to keep their jobs working in "hazardous" areas of the company. Five women, faced with the choice between their jobs and their fertility, underwent surgical sterilization in order to maintain their employment and later successfully sued the company on charges of gender discrimination.[3] Other companies which have required women to prove their infertility are Eli Lilly, B.F. Goodrich, Goodrich Chemical, and Bunker Hill Company of Idaho.[4] Until the Johnson Controls decision, the courts had maintained that such restrictive policies are illegal.

Second, more popular exclusionary policies restrict "women of childbearing age" (as defined by the company) from work which the company deems hazardous to women's reproductive health. Eastman Kodak, St. Joseph Zinc, Union Carbide, Dow Chemical, Firestone Tire, General Motors, and Monsanto have all established exclusionary policies which limit or restrict the work of women of childbearing age.[5]

The third and most common form are exclusionary policies which voluntarily or involuntarily exclude pregnant women from doing hazardous work. In 1987, Digital Equipment Corporation instituted such a policy when a study commissioned by them showed that women working in the microchip production rooms ("clean" rooms) experienced a miscarriage rate two times greater than normal. Pregnant women were immediately banned from all areas of work deemed "hazardous" by the company, and free monthly pregnancy tests were offered to women on site. As soon as a woman was identified as pregnant by the company physician, she was pulled from her work in the clean room and transferred into a non-production "service" job.

Across the country, microchip producers followed Digital's lead, banning pregnant women from clean room work and limiting the work of "fertile" women or women of childbearing age. Some companies, such as AT&T, have also instituted "voluntary" transfer policies for pregnant women, who are strongly encouraged to transfer out of their jobs.

The political territory on which these battles are fought is not easily divided by gender or class. Depending upon attitudes towards gender differences, and short- and long-term political strategies, feminists can find themselves on both sides of the argument. The following sections explore the two competing approaches in the contemporary debate.

"Protection?"

Advocates of protection argue that the biological differences between men and women require their differential treatment in the workplace. Historically, this has meant restrictions on night work, lifting weight, or the number of hours women could work. Today, restrictions are tied more closely to pregnancy—from maternity leave to altering job responsibilities for pregnant women. Proponents of protectionism argue that pregnant women are at higher risk in the workplace because of the physiological changes which occur during pregnancy. From this point of view, the recognition of difference is necessary to the achievement of equity, for to treat women the same as men when they are different places women at a disadvantage.[6]

Most advocates of fetal protection policies, however, are not feminists but corporate businessmen who employ women at hazardous work. From the "protectionist" perspective, policies which exclude pregnant or fertile women are part of a continuum of efforts to modify workplace policies in accord with women's childbearing ability. Corporate executives argue that exclusionary policies are simply an extension of such concerns for pregnant women and their children.

Armed with both scientific data and the morally charged language of protecting motherhood, corporate advocates of exclusion argue that women are more vulnerable than men to hazards on the job. Epidemiological studies have focused almost entirely on hazards to the female reproductive system, weighing the "scientific" evidence in favor of protectionism for women only. [7]

Advocates of exclusion, such as businessmen and members of the medical and legal communities, focus almost exclusively on the risk to *fetal* health. As a representative of DuPont stated, "When we remove a woman, it is not to protect her reproductive capacity, but to protect her fetus."[8]

A fetus may be vulnerable to substances "safe" for the pregnant mother. Because a fetus is at highest risk in the first six weeks after conception, when a woman may not know she is pregnant, advocates of exclusionary policies argue that policies should exclude fertile as well as pregnant women. Furthermore, businessmen argue that they must limit their liability through exclusionary policies. As Dr. Robert Klyne of American Cyanamid argued, "The ideal is that the workplace has to be safe for everyone—the man, the woman and the child. In the real world that's totally unachievable without emasculating the chemical industry."[9]

The focus on fetal rights has significantly changed the nature of the debate. Some advocates of exclusion draw a sharp distinction between the interests of the fetus and the interests of the woman. In fact, defenders of fetal protection policies pose the debate as a conflict between women's rights and fetal rights.

Equity?

Opponents of exclusion question the scientific evidence used to "prove" gender difference, namely, that fecund women, but not men, have a special susceptibility to work hazards. They argue that epidemiological studies have been skewed by identifying procreation only with women. The studies that have been done of men show that substances which present a risk to women pose similar risks to men.[10] Substances which pose reproductive risks are often carcinogenic and present a risk to both female and male workers. Substances such as DBCP and solvents are reproductive hazards to men, causing male infertility by damaging sperm, altering genetic material, or causing impotence.[11] Men can also pass hazardous chemicals on to women directly through their seminal fluid. Studies of the wives of dentists, for example, have shown a higher miscarriage rate due to their husbands' exposure to anesthetic gases.[12]

Advocates of the equity approach argue that biological risks are more similar than different, and that the differences that do exist are not substantial enough to warrant the exclusion of all women from hazardous worksites. In some cases, as with lead and radiation, company policies apply only to women, even though the risk to men is well known.

The exclusion of only pregnant women also fails to address the harm done to the female or male reproductive systems *before* conception, through mutagenic substances which damage genetic material in both men and women.

The underlying bias of "fetal protectionism" becomes clear when one looks at how the business community and the state have dealt with known male reproductive hazards. When DBCP was discovered to cause infertility in men working in a chemical company in California in 1977, the company was immediately shut down and the chemical banned from all further use. The chemical, not the men, was removed from the production process.[13] By contrast, in that same year, the Bunker Hill Co. of Idaho required that women working with known reproductive hazards prove they were sterile before permitting them to keep their jobs.[14]

Knowledge of male reproductive hazards has not always led to the protection of men. On the contrary, in most companies the exclusive focus on pregnant women has led to a complete lack of concern for and attention to male hazards.

Like their historical sisters who opposed gender-specific protective labor legislation, opponents of exclusion argue that women as a class pay too high a price for protection. Anecdotal evidence suggests that women working in male-dominated industries face demotion or dismissal at pregnancy. In one study of a chemical company, women's wages dropped dramatically and women workers lost all seniority benefits after an exclusionary policy was instituted.[15] As a woman in one company stated when faced with the choice between sterilization and loss of her job, "It seemed that you could have a tubal ligation in a very short period of time. It cost about $800 and it seemed to be less than what one would pay for an employment agency to find you a job!"[16] Opponents of protection argue that women who become pregnant while working in hazardous occupations, such as microchip production, often lose their jobs if the company cannot find "suitable" work for them to do. This means not only loss of pay, but loss of health insurance in the middle of a pregnancy.

Opponents of fetal protection policies argue that gender-specific policies are only feasible in workplaces where women are in the minority and can be easily replaced by men. Protection is an illusion, they argue, one that is skewed by gender, race, and class. Women who are exposed to toxins in low-wage assembly line jobs cannot be subjected *en masse* to the same kind of "protections" given women in male-dominated industries. Hospital workers, for example, work with known reproductive hazards such as ethylene oxide (used to sterilize equipment), radiation, chemotherapeutic drugs, and anesthetic gases. Women farmworkers—especially migrant workers—are also chronically exposed to pesticides with no concern for their health or fetal health.[17] Women in the electronics industry in assembly line production jobs work with acids, solvents, and radiation with little concern shown by their employers for their health.

The patterns of protection display the bias of fetal protectionism. Where women compete with men, they may be excluded; where they remain in traditional female occupations, they receive no protection at all.

Finally, advocates of the "equity" paradigm argue that what fetal protection policies protect best is corporate liability. By excluding women from hazardous jobs, companies have opted to risk discrimination suits, rather than tort liabilities for miscarriages or birth defects. As one corporate lawyer put it, "It was easier to deal with union protests over the exclusion of women than with a damage trial in 1990 where a jury would be confronted by a horribly deformed human being."[18]

As the number of women in "heavy" industries increases and as knowledge of female reproductive hazards expands, the practice of exclusion will become more widespread. Equity advocates argue for a safer workplace for all workers, rather than one which focuses so exclusively on the risk to fetal health. Alternatives proposed include gender-neutral policies which protect all "potential parents" in the workplace (and hence, fetuses). Policies should remove the hazard, not women workers. Policies which remove pregnant women from the workplace remove the incentive for corporations to eliminate hazards by removing the threat of lawsuits at low cost to employers.

The Federal Response

Since Title VII of the Civil Rights Act was passed in 1964, protective legislation for women only—restrictions, for instance, on hours or lifting weight—has been ruled illegal by the courts.[19] The most clear-cut cases of discrimination involve the dissimilar treatment of men and women solely on the basis of sex. This form of direct discrimination, where men and women are treated differently by workplace policies, violates the conditions set out under Title VII. Women have thus been able to sue for discrimination in cases, for instance, where physical tests for jobs can be proven to (1) discriminate against women as a class and (2) be unnecessary to the performance of the job.

But a major area of controversy still exists in cases where dissimilar treatment of men and women is based upon "real" biological differences between the sexes.[20] While the Pregnancy Discrimination Act of 1978 prohibited discrimination on the basis of pregnancy or childbearing capacity, the federal judiciary has not clarified the extent to which biological differences *can* be used to justify the differential treatment of men and women in the workplace. Not until the 1989 Johnson Controls decision had a federal court explicitly upheld a fetal protection policy which required proof of sterilization as grounds for women's employment, reflecting a significant change in the direction of court thinking.

In response to the controversy generated by the Digital study (cited above), the Equal Employment Opportunity Commission (EEOC) again issued guidelines on reproductive hazard policies in October of 1988. "It is the Commission's position," the guidelines state, "that employers are prohibited from establishing policies that exclude from the workplace members of one sex but not the other because of a reproductive or fetal hazard, unless that policy can be justified by reputable objective evidence of an essentially scientific nature."[21] The guidelines thus prohibit blanket exclusions of women unless scientific evidence shows that the hazard affects only women and that no less discriminatory alternative is available.

While presumably banning the most blatant forms of discrimination, the EEOC guidelines leave a large opening for exclusionary policies where scientific uncertainty exists about the risks to men. It is precisely through this opening that the court upheld the Johnson Controls policy, citing the EEOC guidelines to justify the exclusion of all women from work with lead. Even though lead, the "substance of concern" at Johnson Controls, is a known male reproductive hazard, the courts upheld the policy based on the presumption that the fetus, not the woman, was at higher risk.

Johnson Controls is not alone in this trend towards exclusion. A recent survey in Massachusetts found that 47 percent of the large chemical and electronics companies surveyed had some form of exclusionary policy in place.[22] Many of these restrictions violate both the EEOC guidelines as well as the standards for discrimination set out in Title VII of the Civil Rights Act.

Sameness, Difference, and Gender Equality

The controversy surrounding fetal protectionism poses a paradox for feminists: to ignore difference is to risk placing women in a workplace designed by and for men. But to design "special" policies for women is to reinforce those assumptions and economic structures which form the foundation of women's inequality in the workplace.

It is true that fetal protection policies are fundamentally flawed because they are based on the traditional assumptions about women, motherhood, and work which underlie gender inequality: that women *are* primarily responsible for childbearing and childrearing (thus the lack of concern for and research on the impact of paternal exposure); that *all* women are ready, willing, and able to procreate (thus the exclusion of women as a class from hazardous jobs); that women are not *rational* about pregnancy (thus the need for the imposition of external controls from government or business); that women are not an *essential* part of the workforce and will not be harmed by loss of work (thus the failure to protect women from loss of wages or seniority when excluded from jobs).

A challenge to fetal protection policies is a challenge to the physical and ideological separation of women's roles as workers and mothers. In

U.S. history, when women's needs as workers have collided with women's needs as mothers, the state has historically come down on the side of motherhood and a traditional gender division of labor.

Alternative policies must transcend this dichotomy and address the ways in which work and motherhood intersect and conflict for women. Fetal protection policies force women into unacceptable trade-offs. In order to get some safety, women must give up their right to higher paying jobs. In order to break into the masculine workplace, women must give up their ability to have and raise children. Women clearly have won the right to enter the male workplace. But the question remains: at what cost to women?

In the truly equitable workplace, the conflict between work and parental responsibilities must be transcended for men *and* women. An alternative definition of gender equality which can recognize and incorporate difference would require that *all* of the specific needs of pregnant women be addressed by workplace policies, not just those that pose a liability risk to employers. Gender equality might then require policies which, first, greatly reduce toxic exposures to all workers, which provide flexible sick leave policies for pregnant women, or which modify work routines (like lifting or standing) for pregnant women.

Advocates such as Dr. Maureen Paul at the University of Massachusetts Medical Center have rightfully called for removing the toxins, rather than women, from the hazardous workplace. Dr. Paul proposes a comprehensive and effective strategy including worker education, temporary job modifications for pregnant women and "potential parents," or voluntary job transfers with retention of wages and benefits. These solutions would adequately address both concerns of health and concerns of discrimination. The creation of a fully informed workforce, combined with voluntary transfer policies, might also relieve corporations of their fear of liability suits.

The challenge is to transform the ideological terms of the debate to expose the gender-biased assumptions about women, work, and motherhood which underlie fetal protection policies. Alternatives must squarely challenge the presumption that either the state or corporate managers have a greater investment in the protection of fetal health than do women themselves.

Notes

1. *New York Times* 10/3/89.
2. Equal Employment Opportunity Commission and Office of Federal Contract Compliance Programs. "Interpretive Guidelines on Employment Discrimination and Reproductive Hazards." *Federal Register* 45, (Friday, February 1, 1980): 7514.

3. Williams, Wendy W. "Firing the Woman to Protect the Fetus: The Reconciliation of Fetal Protection with Employment Opportunity Goals under Title VII." *The Georgetown Law Journal* 69 (1981): pp. 641-704.

4. Terry, Jane. "Conflict of Interest: Protection of Women from Reproductive Hazards in the Workplace." *Industrial and Labor Relations Forum* 15 (January 1981): p. 50.

5. Bayer, Ronald. "Reproductive Hazards in the Workplace: Bearing the Burden of Fetal Risk." *Milbank Memorial Fund Quarterly Health and Safety* 60 (Fall 1982): p. 635; Bertin, Joan E. "Reproductive Laws for the 1990's: Proposed Legislation Regarding Reproductive Health Hazards in the Workplace" (unpublished paper), p. 2; Williams, Wendy W. "Firing the Woman to Protect the Fetus: The Reconciliation of Fetal Protection with Employment Opportunity Goals under Title VII." *The Georgetown Law Journal* 69 (1981): p. 647, note 27.

6. Segers, Mary C. "Equality, Public Policy and Relevant Sex Differences." *Polity* 11 (Spring 1979): pp. 319-339.

7. Rosenberg, Michael J., Paul J. Feldblum, and Elizabeth G. Marshall. "Occupational Influences on Reproduction: A Review of Recent Literature." *Journal of Occupational Medicine* 29 (July 1987): pp. 584-591.

8. Bayer, Ronald. "Reproductive Hazards in the Workplace: Bearing the Burden of Fetal Risk." *Milbank Memorial Fund Quarterly Health and Safety* 60 (Fall 1982): p. 636.

9. Terry, Jane. "Conflict of Interest: Protection of Women from Reproductive Hazards in the Workplace." *Industrial and Labor Relations Forum* 15 (January 1981): p. 48.

10. Stein, Zena A., Maureen C. Hatch, and guest editors. "Reproductive Problems in the Workplace." *Occupational Medicine: State of the Art Reviews* 1 (July-September 1986): pp. 361-539.

11. Ashford, Nicholas A. and Charles Caldart. "The Control of Reproductive Hazards In the Workplace: A Prescription for Prevention." *Industrial Relations Law Journal* 5 (1983): p. 557.

12. Timko, Patricia. "Exploring the Limits of Legal Duty: A Union's Responsibilities with Respect to Fetal Protection Policies." *Harvard Journal on Legislation* 23 (Winter 1986): p. 165, note 38; Bertin, Joan E. "Reproduction, Women and the Workplace: Legal Issues." *Occupational Medicine: State of the Art Reviews* 1 (July-September 1986): pp. 498, 503.

13. Bertin, Joan E. "Reproduction, Women and the Workplace: Legal Issues." *Occupational Medicine: State of the Art Reviews* 1 (July-September 1986): p. 500; Terry, Jane. "Conflict of Interest: Protection of Women from Reproductive Hazards in the Workplace." *Industrial and Labor Relations Forum* 15 (January 1981): p. 45.

14. Randall, Donna M. "Women in Toxic Work Environments: A Case Study and Examination of Policy Impact." *Women and Work* 1 (1985): p. 259.

15. Randall, Donna M. "Women in Toxic Work Environments: A Case Study and Examination of Policy Impact." *Women and Work* 1 (1985): p. 263.

16. Randall, Donna M. "Women in Toxic Work Environments: A Case Study and Examination of Policy Impact." *Women and Work* 1 (1985): p. 269.

17. Barreto, Julie. "Women Farmworkers in California." *Golden Gate University Law Review* 10 (Summer 1980): p. 1133.

18. Randall, Donna M. "Women in Toxic Work Environments: A Case Study and Examination of Policy Impact." *Women and Work* 1 (1985): p. 268.

19. Williams, Wendy W. "Firing the Woman to Protect the Fetus: The Reconciliation of Fetal Protection with Employment Opportunity Goals under Title VII." *The Georgetown Law Journal* 69 (1981): p. 655, note 93.

20. Kenney, Sally J. "Reproductive Hazards in the Workplace: The Law and Sexual Differences." *International Journal of the Sociology of Law* 14 (1986): p. 412;

U.S. Congress, Office of Technology Assessment, *Reproductive Health Hazards in the Workplace,* (Washington, D.C.: U.S. Government Printing Office, OTA-BA-266, December 1985), p. 240.

21. Equal Employment Opportunity Commission, "Policy Guidance on Reproductive and Fetal Hazards," Oct. 3, 1988.

22. Daniels, Cynthia, Maureen Paul, and Robert Rosofsky. "Family, Work and Health Report." Department of Public Health, Commonwealth of Massachusetts, 1987.

"United We Are Going to Get Somewhere": Working Together for Lesbian/Gay Liberation and Reproductive Freedom

Shelley Mains and Stephanie Poggi

As lesbians who have worked together for many years in the reproductive rights and gay movements, we periodically get together and bemoan the disappointments of our political efforts. Common themes have been the difficulties of coping with lesbian/gay invisibility in the struggle for abortion rights and sexism in the movement for gay/lesbian liberation.

At the same time, we've also marvelled at the links we've seen develop between the movements. We're encouraged when gay male AIDS activists show up at abortion rallies and articulate a brilliant defense of reproductive freedom. We're thrilled when college reproductive rights supporters prominently place the demand for gay/lesbian parenting rights on their snazzy T-shirts.

In writing this article, we hope to explore what the reproductive rights and gay liberation movements have in common, why they come into conflict, and how (and if) they can become stronger allies in the future. We feel somewhat ridiculous talking about the "two sides"—as if they are separate, monolithic entities. Obviously there's a lot of overlap of personnel (like us), and an incredible variety of perspectives. For purposes of this brief discussion, however, we've chosen to identify each movement by general goals and agendas.

Common Theories, Shared Realities

[My gay male lover, Gary, and I] spotted some [Operation Rescue picketers at an abortion clinic]...We walked past the group and took up residence against a tree [nearby] and began necking. We kissed and we billed and we cooed and we talked to each other about how much we loved each other, all without giving the [picketers] so much as a glance.

Their resolve began to quickly melt. Within two minutes, a young mother ushered her two children away from the scene lest our evil influence corrupt them. Then, a woman used her placard to try and shield the picketers from the view of our amorous display. We moved to just the other side of the placard and intensified our efforts. The woman quickly skulked back to the safety of her heterodyne peers.

—Letter to the editor, *Gay Community News*, January 22, 1989

Even the most flamboyant pair of queens could probably find a preferable place to kiss than amidst a throng of anti-abortion activists. The gay men at the Operation Rescue demonstration were doing more than satisfying an urge for intimacy or exhibitionism: they were making a graphic statement about the links between the reproductive freedom and gay liberation agendas.

Our movements share a theoretical basis. Talk to supporters of either movement, and before long you're likely to come to a feminist critique of sex roles. Reproductive rights activists argue that the fact that women have reproductive equipment doesn't mean that every woman must give birth; we also argue that biology does not dictate that only women can nurture children. The social norms that proscribe women's activities outside the home in turn keep men focused on breadwinning, competition, and power. According to this framework, abortion destroys the social fabric because it allows women to escape their maternal destiny. Likewise, these norms preclude male-to-male intimacy. Men who relate emotionally challenge traditional roles: they are seen as acting like women and voluntarily giving up power for second-class status. Lesbians represent a social aberration as well, for women whose primary sexual and emotional connections are to women are able to resist dependence on men's sexual, social, and economic power. Informed by feminism, the reproductive freedom and gay liberation agendas aim for more than the acquisition of rights. Both movements call for a dismantling of traditional sex roles and for a radical change in social norms.

Even if we activists don't often stop to ponder these theoretical ties, the Right links us in a cohesive theory. In fact, they sometimes see us as one and the same: at a recent Operation Rescue demonstration, an anti-abortion activist's child pointed to a heterosexual pro-choice marshall and asked her mother, "Why is that lady wearing a purple armband?" "That's how you can tell who the lesbians are," snapped the mother, snatching her child away from what she clearly saw as an indistinguishable swarm of murderers and perverts.

Gay men, lesbians, and supporters of abortion rights blur in the eyes of social conservatives because we're seen as a monolithic threat to a reactionary but powerful notion of the "Traditional Family," idealized as a haven of emotional security and moral development, and as the cornerstone of society. The "decline of the family" is seen by the Right as the cause of society's ills, and favored scapegoats are those who challenge the ideology of the nuclear family by their very existence, as well as through ongoing political struggle. A backlash has ensued, creating a climate in which people living with AIDS and women with unwanted pregnancies are thought to "get what they deserve" for immoral sexual acts and are seen as undeserving of treatment, while explicit safe sex materials are censored or lose funding.

It's open season on social outcasts, as appalling stories of hate crimes in the daily press remind us. At its most extreme, this scapegoating of social deviants is evident in the rise of neo-Nazi organizations which propose social and economic salvation through systematic violence—not only against gay people and non-conforming women, but also against non-whites, non-Christians, and, indeed, non-fascists. As we respond to these attacks, the demand for control over our bodies represents a common denominator between reproductive freedom and gay/lesbian liberation.

At its most watered-down, this demand surfaces in calls for privacy, whereby women, gay men, and lesbians insist that it should be up to us, as responsible adults, to decide what we will do with our bodies in such sanctums as the bedroom or the doctor's office. But many of us are demanding more, in the name of control, than the narrow right as individuals to do our "dirty" business behind closed doors. We are publicly calling for full sexual liberation for all people. This means a society that ensures a woman's right to have—and, crucially, to enjoy—sex when and with whom she pleases, without facing violence or the consequences of an unwanted pregnancy; it also means a society that ensures her right to refuse sex as she chooses.

Such a society must guarantee gay men and lesbians the right to be publicly (as well as privately) intimate without fear of being stigmatized, losing a job, alienating friends and family, or risking physical attack. Sexual liberation means that adolescents must have the opportunity to develop confidence and decision making skills so they can choose whether to experiment with heterosexuality and/or homosexuality or to remain celibate, without shame or punishment, and armed with necessary information about sexually transmitted diseases and birth control.

While the reproductive rights movement is usually associated with preventing and ending unwanted pregnancies, many champions of reproductive freedom also demand that persons who wish to parent have the opportunity to realize their desires. Currently many women face economic barriers to becoming parents; this is as serious an infringement on reproductive freedom as are restrictions on abortion access. In this economic context, many women are essentially forced to "choose" to be sterilized, because federal government funds support sterilization but will not pay for abortions. At the same time, women have been blatantly sterilized against their wills. In these ways, the state and the medical establishment send powerful messages about who is fit to parent. The movement for reproductive freedom seeks to re-examine the notion of who can and should parent, and to ensure that a diverse range of persons wishing to be parents has the economic and social support to do so. As more and more gay men and lesbians seek to become parents—whether through pregnancy, adoption, or co-parenting and extended family arrangements—this becomes another tie that binds the movements.

In fact, gay men and lesbians share many experiences with those who are hardest hit by restrictions in reproductive rights. Whatever the backgrounds and overlapping identities of lesbians and gay men, we often find it easy to identify with and support the demands for reproductive freedom of people who are poor, young, disabled, or people of color. We all face substantial barriers to becoming parents in a society which still widely venerates the Ward and June Cleaver image of parenthood. For gay men and lesbians, such obstacles include the "married-only" requirement at many sperm banks, the regulations thwarting gay/lesbian foster care and adoption in various states, and the difficulties gay/lesbian workers face in extending their "family" insurance coverage to lovers and children. Working-class lesbian parents in particular share the economic difficulties of single heterosexual mothers in trying to make ends meet with only a fraction of the earning power of a man. These similar experiences of oppression give our movements a basis for learning from each other and ultimately joining together.

Lessons from Gay/Lesbian Liberation

While the gay/lesbian liberation and reproductive rights movements share some common themes (and enemies), each has also developed according to its own specific history. As allies, our movements can exchange hard-learned lessons, skills, and insights, so we can avoid repeating one another's past mistakes and thus be more effective in our future work.

What do the experiences of gay and lesbian organizing offer the reproductive rights movement? Over the years the abortion rights movement has backed off from talking explicitly about sex; we talk about less carnal concepts like "choice," "freedom," "justice," and "privacy." This leaves it to the Right to control public discussion of sexuality and to shape it in terms of Christian morality.

Lesbians and gay men, even when some of us want to, can't escape talking about sex because our public image centers around our sexual preference. While many gay efforts have been focused away from sex and toward diffuse concepts like "civil rights" and "pride," it's proven difficult to keep the "sex" out of "homosexuality." Ask any gay or lesbian speaker who's given a presentation in a school or a community group, and they will tell you that however painstakingly they discuss sex role stereotypes or the right to privacy, the burning question the audience always gets to is, "What do you do in bed?" Thus, as individuals, "out" gay men and lesbians often become relatively comfortable talking about sexuality in various forums; perhaps this is why disproportionate numbers of lesbians and gay men seem to end up working in areas like sexuality counseling, family planning, and sex education. The reproductive rights movement can look to lesbian/gay liberation as a model for bringing sexuality into public discussions, rather than ceding our "sexual turf" to the Right by talking about reproductive freedom as an abstract concept divorced from sex.

In the realm of practical organizing, gay men and lesbians can offer the reproductive rights movement new strategies. In Boston, for example, many lesbians are involved in affinity groups, a decentralized system of organizing which became popular in this country through the anti-nuclear movement and has been kept alive particularly among lesbian feminists. As reproductive rights organizations have sought to "call out the troops" to fight Operation Rescue, to protest Supreme Court decisions, and to perform various acts of visibility, we've often relied on the organizing strength and energy of our sisters in affinity groups.

Similarly, as AIDS activism has increased, particularly among gay men, the reproductive rights movement has welcomed a shot of new energy. While for decades we've been talking about issues like sex and health care access in the context of the abortion issue, groups like ACT-UP have burst onto the scene, raising the same issues in terms of AIDS, and raising them with the kind of enthusiasm, style, and urgency that recalls the pre-*Roe* era of abortion activism. We've been buoyed up by the example of AIDS activists, and perhaps some of their style has even rubbed off on us as our own actions become more massive, more angry, and more confrontational in response to continuing attacks on our reproductive rights.

Lessons from the Reproductive Rights Movement

Lessons from the reproductive rights movement can also inform lesbian and gay organizing. For example, feminists who have come to question a strategy based on the right to privacy have a lot to share with gay activists struggling to overturn sodomy laws. While many proponents of reproductive rights continue to rely heavily on "privacy" ideology, a growing number of activists—particularly women of color and working-class women—have pushed the movement to recognize the limitations of this approach. Given the economic oppression of the majority of women, privacy most often means the dubious right to be left to our own devices in a society stacked against us. We have seen over and over again that support for abortion rights on the basis of privacy translates into opposition to public funding.

Women know from first-hand experience that privacy has often been a kind of hell for us—where women are isolated and where abusers can count on immunity. Enormous numbers of women continue to be attacked in our homes by people close to us, and enormous numbers of women work against battering, incest, and marital and date rape.

Just as activists for reproductive freedom need to hold out for more than individual rights, gay activists must demand more than freedom from government interference. Pressures within many gay communities, as well as external influences, support this shift in priorities. Over the last several years, movements of lesbian/gay people of color have sought fundamental changes in society and have urged mainstream gay circles to challenge race and class oppression within the gay movement. The devastation of the AIDS epidemic has also changed the political priorities of many gay men. Gay men who believed their material resources would cushion them from certain kinds of discrimination have discovered—in the most brutal way—that the government will let them die along with IV drug users and people of color. Government response and community empowerment—not privacy—are the rallying cry. Finally, censorship not only of lesbian/gay sexual imagery, but also of explicit safer sex education, unequivocally demonstrates the life-and-death importance of freedom to publicly express our desire.

The feminist self-help movement has also offered a model for gay activists with AIDS who have been building a self-help network—although some AIDS activists have been slow to acknowledge their feminist precursors. For example, the Jane Collective, a group of lay women who trained themselves in abortion techniques and illegally provided abortions for 11,000 women before 1973, set a pattern that has been revived by people with AIDS (PWAs) who have formed research initiatives, alternative treatment groups, drug-buying clubs, and other underground networks. Similarly, feminist health activists laid the foundation for people living with AIDS to push the limits of the traditional relationship between doctor and "patient" by demanding control of treatment. It's no surprise to feminists that doctors might not have all the answers, and that we must become our own experts. *Our Bodies/Our Selves,* self-cervical exams, home menstrual extraction, the feminist health center network etc., are institutions of feminist empowerment that emerged from women's need to literally take our bodies into our own hands.

Points of Conflict

The movements for gay liberation and for reproductive rights have often run in tandem, but have also suffered fits and starts of hostility and missed connections. While the political limitations of each movement account for some of the problem areas, gay people and reproductive rights activists are frequently pitted against one another by outside forces. Our relative lack of legitimacy and financial power in society can make us desperate for visible gains—and leave us little leverage to protest attacks on our sometime allies. The following anecdotes illustrate some of these difficulties and attempt to offer models for constructive cooperation. On January 22, 1986, Massachusetts Governor Michael Dukakis headed for the podium at a Boston event commemorating the Supreme Court 1973 decision to legalize abortion. As he reached the dais to declare his support for abortion rights and his opposition to Question #1, a ballot item that would have cut off state Medicaid for abortion, 30 lesbians and gay men in the audience stood and turned their backs to him.

Why were gay people, all of whom supported the Governor's position on abortion, turning their backs? Well, the signs they wore read "Foster Equality." The pro-choice Governor had enacted a policy six months before that virtually prohibited lesbians and gay men from being foster parents, and that stressed the "traditional" family with the woman staying at home as the best setting for children. The policy, which was considered responsible for a new wave of attacks on lesbians and gay men in the state, was opposed by social workers, Black, Latino, and Asian community leaders, civil liberties advocates, and many reproductive rights activists.

The event at which Dukakis spoke was organized by the steering committee of a statewide group called the Coalition for Choice, which included mainstream organizations such as Planned Parenthood, the League of Women Voters, and the state affiliate of the National Abortion Rights Action League, as well as the more radical Reproductive Rights Network (R2N2), which defines its politics to encompass a demand for sexual freedom. Most members of the steering committee said they saw no contradiction in inviting the anti-gay Dukakis to a pro-choice event.

At the time, some lesbians within R2N2 and Boston NOW said they felt lesbian/gay parenting issues had been trivialized and traded away.

Some felt that R2N2 should resign from the steering committee rather than go along with inviting Dukakis. Other lesbians felt that foster care could be fought for in other arenas, and need not be an issue at this particular event.

This controversy illustrates the unclear place of lesbian/gay concerns within the reproductive rights movement. While "abortion" remains a dirty word in some quarters, we "queers" are dirtier still. Do groups like Planned Parenthood not even grasp the relationship between foster care and abortion, or do they believe a link to gay issues will hurt their cause? Groups like R2N2 that consciously make the links are the exception. And, as we've illustrated, how to support lesbians and gay men has been controversial even within such an organization.

At a commemoration of the *Roe v. Wade* anniversary on January 22 in an Eastern city some years ago, seven women—performers and speakers—appeared on stage before a packed crowd. Six of the seven were lesbians. Only one let her sexual preference be known.

Not only don't our issues always get addressed, but lesbians also have a hard time making ourselves visible, despite our omnipresence in the movement. The lesbians at this particular January 22 event "chose" not to come out, and their reasons for remaining closeted no doubt have to do with more than the atmosphere of reproductive rights organizations. But our movement must more seriously address heterosexism—not only by publicly recognizing lesbians as major players, not only by addressing reproductive freedom for lesbians—but also by challenging heterosexism at large. This means learning about issues apart from reproductive rights that affect lesbians and taking action on them. A related issue rarely addressed is the often subtle heterosexism of the "social culture" of our groups. Even some of the most hip heterosexual women working with us too often presume heterosexuality—and monogamy—and usually leave sexual freedom at the periphery of the agenda. When straight women talk about marriage, in-laws, or the other "joys" of heterosexuality without acknowledging "straight privilege," they foster the kind of heterosexism we deal with in almost every other area of our lives. Like women of color, working-class women, disabled women, old women, and very young women, lesbians still face the task of creating spaces where we feel comfortable and where our experiences are valid. Heterosexual women must take a leading role in helping to make room for lesbians to feel as free to talk about our lovers, friends, and coming out experiences as they do about their boyfriends, husbands, and families.

We've also found that lesbians in reproductive rights organizations are often looked to as the repositories of expertise on all things gay. Even if we are childless individuals, we're assumed to have the latest statistics on the "lesbian baby boom." When a discussion focuses on AIDS—whether concerning homophobia, IV drug use, or women's reproductive health—the lesbians are assumed to know the most, care the most, and have the best developed political line. Of course, in many cases we do know or care or think more about these issues than our straight sisters. But this is part of the problem. Only when gay issues are no longer "ghettoized" (and in the particular case of AIDS, when AIDS is no longer seen as "just a gay issue"), and only when issues like AIDS and gay parenting are taken at face value as legitimate reproductive rights issues—can we lesbians take on whatever reproductive rights work interests us most. Until then, we'll be forced to pursue issues because we're stuck with them by others in our organizations, or because we're reluctant to let go for fear that others won't do "our" issues justice.

At the same time we're working for recognition in the reproductive rights movement, we confront pressure in the lesbian/gay movement to be gay- or lesbian-identified, rather than woman- or feminist-identified. Gay men may ask us why we care about this problem of straight women (abortion), and other lesbians have expressed resentment that lesbians continue to work on almost everything under the sun except lesbian-specific issues. Within our own social/political circles, we sometimes feel that reproductive rights activism is seen as necessary drudge work—it's important, but so boring.

Even when allies in the lesbian/gay liberation movement whole-heartedly join reproductive rights work, conflicts can develop over who controls the strategy and message. For example, gay men recently organized a safer sex demonstration with a giant dildo prop at a Boston abortion clinic under attack by Operation Rescue. Feminists, including many lesbians, who had been coordinating clinic defense for months, found this action problematic because the enormous symbol of male genitals may have been upsetting to women going in to get abortions, some of whom may have been raped. On the other hand, the women clinic activists supported the demonstration's pro-sex message and its creativity. Some said they would have welcomed a chance to work out an alternative action with the gay men ahead of time.

Cause for Hope: Solidarity and Visibility

There are certainly plenty of examples of solidarity between the lesbian/gay and reproductive rights movements. We'll focus on a particularly exciting one here: the consistent support of reproductive rights in *Gay Community News,* a newspaper with which we've both been involved for many years. This support has developed over time: in the 1970s, reporters covered reproductive rights, but had to make sure an out lesbian explicated the links to gay issues in every story. By 1982, the staff of men and women exhorted readers to attend the Cherry Hill abortion demonstration in an editorial—and reporters didn't have to explain why reproductive rights were relevant in a gay paper.

In 1984, when the largest gay PAC—the Human Rights Campaign Fund—honored Boston Mayor Ray Flynn for signing a human rights ordinance into law, *GCN* wrote an editorial in opposition. Flynn did not deserve an award for his work on behalf of human rights, argued the *GCN* staff, because he opposed abortion rights and, as a state legislator, had even sponsored a bill to deny Medicaid funding for abortions. Further, the Mayor is known to have been an active leader against busing in the 1970s. By refusing to let gay needs be separated from other needs, the paper set an example for other lesbian/gay groups and continues to educate readers about the issue.

Working together for both reproductive freedom and lesbian/gay liberation is no small feat. Indeed, the efforts of activists in both movements to translate social visions into concrete coalition strategies is part of the essential work of liberation struggles around the world. When we feel frustrated in this difficult organizing, we can often find hope by listening to other activists forging similar bonds. Simon Nkoli, a gay, Black, South African anti-apartheid activist, makes a compelling case for breaking through the barriers between liberation movements, and he sees lesbian and gay visibility within these movements as crucial:

> What will lesbians and gay men say if people ask us: "What did you do to bring a change in South Africa; where were you during the battle?" Will we say, "We were with you but we didn't want you to know that we were there?" That would be a foolish answer. The same applies to organizing in the gay/lesbian community. When gay people come out of the closet, they tend to say, "Okay, let's fight for gay/lesbian rights," and isolate that liberation struggle. But if we isolate this struggle, it will be the same thing as women isolating their struggle, or youth or workers. Let's bring all of these issues together, and united we are going to reach somewhere.

Reproductive Rights Position Paper: National Black Women's Health Project

The National Black Women's Health Project (NBWHP) of Atlanta, Georgia, was founded as a self-help and health advocacy organization to improve the chronically poor and declining health status of Black women and their families. Today it consists of a network of 88 developing and established chapters in 24 states, serving a broad-based constituency of almost 2,000 members. The purpose of the NBWHP is the definition, promotion, and maintenance of health for Black women, including full reproductive rights and the essential authority of every woman to choose when, whether, and under what conditions she will bear children. Because too many single family households in the United States are headed by Black women living in poverty, possessing fewer educational and job training opportunities, enduring inadequate, often non-existing child care services, subject to substandard housing conditions, and lacking access to appropriate health services of any kind; because more than half of all Black children are poor, born of mothers receiving inferior, if any, prenatal care, suffering the highest rate of infant mortality and neonatal deaths in the Western world; and because we lack fail-safe birth control methods, lack adequate human sexuality education, and suffer also the highest rate of teenage pregnancy in the Western world, we firmly insist upon continued access to safe, legal, and affordable abortion. Restrictive abortion laws exacerbate the low socioeconomic status of women of color, and the passage of such will further impugn the dignity of Black womanhood, leaving sterilization as the only publicly funded and permanent birth control method available to women of color. The lives of Black and other women of color will be disproportionately damaged, as we are forced to rely on publicly funded health facilities where they exist.

NBWHP is further committed to establishment of environments that will encourage Black women to initiate and continue dialogue on the full range of reproductive rights issues. This dialogue will increase our knowledge base, influence our attitudes, and shape our behavior. This can be visualized as follows:

NBWHP	Demonstrated	Confidence	
Self-help +	Knowledge and +	to act based =	EMPOWERMENT
Process	skills	on knowledge	
		and skills	

Reproductive freedom is an essential part of every woman's personal empowerment.

Vision Statement:
Women of Color Partnership Program

The Women of Color Partnership Program (WOCPP) was created by the Religious Coalition for Abortion Rights in 1985 as a vehicle by which African-American, Latin American, Asian-Pacific-American, Native American, and all Women of Color in this country can become actively involved, as decision makers, in the reproductive choice movement.

This program seeks to identify and address not only reproductive rights issues but also reproductive health care concerns from the unique perspectives of Women of Color. The WOCPP has initiated a number of forums through which we, Women of Color, can converse, share ideas, develop and distribute resources, and promote our own views and public policy objectives on issues concerning comprehensive reproductive health care.

We envision our work to include:

Broadening the agenda of the pro-choice movement to encompass a full range of comprehensive reproductive health issues such as: (1) the right to choose or not to choose abortion; (2) family planning and all methods of birth control; (3) teen pregnancy; (4) prenatal care; (5) child care; and (6) medical abuses against Women of Color;

Promoting the education of Women of Color around reproductive health options as a key aspect of our quality of life and that of our families;

Building a partnership and agenda among all Women of Color which incorporates our political and social organizations and our individual faith perspectives;

Expanding the pro-choice movement to reflect the diverse needs, views, and aspirations of Women of Color and our families; and

Insuring that access to comprehensive reproductive health care options is not denied to anyone.

The Women of Color Partnership Program will serve as the foundation on which to build a united multi-cultural coalition. It is our hope that the WOCPP will also serve as a conduit through which we, Women of Color, will feel empowered to speak out against the threats to our physical, spiritual, emotional, and intellectual well-being.

Statement of Asian-Pacific Women on Reproductive Health

This statement was presented originally to the "In Defense of Roe" conference, April 7-8, 1989, Washington, D.C., sponsored by the American Civil Liberties Union and the Religious Coalition for Abortion Rights.

This is a historic moment for us. Recognizing the context of a tradition of family and community, including alternative lifestyles, we, as Asian-Pacific American women, underscore the importance of a reproductive health agenda for our communities.

One definition of reproductive health includes issues of access to health care, abortion, sterilization, pre- and postnatal care, issues of AIDS, forced abortions, teen pregnancy, and sex education.

The particular needs of our community can only be met through bilingual and generation-sensitive information and sex education. It is also necessary for us to confront the sexual objectification of our peoples, e.g., military prostitution, sex tourism, mail order brides, geishas, and other exotica.

An acute problem for our community is our invisibility in statistical and census data which lump Asians in the category of "other." Because of the inadequate data and resources, effective policy making is hampered. The stereotyping and historical disenfranchisement of us blocks our full and equal participation as people of color.

Because of our close links with our countries of origin, any reproductive health policy must consider the global impact on Asian women.

We are committed to confronting racism within our own communities and other communities of color, and we demand the same respect.

We request sensitivity from all of you in recognizing the difficulty of organizing around this issue in our very diverse communities.

Developing a Reproductive Rights Agenda for the 1990s[1]

Kathryn Kolbert

This is a call for a reproductive rights agenda for the 1990s. It suggests a process for developing a comprehensive approach to reproductive rights issues and outlines an agenda that can serve as a starting point for further discussions. Defining our goals is essential to achieving them. By taking the time now to articulate our vision of the future and grapple with the many hard questions that surround reproduction—questions about sexuality, childbearing, and parenting—we can develop and build a consensus about the basic premises of our work. We will then be better able to set priorities and develop collective strategies to achieve our goals.

The time is ripe for this type of discussion. For many feminists working for social change in the 1960s and 1970s, the ability of women to decide whether, when, and with whom they would have children was crucial in determining the course of their lives. Therefore, the struggle for legal birth control and abortion emerged as a critical issue. Later, widespread problems of sterilization abuse and teenage pregnancy made it clear that reproductive freedom meant more than eliminating criminal prohibitions on birth control and abortion; it involved a wider range of issues. The movement for reproductive freedom grew to include actions to help women who faced obstacles acquiring safe and effective birth control methods, obtaining publicly funded abortions, and withstanding efforts to compel their sterilization, as well as organizing on behalf of women who faced obstacles delivering healthy babies, escaping reproductive hazards in the workplace, obtaining comprehensive sex education, gaining access to new reproductive technologies, and meeting their work and parenting obligations.

We are today at a critical juncture in the feminist movement. With the Democrats regaining control of the U.S. Senate, opponents of abortion losing major battles for legislation and public support, and, most importantly, women's groups reaching a new understanding about the need for concerted, affirmative political action, we have an opportunity to take the initiative and define a new direction for public policy debates on reproductive rights. On the other hand, proponents of reproductive freedom face numerous legislative and administrative battles to preserve existing rights without support from the federal judiciary. Fighting effectively in this context requires us to understand and articulate better what reproductive choice really means.

Reproductive freedom means the ability to choose whether, when, how, and with whom one will have children. Choice means not only having a legal option, but also the economic means and social conditions that make it possible to effectuate one's choice. Reproductive freedom is necessary if all persons are to lead lives of self-determination, opportunity, and human dignity. Because women have historically been defined by and valued almost entirely for their reproductive capacities, and all persons, especially women, have been expected to express their sexuality in ways that satisfy society's norms for childbearing and childrearing, the fight for reproductive choice is essential if women are to become full and equal partners with men in this society, and is a crucial part of a larger struggle for liberty and equality.

The process for developing a reproductive rights agenda for the 1990s must be inclusive. Only by hearing from women with a wide range of life experiences are we likely to understand that lack of access to abortion contributes to sterilization abuse, that lack of comprehensive sex education and birth control contributes to high abortion rates as well as to premature and low-birthweight babies, that less than full health coverage for all persons raises the level of infant mortality and makes technologies of fertility a privilege of the upper class. More importantly, finding the basis to unite in broad coalitions focused on reproductive rights is essential to gaining sufficient power to win many of the critical political battles.

The process must be as inclusive as possible, and the dialogue must be genuine. All of us need to hear from battered women and to understand how the dynamic of their abuse denies them autonomy in reproductive matters. We need to hear from Black women and to understand the long history of their deprivation of reproductive freedom, from the days of slavery through the eugenics movement, including their exclusion from the adoption process and their subjection to involuntary sterilization. Poor women can detail the inadequacies of the welfare system and minimum wage jobs that force them to raise their children in poverty and make them reluctant to carry their pregnancies to term. Rural women can relate the difficulties they experience when they must travel long distances for family planning, abortion services, or maternity care. Hispanic women can tell us about their experiences as the subjects of experiments with the pill, as migrant workers exposed to pesticides, and as victims of sterilization abuse. Native American women can describe their experience with sterilization abuse, lack of health care services, and termination of their rights to their children. Lesbians and gay men can recount the discrimination they have suffered when attempting to retain or regain custody of their children, trying to adopt or become foster parents, or using alternative methods of reproduction. Unmarried couples and inter-racial or even inter-generational couples can describe the stigma of living and bearing children in relationships that do not comform to societal norms. All of us need to hear the voices of disabled women, who can convey their difficulties being seen as sexual beings and the obstacles they face in seeking to reproduce. Separated and divorced women can share their frustrations at how trying to secure child care, flexible working hours, parental leave policies, and comprehensive health insurance constrains their reproductive choices and adds to the stresses of childrearing.

Developing broader-based coalitions that reflect the diversity of women and a wide spectrum of reproductive experiences will enable us to expand both our ranks and our success, and to nurture choice as a basic social value. We will also be better able to define and explain our goals in ways that make sense to political allies—from health care professionals to corporate managers to welfare recipients or the countless people who may personally oppose abortion but embrace the principles of personal choice. We must be cautious, however, to remember that reaching out means more than just talking to new audiences and inviting them to join us. It means trying to understand different perspectives and concerns, working collaboratively, sharing power, and doing all we can to make our movement diverse and mutually respectful—just as we want our society to be.

Our dialogues and coalition-building may take a variety of forms. Organizations, particularly large national ones, need to find ways to discuss and debate the issues within their membership. For example, NARAL's efforts to listen to the voices of women through its "Silent No More Campaign" and new efforts to outline a "Reproductive Bill of Rights" have had the result that activists throughout the heterogeneous organization have been hearing one another's experiences and discussing the basic principles of reproductive choice. Likewise, NOW's Women of Color Conference on Reproductive Rights facilitated genuine learning and dialogue among women of very different backgrounds and helped to ensure that policy demands which are developed and supported by NOW will reflect the needs of women of color.

On the state level, the experience of Women's Agenda in Pennsylvania is instructive. Through extensive discussion among diverse groups of women and organizing efforts that targeted statewide legislative priorities, over $74 million in new money was generated in the last three years for women's and children's programs, as well as welfare grant increases, reforms in maternal and child health programs, and abortion rights. Although reproductive rights issues often have been lost or compromised away in similar economic justice efforts in other states, Women's Agenda has demonstrated that the issues surrounding economic justice are closely related to and cannot be separated from reproductive rights issues.

The reproductive rights agenda for the 1990s which follows is offered as a starting point for discussion and with the hope that it will lead to consensus on basic principles and creative exploration of a full range of policy alternatives. Where the need for particular policies is already clear, the discussion should concentrate on preserving existing gains and implementing new policies in our law and social institutions. Where issues are less clear, or where the issues have yet to be the subject of thoughtful deliberation by a wide range of activists, like those emerging in the context of new reproductive technologies, it makes sense to broaden discussion of these issues and propose a variety of options that meet our underlying principles.

Once basic principles are agreed upon, we need to examine the full range of tactics available to achieve our policy goals. There are an untold number of ways that we can make our voices heard and our objectives a reality if and when we set our minds to it. Lawsuits, legislative advocacy, demonstrations, sit-ins, and speak-outs are only a few of the strategies we can and must use to win. But we must not dissipate our energies in disputes over strategies. Rather we must encourage different individuals and organizations to approach problems in different ways and, where necessary, to coordinate programs and activities.

Because of the heightened assault on women's reproductive rights, most activists find themselves barraged by the sheer volume of work necessary to preserve the limited gains for safe and legal birth control and abortion that we have won in the last 20 years. There is legitimate fear that widening the reproductive rights agenda to issues beyond birth control and abortion will dilute the struggle for rights that are so clearly in jeopardy. These fears are realistic and not without merit. But if we are ever to win the long-term effort to achieve reproductive choice, we must widen our base of support and avoid being isolated as a "fringe movement." We can do this most effectively by drawing the connections among a full range of reproductive rights issues and better utilizing the energy of activists who do not now understand their organizing efforts to be part of a wider struggle for reproductive choice. By taking the time and initiative to define our agenda, rather than responding to the pressures of the Right, we may move a little closer to gaining the reproductive autonomy that we want so dearly.

A Reproductive Rights Agenda for the 1990s

Introduction

Women's ability to control whether, when, with whom, and under what conditions they will have children—in short, women's power to control their fertility—is essential if women are to participate fully and equally in society. Only with the freedom to control their fertility are women free to learn and grow, to better themselves, to establish a home and family, to follow their dreams, or to express themselves and contribute as mothers, workers, artists, activists, scientists, or in whatever roles they choose.

To make truly voluntary decisions about their sexuality, childbearing, or parenting, women and men need access to sex education and counseling and affordable, comprehensive health care for themselves and their children. Women also need protection from unnecessary or invasive medical procedures and sterilization abuse, from family violence, and from hazardous workplace conditions.

Unless parents are able to ensure that adequate food, clothing, and shelter and quality child care and education are available for their children, their reproductive choices are limited. A fair and equitable welfare system and jobs that pay a living wage are critical to this effort.

When we think of how many women and families are now denied some or all of these rights because their income is too low or the color of their skin is too dark; because they live in rural communities, have physical disabilities, or have relationships with others of the same sex; or because they are uninformed, fearful, or stigmatized, we realize that the policy agenda for a pro-choice society is a very long one.

In a society based on gender equality, one that accepts the personhood of women by valuing their ability to be parents, to undertake meaningful work outside the home, and to have proud aspirations for their lives—one that encourages men similarly to combine work and nurturing roles—the bearing and rearing of children would not so often amount to a confining loss of opportunities for women. Such a society would foster the conditions that make true reproductive choice possible. Such a society would maximize reproductive choices and life options for all women and their families.

1. Freedom and Legal Rights to Make Voluntary Decisions

Our law and social institutions must enable women to make voluntary, thoughtful, and deliberate choices about their own sexuality, childbearing, and parenting and must respect the decisions that women make for themselves and their families.

All persons must have the legal right to make voluntary and informed decisions. Our legal system cannot be used to deprive women of equal access to a full range of reproductive options. Nor can it be used to coerce women's reproductive behavior or choices, regardless of age, ancestry, creed, disability, economic status, marital status, national origin, parental status, race, sex, or sexual orientation.

2. Comprehensive, Quality, and Affordable Health Care and Human Services

A. A Full Range of Reproductive Options

Women must have access to existing methods of safe, quality birth control, and medical research must develop better, safer methods. Men as well as women must assume responsibility for birth control, and technologies must be developed that will enable them to do so.

Women who find themselves pregnant must have access to quality counseling to determine their reproductive choices. If they choose to terminate their pregnancies, they must have access to safe and affordable abortion services at or near their homes or jobs.

Women who choose to carry a pregnancy to term must have access to quality prenatal care, genetic screening and counseling, childbirth and postpartum care, and pediatric care for their children.

Pregnant women, especially poor women and women in Black, Hispanic, and Native American communities who are experiencing a crisis of drug and alcohol abuse, must be provided reproductive health and maternity services in an environment that is supportive and free of stigma. They must be fully informed of the risks to themselves and their infants in a way that is caring and nonpunitive and that helps them to deal with additional problems of poverty, poor housing, and male violence.

All women must have access to confidential and quality care for sexually transmitted diseases. Women who are HIV positive or at risk for AIDS who are or may become pregnant have the same right to noncoercive counseling and choice as women with other disabilities or possible fetal impairments. AIDS testing, like prenatal diagnosis, should be offered on an anonymous or confidential and voluntary basis and within a program of counseling and education that respects all persons' rights to express their sexuality.

B. Comprehensive Care

Because reproductive choice includes the ability to care for as well as bear children, comprehensive health care and human services must be available to all families. Whether offered through the Medicaid program, private insurance, or a national health plan, the services must be physically accessible—to disabled and rural women, to those dependent on public transportation, to those who work nights—and must be affordable to all.

C. Safe and Quality Care

Health and human services including all reproductive health services should focus on health, wellness, and the prevention of problems, as well as on the cure and amelioration of problems, and should be provided in a culturally supportive manner, in an environment that is free from violence, deception, and fraud. Women should define their own needs and be enabled through the use of these services to make positive changes in their lives.

Medical practitioners must not adopt unnecessary or invasive practices that endanger women's lives or health and must not use their power or authority to coerce reproductive decisions. For example, procedures such as sterilization, hysterectomy, amniocentesis, ultrasound, Caesarean section, or electronic fetal monitoring should be used only when medically appropriate. To prevent further medical abuse, the crisis in malpractice and liability insurance which has forced medical practitioners to adopt unnecessary or invasive practices in order to protect against legal liability must be addressed without leaving women unprotected.

D. Informed Consent and Informed Refusal

Principles of informed consent and informed refusal must be an intrinsic part of the decision making process and must be backed up by supportive counseling. Only when women have full knowledge about the ramifications of accepting or rejecting a particular health option, including explanations of medical procedures and their risks and benefits in understandable terms in the woman's own language, can decisions be voluntary. At the same time, women must have the option of refusing particular types of information—e.g., the sex of the child after amniocentesis. In addition, informed consent must not become a pretext for harassment or discouragement of a particular reproductive choice, such as abortion or sterilization.

3. Sexuality, Reproductive, and Life Skill Education

Women, particularly teenage women, often become pregnant because they lack essential knowledge about sex, pregnancy, and contraception. Persons of all ages must have sufficient information about their sexuality and reproductive health to make intelligent decisions about sexuality, childbearing, and parenting. Information about how their bodies work, varied forms of sexuality, contraceptives, and sexually transmitted diseases must be provided to all persons at accessible locations, in a manner that is understandable and age-appropriate. Men as well as women must be taught that they have equal responsibility to be well informed about and to participate fully in choices related to sexual behavior, reproduction, and parenting.

As society grows increasingly concerned about the transmission of AIDS, women and men should be fully informed about the risks and pathology of AIDS and the necessity of using condoms or other "safe sex" practices. Public education campaigns to prevent AIDS should be administered in a context that respects all persons' needs to express their sexuality, both inside and outside the traditional framework of marriage and heterosexuality.

But education about sexuality and reproduction is only a part of the solution. Women, especially young women, often choose to become mothers because they have no realistic possibilities of advancement in society. Our educational system must provide women with the opportunity to set ambitious goals for their future, and the background to make these goals a reality, enabling women to choose motherhood when it is the best choice for them.

4. Freedom to Express One's Sexuality, and to Adopt Varied Family Arrangements or Lifestyles

If women and men are coerced or socialized into heterosexual relationships, or if childbearing or childrearing is permissible only within heterosexual relationships, then people's ability to make intimate decisions about reproduction, as well as about sexuality and parenting, is constrained. Society must not discriminate against, stigmatize, or penalize persons on the basis of their sexuality or sexual preference. Moreover, varied forms of sexual expression including heterosexuality, bisexuality, and homosexuality must be accepted as normal human responses, with positive meaning and value.

Women must be as free to say no to sexuality, childbearing, and parenting as they are to choose these options. Women must be free to express their sexuality in whatever noncoercive forms they choose, without recriminations, without effect on their value in our society or their self-esteem, and without fear of becoming pregnant if they do not wish to be so.

Varied forms of family and living arrangements must be acceptable choices. When women choose to parent outside of marriage, or to live collectively or inter-generationally, these choices must be respected. The legal barriers to and social stigma of unwed parenthood, inter-racial childbearing, or lesbian motherhood must be eliminated if true reproductive choice for all women is to be an option. Moreover, since pressure to have children is often brought about because there are few other acceptable adult-child relationships, we must encourage alternative forms of adult-child interaction.

5. Economic Equity and Reproduction

In order that all persons have equal opportunity to become parents, they must have the means to do so. The economic barriers to alternative forms of reproduction, such as the cost of adoption, donor insemination, in vitro fertilization, or embryo transfer must be lessened for low-income women through fee reduction or subsidies.

If we want a society in which children are truly an option, women must have the economic means to raise their children—to provide adequate food, clothing, and shelter and quality child care and education. We must work to eliminate the feminization of poverty that today so limits women's reproductive options and work to create jobs and a welfare system that afford dignity to all. Without an economy and social services that support women, women are unable to support their children and families; responsible parenting is possible only in a society that provides the necessary resources for parents.

Public policies must be enacted that will ease the burdens of working parents, caught between responsibilities of job and home. In addition to quality, affordable child care services, a reproductive rights agenda requires gender-neutral pregnancy and child care leave provisions and flexible work schedules available without penalty to fathers as well as mothers. To make these provisions available to all working parents and not just the most privileged, leave time must be paid. Corporate and governmental employers should be encouraged to initiate internal education programs, similar to those currently underway regarding sexual harassment, to change employee attitudes about male and same-sex partner participation in prenatal and child care tasks.

6. Freedom from Violence

Because fear of violence by a spouse or partner and fear of sexual assault limit everyone's ability to make intimate decisions, all persons must be free to choose whether, when, and with whom they have sex and have children, and to raise their children without fear of sexual assault, abuse, violence, or harassment in their homes, on the streets, or at their jobs.

7. Freedom from Reproductive Hazards

All persons must be free from reproductive hazards within the environment, in their homes, and at their workplaces. Rather than attempting to repair the effects of reproductive hazards by treating infertility or disease or by banning fertile women from hazardous work-sites (and consequently from higher paying jobs), we must eliminate the hazards.

8. Family Law and Services

In order to enable all persons to freely form the arrangements in which they parent, they must be able to establish and terminate these arrangements without economic and social penalty. Fair and equitable divorce, child support, and child custody laws must be available and enforceable by women whose marriage or other family arrangements have dissolved or proven inadequate. In the event of the death or disability of both of a child's parents, governmental and community resources must provide for the well-being of the child. In the event of child abuse or neglect, governmental and community resources must provide necessary medical, social, and legal services to keep families together.

9. Political Participation

All persons must have the full right to express their views and, through organized, collective, and nonviolent action, to work actively for positive, systematic changes that will guarantee reproductive choice. Women must have the opportunity to be involved at all levels of the political process and within all political parties and be encouraged to take positions of leadership.

Notes

1. Copyright © 1988, Rutgers The State University. All rights reserved. Printed by permission. Request for permission to reprint this article should be addressed to: Nadine Taub, Director, Women's Rights Litigation Clinic, School of Law, Rutgers The State University, 15 Washington Street, Newark, New Jersey 07102.

Reproductive Rights and
Coalition-Building[1]

Byllye Avery

This is the first time women of color have come together to talk about defending abortion rights. We are herstory—we are writing it right now. So we don't have models. Society has set us up to continue to function away from each other, not understanding each other, not coming together. Some of us are still real confused. Some of us are saying "Black women." Others are saying "African-American women." Some of us don't know the difference between Latinos and Hispanics and some of us can't tell the difference between a Japanese and a Chinese woman. We don't know those things yet. Some of us are confused about whether to say "Indians" or "Native Americans." We don't know what to say because we don't know if we're hurting somebody's feelings. These are basic dialogues that we have to have within our diversities so we learn how to work together. And we haven't even gotten to the class lines yet.

We need first to understand the meaning of the word respect—for ourselves and for others wherever they are. People are here [at the "In Defense of Roe" conference] because we are working for the same cause. It doesn't mean that everybody has to be in the same place. Coalitions build and go along a continuum, and we need to have people who are at all places along that continuum. You will meet a woman who might say to you, I personally can't have an abortion. And she might be having baby number 31. And you can believe that that woman really needs to have an abortion rather than baby number 31. But you need to respect her choice and, by respecting hers, she can support you around your abortion decision.

We are building coalitions here and we are going to have to work for issues that will lead to the end goal. You may wonder how we will get there. Some groups will have to organize around health in general and then move from there. Some groups will have to organize around sex education and move from there. But at least there will be a place to have a dialogue. There are a whole mess of people out there that nobody is talking to and they don't know what to do. We cannot wait and talk only to the very pure.

Our analysis, which will be put into practice through effective coalition-building, must always be done around the sisters who are forced to function on the bottom of the society—that is, the sisters who have the lowest income, who have the least access to services, who have the hardest time. They are who we need to hear from. What does "reproductive rights" mean to you? If we're talking about using RU-486, what does that mean for the sisters on the bottom? For some sisters it might mean that all they need is a drug to take care of any problems that come up. But what about the sisters who don't have means to deal with problems? If we do the analysis and operationalize our work around the folks on the bottom, we will lift up the whole heap as we move the women on the bottom.

If we can work out a way to operate, we can use this when we go back to organize the diverse people at home because we are a microcosm of our communities and these are lessons we need to learn. Folks have made it possible for us to be together and talk. Sisters, let's capitalize on it and move forward!

Notes

1. Presented at the "In Defense of Roe," conference, April 7-8, 1989, Washington, D.C., sponsored by the American Civil Liberties Union and the Religious Coalition for Abortion Rights.

Notes on Contributors

JACQUI ALEXANDER is Professor of Sociology at Brandeis University in Waltham, Massachusetts. Her scholarship focuses on third world feminism, especially women in the Caribbean. She is also involved in the feminist movement and in political struggles for lesbian and gay freedom.

HORTENSIA AMARO is Associate Professor of Social and Behavioral Sciences at the School of Public Health and the Department of Pediatrics, Boston University School of Medicine. She is co-founder and President of the Latino Health Network of Massachusetts and serves on the Governor's Task Force on AIDS. Her research and public health advocacy focus on substance abuse, HIV infection, and reproductive health among Latina and Black women.

ADRIENNE ASCH writes on bioethics issues, with particular interest in their ramifications for women and minorities such as people with disabilities. She is a former member of the Board of Directors of the National Abortion Rights Action League.

BYLLYE AVERY is Director and founder of the National Black Women's Health Project in Atlanta, Georgia. She was also the recipient of a MacArthur Foundation award in 1989.

SUSAN BAILEY has an M.A. in English from the University of New Orleans. She has taught at the University of California at Berkeley and is currently doing graduate work in chemistry at Mills College in Oakland, California.

ANN BAKER founded the 80% Majority Campaign, which provides information and materials to grassroots activists. She assists clinic directors and activists in responding to Operation Bully and in state legislative battles. The Campaign publishes *The Campaign Report,* an eight-page newsletter that comes out twice a month. For further information, contact: The 80% Majority Campaign, P.O. Box 971, Hightstown, New Jersey 08520. Phone: (609) 443-8780.

JACQUELINE BERRIEN is a staff attorney at the Women's Rights Project of the American Civil Liberties Union in New York City.

MARIAN BLACKWELL-STRATTEN is a disability rights advocate and para-legal associated with the legal training and technical assistance programs of the Disability Rights Education and Defense Fund since 1982. She is a disabled woman and a feminist.

ANGELA BONAVOGLIA is a freelance writer, a contributing editor of *MS. Magazine* and Director of Development and Communications for the MS. Foundation for Women. Her book about the abortion experiences of influential American women entitled, *The Choices We Made,* will be published in 1991 by Random House.

MARY LOU BRESLIN is Acting Director of the Disability Rights Education and Defense Fund. In this capacity, she is spokeswoman for the rights of disabled children and adults. She is also a disabled woman.

SARAH BUTTENWEISER is a writer and political activist in western Massachusetts, working for the Civil Liberties and Public Policy Program at Hampshire College. She is a former counselor at an abortion clinic and currently runs a post-abortion support group.

MARGARET CERULLO is Professor of Sociology at Hampshire College in Amherst, Massachusetts. She is a long-time activist in the feminist and gay and lesbian movements.

CONNIE S. CHAN is Professor of Human Services at the College of Public and Community Service, University of Massachusetts, Boston. She is an activist in the Asian-American community and in the women's movement.

LYNN S. CHANCER teaches sociology at Barnard College and is the author of a forthcoming book on sado-masochism.

RHONDA COPELON is Professor of Law at City University of New York School of Law. She argued *Harris v. McRae* in the U.S. Supreme Court. For 12 years she was a staff attorney at the Center for Constitutional Rights where she is currently Vice President and a volunteer attorney.

SHARON COX is a writer/poet from Roxbury, Massachusetts.

CYNTHIA DANIELS has been active in political organizations working on women's health issues. She worked for the state as a "feminist guerrilla" within the state bureaucracy and currently is writing a book, *Fetal Rights and State Power,* about the politics of fetal protectionism and feminist theories of the state.

JANEAN ACEVEDO DANIELS is an attorney in California. She researched and wrote the article that appears in this volume while she was a law clerk for the National Health Law Program, Los Angeles, California.

ANGELA DAVIS is an internationally-regarded writer, scholar, lecturer, and fighter for human rights. Her books include *If They Come In the Morning: Voices of Resistance; Angela Davis: An Autobiography;* and *Women, Race and Class.*

LANI DAVISON is Associate Director for Planning and Program Development of the Hispanic Health Council and Director of the Mujeres en Acción Pro Salud Reproductiva Project.

DÁZON DIXON is the founder and Director of SISTERLOVE: Women's AIDS Project. She is a member of and consultant for the National Black Women's Health Project, and formerly a project director for the Feminist Women's Health Center in Atlanta, Georgia.

MICHELLE FINE is Professor of Psychology in Education and Women's Studies at the University of Pennsylvania, and a feminist activist concerned with adolescent females.

JOAN FISHBEIN lives in Augusta, Georgia. She is a graduate of Vassar College and recently received an MFA from Warren Wilson College. Her poetry has appeared in *Helicon Nine; The Devil's Millhopper;* and *The Kennesaw Review.*

CÁNDIDA FLORES is the Executive Director of the Hispanic Health Council, and a Board member of the Hartford Permanent Commission on the Status of Women.

MARLENE GERBER FRIED is Director of the Civil Liberties and Public Policy Program at Hampshire College. She is a long-time reproductive rights activist with the Boston Reproductive Rights Network (R2N2) and a co-founder of the Abortion Rights Fund of Western Massachusetts.

SHERRILYN IFILL is Assistant Counsel, NAACP Legal Defense Fund, New York, New York.

"JANE" was a member of the Jane Collective in Chicago. She is currently writing a book about Jane.

SABRAE JENKINS is Director of the Women of Color Partnership Program of the Religious Coalition For Abortion Rights.

BRENDA JOYNER is Co-Director of the Tallahassee Feminist Women's Health Center.

KATHRYN KOLBERT is an attorney with the Reproductive Freedom Project of the National ACLU. She argued *Thornburgh v. ACOG* in the U.S.Supreme Court and co-ordinated the friend-of-the-Court briefs in Webster v. Reproductive Health Services.

REVA LEVINE is a social worker and former abortion counselor, and runs a post-abortion support group.

SHELLEY MAINS is an activist in both the reproductive rights and lesbian and gay movements. She is a writer who frequently contributes to *Gay Community News* and *Sojourner.*

ARLENE BYRNNE MAYERSON is Directing Attorney for the Disability Rights Education and Defense Fund.

JUDY NORSIGIAN is Co-Director of the Boston Women's Health Book Collective and co-author of *Our Bodies, Ourselves*. She is a Board member of the National Women's Health Network.

ROXANNA PASTOR is an activist in the anti-interventionist and reproductive rights movements. She is currently living in Mexico.

CYNTHIA PETERS works for South End Press. She has recently returned from a year in Nicaragua, where she was working with Editorial Vanguardia under the auspices of the Publishers Support Project.

STEPHANIE POGGI is an activist in the reproductive rights and lesbian and gay movements. She is a writer working, until recently, at *Gay Community News* as News and then Features Editor.

LAURA PUNNETT is a long-time activist for women's health and workers' rights. She is currently Professor of Work Environment at the University of Lowell, Massachusetts, studying the health effects of physical work stress.

ENID MERCEDES REY is Coordinator of Cosas de Mujeres and the Women, Health and Development Unit of the Hispanic Health Council. She has worked with Magdalena de Leal and the Casa del la Mujer in Bogota, Colombia.

MIGDALIA RIVERA is a psychotherapist with the Hartford, Connecticut public schools. She has worked on health and mental health issues affecting Puerto Rican women for 15 years.

LORETTA ROSS is Program Director with the National Black Women's Health Project. Formerly she was Director of Women of Color Programs for the National Organization for Women.

MARÍA SERRANO is a health educator. She has worked for the past 10 years with Puerto Rican women doing community education, outreach, and counseling.

BEVERLY SMITH is the Prevention and Education Program Planner for the Boston AIDS Consortium. She is a long-time activist in various movements focusing on justice for people of color.

SUSAN TRACY teaches history at Hampshire College in Amherst, Massachusetts.

ALICE WALKER is the author of novels, short stories, and essays, including *The Temple of My Familiar* and *The Color Purple*.

ELLEN WILLIS is a writer with the *Village Voice* in New York City.

Index

A

80% Majority Campaign 179
Abortion
   accessibility 4, 7
   clinics 10-11
   decriminalization 33
   erosion 12
   health care 13
   illegal 24, 84, 89-90, 139, 148,
      200
   isolation 125
   legal 122, 139, 192
   legal right to 6-7, 15-17, 50, 90
   Medicaid funding 5, 24, 46, 75,
      154, 206
   notification law 171
   parental consent 168, 173
   parental notification 48, 173
   privacy 29, 33-40, 56, 169, 286
   public 4
   safe 2-3, 5, 15, 182
   spontaneous 148
   spousal consent 4, 46
Abortion Action Coalition 86
   Third World Women's
      Committee 86
Adolescent Pregnancy and
   Parenting Services (NY) 115
AIDS Discrimination Division of
   the Law Enforcement Bureau of
   N.Y. Commission on Human
   Rights 248, 252
AIDS 12, 85, 127, 159, 228
   activism 281, 285
   AIDS-Related Complex (ARC)
      253

AZT 249
   counseling 250
   epidemic 246
   HIV infection 245-246, 248
   HIV positive 85, 252
   HIV testing 248-249
   in women 247-248
   prevention 229, 253
   transmission 248-249
   virus 148
   Women and Aids Conference
      86
Akron Center for Reproductive
   Health v. City of Akron 46
Agency for International
   Development 107, 109
Alabama Court of Civil Appeals
   166
Allen, Lillie 79
American Birth Control League
   20-21
American Civil Liberties Union
   169, 266
   Reproductive Freedom Project
      24, 167
American Cyanamid 272-274
Americans United for Life Legal
   Defense Fund 168
Amigas Latinas en Acción (ALAS)
   221
Asian-Pacific American Women
   147, 293

B

Baird v. Bellotti 28, 46, 169
Bangladesh 53

Baulieu, Etienne-Emile 198
Bean, Dr. Xylina 263
Beers, Greg 169
Benshoof, Janet 167-168
Birch, Guy Irving 20
Birth Control Federation of
America 21
Birth Place 77
Black Women's Council on AIDS
86
Blackmun, Justice Harry 27, 35
Bork, Robert 30
Boston City Hospital 83
Bowers v. Hardwick 28-29, 33,
35-37, 47
Bradley, Senator William 267
Bunster-Burotto, Ximena 57

C

Carolina Women's Clinic 190
Caesarian section 36, 224, 249,
255-259
emergency 250
court-ordered 255-260
Chastity Bill 3
Chavkin, Dr. Wendy 263-264
Chicago Women's Liberation
Union 94
Child Welfare League of America
170
Children's Defense Fund 267
Christian Action Council 209
Civil Liberties Union (MA) 7
Civil Rights Act 277
Civil Rights Restoration Act 155,
276
Clergyman's Council on Problem
Pregnancies 88
Coalition for Choice 7, 287
Collier, Dr. Maxie 266
Colonization 52, 108, 221
Comissión Feminíl Mexicana
National 222
Comité de Mujeres
Puertorriqueñas Miriam Lopez
Perez 222, 227
Committee to End Sterilization
Abuse (CESA) 109

Commonweal 132-134, 136
Contraceptives 45, 53
IUD 53
Pill 53
Cook County Hospital 93
Corea, Gena 49
Cosas de Mujeres 223, 227, 230
Cox, Nial Ruth 22
Crew, J. Wynell Brooks 163

D

Daly, Mary 101
de Beauvoir, Simone 114
Decade for Women 52, 55
Department of Health, Education
and Welfare 17, 24
Department of Health and Human
Services 17, 23, 153-154, 225
Department of Public Health (CA)
24
Depo-Provera 22
Derzis, Diane 162, 164, 166
D & C (dilation & curettage) 99,
198
Doe, Baby Jane 234, 241, 242
Doe v. Bolton 16, 45
Downer, Carol 207

E

Ehrenreich, Barbara 116
Eisenstadt v. Baird 34, 45
Enloe, Cynthia 57
Equal Employment Opportunity
Commission 276
Equal Rights Amendment 3
Eugenics Society 20
Everywoman's Center 122

F

Fair Housing Act 155
Federation of Feminist Women's
Health Centers 111, 207, 211
Feminist Women's Health Centers
107, 199
Tallahassee 205, 207
Fetal protection policies 272-278
Fetal Rights 269-274

First National Conference on
  Black Women's Health Issues 78
Francke, Linda Bird 118
Franke, Katherine 248

G

Gainesville Women's Health
  Center 75
Gay Community News 189-190,
  282, 289
Gay rights 9
  movement 33, 192, 281-284
Genocide 85, 141, 185
Gordon, Linda 17
Grimke, Sarah 18
Griswald v. Connecticut 34, 45
Guttmacher Institute 170

H

Hamer, Fannie Lou 65
Harper, Ida Husted 19
Harris v. McRae 12, 28, 38
Healthy Birth Act (1989) 267
Helms Amendment 54
Hispanic Health Council on
  Puerto Rican Women and
  Reproduction (Hartford,
  Connecticut) 222, 224, 225,
  228-229
Hodgson v. Minnesota 48
Hoechst Corporation 201
Howe, Julia Ward 19
Human Life Amendment 4
Human Rights Campaign Fund 290
Hyde Amendment 4-5, 7, 12, 24,
  116, 149, 155, 210, 252

I

Incest 148, 170·
Indian Health Care Bill 155
Indian Health Service 149
Indian Health Services Hospital
  23, 63
Infanticide 17
International Menstrual
  Regulation Conference 107
International Monetary Fund 55

International Planned Parenthood
  Federation 54

J

Jackson, Jesse 207
James, Kay 168
Jane 93-100, 103
Jayawardena, Kumari 51
Jiménez, Rosie 155
Johnson Controls 271-272, 276-277
Jones, Marcus 163-165

K

Kempton, Murray 116
Kennedy, Arthur 30
King, Martin Luther 185-186
Klassal, Dara 168
Klyne, Dr. Robert 274
Kurz, Martha 170

L

Lamaze 77
La Operación 224
League of Women Voters 7, 287
Leland, Mickey 267
Liederman, David 170
Loesch, Juli 135
Luker, Kristin 115
Lynn, Jr., Lawrence E. 117

M

Macy, Joanna 123-124
Manushi 56
March for Women's Equality and
  Women's Lives 181
Martinez, Bob 205
McDonnell, Kathleen 118
Medicaid 23, 30, 76, 154-155, 158,
  177, 208, 251, 256
Meehan, Mary 135-136
Menstrual
  cycle 102, 202-203
  extraction 101-105, 108
  flow 101
  induction 103
  regulation 105, 107
Midwives 176
Miscarriage 271-272

Mitchell, Joseph 167
Mohanty, Chandra Talpede 51
Montgomery Community Action
  Commission 22
Mortality
  infant 80-81, 152-153
  perinatal 148
Ms. 167, 169-170
Mujeres en Acción Pro Salud
  Reproductiva Project 224-225
Mujeres en Acción Research
  Project 222, 226, 230

N

National Abortion Rights Action
  League (NARAL) 6, 8, 287, 299
National Black Child
  Development Institute 154
National Black Women's Health
  Project 78, 80, 291
National Institute for Drug Abuse
  264
National Latina Health
  Organization 222
National Organization for Women
  (NOW) 7, 97, 210, 287, 299
National Right to Life Committee
  183, 201
National Self Help Convention 105
National Urban League 154
New England Journal of Medicine
  256, 258
New Right 3, 9, 117, 131-132, 190,
  236
Nice, Charles 163, 165, 167
Nkoli, Simon 290

O

O'Connnor, Sandra Day 28, 31,
  119
Ohio v. Akron Center for
  Reproductive Health 48
Operation Bully 179-183
Operation Rescue 1, 5, 10, 116,
  179, 185, 187-190, 281-282, 285,
  287

P

Pap Smear 105-106
Paul, Dr. Maureen 278
Pierce, Dr. Clovis 22-23
Planned Parenthood 7-8, 143, 287
  clinic (Boston) 170
  Federation 168, 171
  International 107
  League of MA 171
Planned Parenthood of Central
  Missouri v. Danforth 46, 169
Pogrebin, Letty Cottin 170
Population Affairs Office 23
Population Control 21, 105, 109
Population Council 107
  information program 107
Post-Abortion Stress Syndrome 123
Pregnancy Discrimination Act of
  1987 276
Progesterone 197
The Progressive 136
Project Life 179
Pro-Life Action Network 179
Prostaglandin 198
Public Health Service 248
Puertorriqueñas 221, 223-224, 228
  Puerto Rican Women 16, 227

R

Radosh, Alice 115-116
Raspberry, William 153
Relf, Minnie Lee & Mary Alice
  21-22
Religious Coalition for Abortion
  Rights 7, 151, 156, 293
Reproductive Rights 6, 14, 33, 283,
  285, 297, 300-302
  Bill of Rights 299
  choices 80, 208
  civil rights 142
  freedom 49, 184, 298
  health services 179
  politics of 127
  rights network 287
Rockefeller Foundation 53, 107
Roe, Conference in Defense of 13,
  307

Roe v. Wade 3, 6-7, 13, 16, 27-31, 33-36, 45, 98, 113-114, 117, 147, 152, 155, 162-163, 168, 177, 186, 256, 288
Roussel-Uclaf 201-202
Routh St. Clinic 199
RU-486 13, 197-203

S

Salazar, Sandra 24
Sanger, Margaret 20
Scheidler, Joe 179
Schering 202
Schultz, Carl 23
Sharples, Vivian 190
Sheeran, Patrick 117
Sidel, Ruth 115
The Silent Scream 113
Simonds, Wendy 115
Smith, Barbara 50
Snelling, Karen 169
Sojourners 135
Southern Poverty Law Center 22, 208
Squeal Laws 3
Steinfels, Peter 131
Sterilization 192, 224
    abuse 25, 53
    forced 193, 284
    involuntary 241, 253
    on demand 156
    voluntary 23
Stoddard, Lothrop 20
Sudden Infant Death Syndrome (SIDS) 81, 158
Summit Medical Center 162, 166, 172
Swaans, Marilyn 170

T

Tallahasseans United for Reproductive Freedom 207, 210
Terry, Randall 180
Thirteenth Amendment 32
Thornburgh v. American College of Obstetricians and Gynecologists (ACOG) 35-36, 47
Title X 155

Trask, Haunani-Kay 57

U

Uri, Dr. Connie 23
U.S. Foreign Assistance Act 54
U.S. Office of Population Control 109

V

Voluntary motherhood 15, 18

W

Wallis, Jim 135
Wattleton, Faye 143
Webster v. Reproductive Health Services 4-10, 12-14, 27-28, 33, 40, 42, 147-148, 155, 179, 205, 227, 252
Westchester Coalition for Legal Abortion 182
Wheatley, Jr., Mickey 189
Williams v. Zbaraz 46
Willis, Ellen 32, 116
Wills, Gary 132
Women of Color Partnership Program of the Religious Coalition for Abortion Rights 293-294
Women, Infants, & Children (WIC) 153, 267
Women's Agenda 300
World Congress of Gynecology & Obstetrics 201

About South End Press

South End Press is a nonprofit, collectively run book publisher with over 150 titles in print. Since our founding in 1977, we have tried to meet the needs of readers who are exploring, or are already committed to, the politics of radical social change.

Our goal is to publish books that encourage critical thinking and constructive action on the key political, cultural, social, economic, and ecological issues shaping life in the United States and in the world. In this way, we hope to give expression to a wide diversity of democratic social movements and to provide an alternative to the products of corporate publishing.

If you would like a free catalog of South End Press books or information about our membership program—which offers two free books and a 40% discount on all titles—please write us at South End Press, 116 Saint Botolph Street, Boston, MA 02115.

Other titles of interest from South End Press:

Abortion Without Apology, Radical History for the 1990s
Ninia Baehr

Women, AIDS, and Activism
ACT UP/New York Women and AIDS Handbook Group

Walking to the Edge: Essays of Resistance
Margaret Randall

Yearning: Race, Gender, and Cultural Politics
bell hooks

Race, Gender and Work: A Multi-cultural Economic History of Women in the United States
Teresa Amott and Julie Matthaei

True Story of a Drunken Mother
Nancy Lee Hall

Not an Easy Choice: A Feminist Re-examines Abortion
Kathleen McDonnell